DISCARDED

DIARY OF
Howard Stillwell Stanfield
1864-65

EDITED BY
Jack J. Detzler

HSS

Howard Stillwell Stanfield

Diary of HOWARD STILLWELL STANFIELD

Overland trip from Indiana to California, 1864 via Virginia City, Montana Territory AND *Sea voyage from San Francisco to New York, 1865 via Panama*

edited by

JACK J. DETZLER

INDIANA UNIVERSITY PRESS
BLOOMINGTON · LONDON 1969

Indiana University Social Science Series No. 25
Indiana University, Bloomington, Indiana

PUBLICATION COMMITTEE

John E. Stoner
Carroll L. Christenson
Robert H. Ferrell

The Indiana University Social Science Series was founded in 1939 for the publication of monographs and occasional papers by members of the faculty.

COPYRIGHT © 1969 BY INDIANA UNIVERSITY PRESS

Library of Congress Catalog Card No. 68-64123

SBN 253-38525-3

Acknowledgments

Many persons contributed their time and thought in the course of assisting me to prepare this book. Professor Robert Ferrell of Indiana University was totally generous with invaluable suggestions, and Professor Oscar O. Winther of Indiana University has been very helpful. Librarians and directors of historical societies were uniformly courteous and co-operative in leading me to the resources of their depositories. I also want to acknowledge the assistance of James Abajian, California State Historical Society Library; Mrs. Clara Beatty, Nevada Historical Society; Miss Mary Dempsey, Montana State Historical Society Library; Richard H. Dillon, Sutro Library, San Francisco; Archibald Hanna, Yale University Library; Miss Helen Mayden, Sacramento Public Library; Dale Morgan, Bancroft Library; Miss Thelma Neaville, Marysville Public Library; and Mrs. Marion Welliver, Nevada Historical Society. Finally, to Mrs. Thomas Stanfield, wife of Howard Stanfield's nephew, I owe a special debt of gratitude for giving me access to Stanfield's journal and diary. (The original MSS are now in the possession of Mrs. Lyndon Kirkley—Mrs. Thomas Stanfield's daughter—417 Greenhurst Drive, Pittsburgh, Pennsylvania.)

Contents

INTRODUCTION 1

ONE | THE TRIP BEGINS 11
Diary 16

TWO | IOWA—A TRANSITION 21
Diary 25

THREE | ENDLESS PRAIRIES 34
Diary 38

FOUR | INTO THE MOUNTAINS 49
Diary 55

FIVE | STAGE TO THE CITY OF THE SAINTS 74
Diary 78

SIX | JOURNEY'S END 87
Diary 90

SEVEN | THE PACIFIC VOYAGE 107
Diary 112

EIGHT | HOMEWARD BOUND 130
Diary 135

Bibliographical Notes 143

Bibliography 166

APPENDICES

The Indiana Train 174

Calendar of Stanfield's Trip 180

Notes 185

Index 227

Illustrations

PHOTOGRAPHS

Frontispiece

Davenport, Iowa 14

William S. Bartlett 18

Virginia City, Nevada 91

MAPS

Stanfield's Journey West x

First Stage of Journey 10

Second Stage of Journey 50

Third Stage of Journey 86

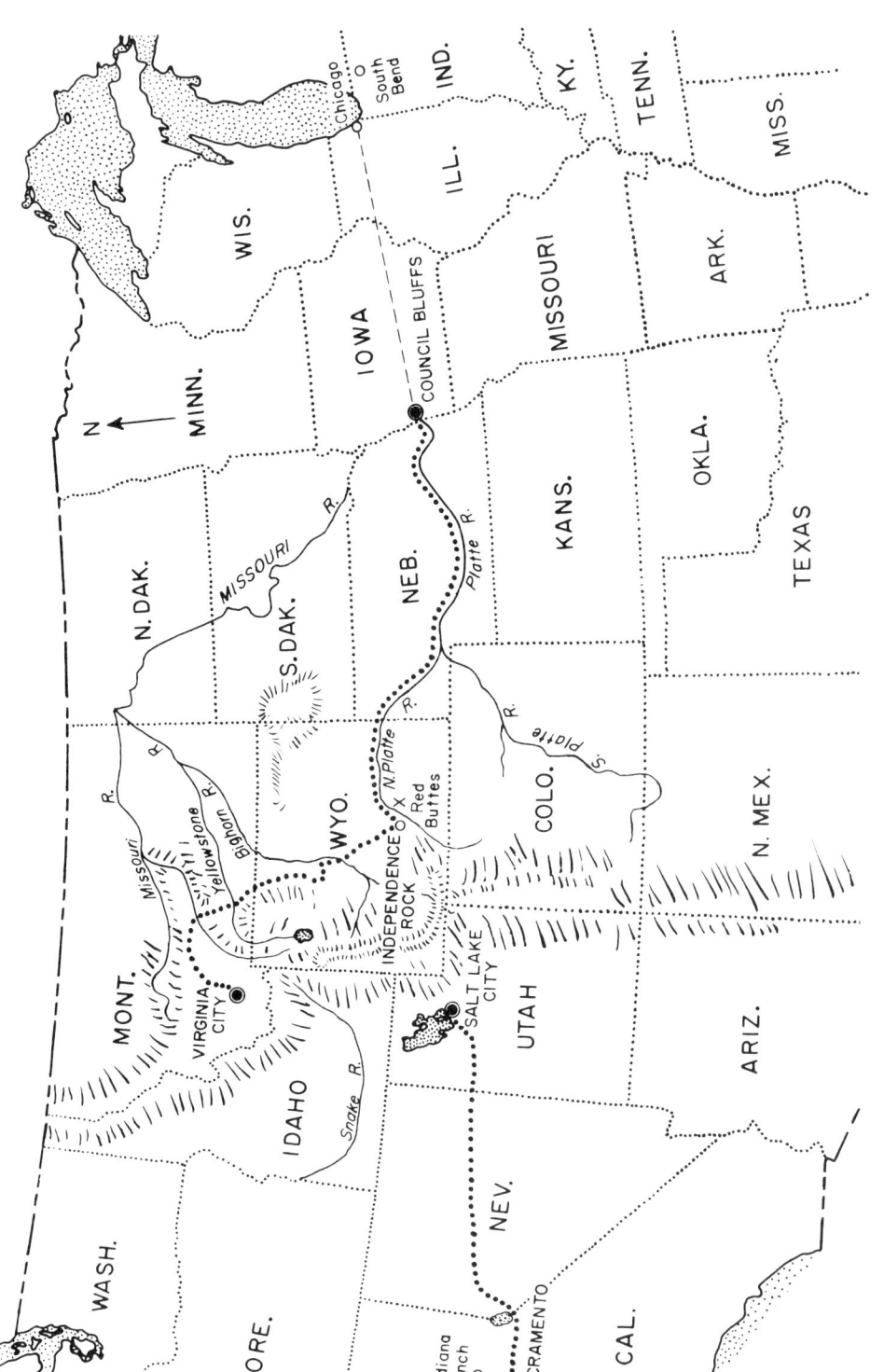

INTRODUCTION

*H*oward Stillwell Stanfield was a bright, active, inquisitive seventeen-year-old who wanted to see something of the world. His older brother was doing just that. Edward had attended Princeton University, and in 1861 he joined the 48th Indiana Volunteers as a First Lieutenant.[1] Howard, who suffered from poor health, could neither attend college nor serve in the army, but after long family discussions he received permission to go west.*

Permission and financial support for his trip west came from Howard's father, Judge Thomas Stanfield.[2] Judge Stanfield, who ruled his family autocratically, seems to have approved the trip in order to compensate Howard for missing college and the army. Other factors may also have influenced the father's decision—California's climate might prove beneficial; the boy had completed his schooling and had earned a vacation; he had no career in mind and might find a profitable business connection; and, finally the trip would give him a chance to become acquainted with relatives already in California.[3]

California was not unknown to the Stanfields. As Howard grew to manhood, his family often had talked of that far-off land. Relatives lived there, and many friends had gone west, attracted by the same promises which drew Howard. Their expectations were of adventure in a frontier society, of health and wealth in a glorious climate.

* Further details of Stanfield's life are given in App. I, pp. 175–76.

Howard's departure was simplified because he had no family responsibilities. As was true of many of the South Bend people he met along the trail, his family was well-to-do. Only the sadness of leaving his family gave him concern.

Stanfield started on his trip with a lifelong friend and neighbor William S. Bartlett, the twenty-one-year-old son of the wealthy merchant, Joseph Bartlett.[4] Young Bartlett was a clerk in his father's store and had helped hold the family together after the death of his mother. While the usual reasons drew young Bartlett westward, the remarriage of his father seemed to assure that his younger brothers and sister would be cared for, and he found in his friend Stanfield the company he sought. Once in California, Will was so favorably impressed by the climate and business prospects that he decided to remain there. He entered the banking business in Oakland and later moved to Los Angeles, where he became a banker and civic leader of prominence.

On the trip new experiences taught Stanfield to appreciate different points of view. Crossing his path were people he had never known before: immigrants, prospectors, Indians, and South Americans. He had also to adapt to new living patterns essential to his existence. He felt for the first time the raw strength of nature both as it threatened life and as it showed its incomparable western grandeur. In these ways Stanfield acquired, one might say by accident, certainly without much design, an education.

In his diary Stanfield recorded his new knowledge, impressions, insights. He did this to retain his South Bend ties—he was in a sense talking to his family—and also because he foresaw that the diary would be a reminder of events he might forget with the years. Then, too, he sensed the importance of the westward movement; his experiences may even have given him a feeling that he was writing an historical document—ponderous though such an idea would probably have seemed to him. Two years after returning to

INTRODUCTION 3

South Bend, he expanded the diary into a journal, and it is the diary supplemented by the journal which appears in the pages that follow. He emerges in them as a person of some charm, an intelligent observer, a good Christian, a philosopher, and a first-rate diarist who could on occasion cover his temporary inadequacies with tongue-in-cheek braggadocio or a jovial remark. His personality fills out his writing, and the reader comes to smile with him in pleasure at a well-turned phrase or to enjoy an occasional roguish observation, as when Stanfield notes that the Missouri River is like all women who change their beds whenever it profits them.

Stanfield's mild nature is apparent throughout the diary. The reader sees a young man on his first trip away from home, trying to be the adventurer. He was often filled with anxiety, as when he hoped the Indians would be peaceful. His uneasiness at the "murder" of the prairie animals demonstrates his gentle way. A further clue to his personality comes from his description of the prairies and mountains; here his writing is, if mid-Victorian, highly sensitive:

After the sun had gone down in all his glory tipping the tree tops with borders of gold, we had a beautiful moon which was nearly full the splendid moon light scenes of the night far eclipsed in magnificence the views by day. The tall noble pines rearing their lofty heads far above us, the gentle rays of the moon shining upon us, through rugged tops, oh that I were a poet; and could do these old mountains justice, by proclaiming their beauties to the world, in inimitable verse, but alas I am nothing, but a poor emigrant, who has no business with such lofty ideas.

Some continental travelers in 1864 undertook the trip unaware that they faced problems comparable to those of 1849. Only experience revealed the enormous hardship of travel through unsettled land. The trail steadily deteriorated until beyond Kearney it became a rutted path without even a stage station where travelers could rest. West of Fort Laramie, cutting northwestward to the Montana gold fields, an entirely new trail had to be broken. The guides hired to lead the settlers through this unmarked land were seldom reliable. The unsuspected problems of survival on the prairies and in the mountains came as a rude awakening.

Most of the immigrants in 1864 looked forward to a friendly reception from the Iowa farmers. They were considered kinfolk, hospitable Midwest people. Disappointment often followed, however, for the behavior of the farmers, who thought the wagon people riff-raff and rootless—raising dust and digging ruts on "good" Iowa roads—was sometimes openly hostile.[5]

Many of the travelers assumed that their trail equipment was superior to that used by earlier settlers, but actually prairie schooners had changed little, although the manufacturers claimed that their wagons were better suited for western travel. The Studebaker wagons were advertised with typical gusto:

> Ho! for Idaho! Emigrants attention! We are making a lot of wagons especially for your wants and we Will Sell Them Cheaper Than any other Concern in this country.[6]

Though advertisers stressed that their equipment eased the burdens of the trip, the immigrant found that the problems with his equipment were identical to those of the forty-niners.

People leaving for the West had confidence that the army would protect them from Indian attacks. Their attitude changed at the sight of the unkempt troops maintaining rundown forts at Kearney and Laramie. This uneasiness was heightened when the fort commanders ordered wagons to travel in trains for protection, and as the immigrants discussed Indian depredations. Indian resentment was clear, too, as the natives approached the wagons for gifts; the placid surface relations during these contacts fooled no one. Troops seldom left the forts, and Indian activities went unchecked.

Over the years immigration had stripped the countryside bare; consequently, the shortage of firewood along the trail was more severe in 1864 than in 1849. Wood was still to be found across Iowa and immediately west of Council Bluffs, but from there to the mountains it was scarce with only scrubby greasewood and sagebrush to be found. Many of the travelers, however, had prepared for this by stowing wood under their wagons, or they used buffalo chips, which were plentiful.

An oppressive hardship of every overland wagon trip was the mentally-dulling monotony combined with the harsh physical demands. Immigrants found the long travel across miles of unchanging landscape both boring and exhausting. On the prairies they had no shelter from the sun, and in the mountains they suffered from cold. Deep ravines, sand hills, and swift rivers delayed the travelers' journey. Nature everywhere was against the immigrants in a frightening challenge to survival.

The wagon immigrant of every generation planned carefully for his animals' welfare since on their well-being depended his own life. Securing the necessary fodder could be a problem. When the route was known to be without grass, grain was stowed away and water used sparingly. Immigrants in a wagon train adopted an orderly camp routine and followed a schedule. Time had to be allocated daily for securing wood, drawing water, cooking, washing dishes, and caring for the animals. The individual had to adapt to the routine of trail life or be left behind. All wagon immigrants were, of course, hard put to secure a normal diet. Food consisted of such staples as rice, corn meal, flour, beans, coffee, tea, dried fruit, pickles, salted pork, and bacon. There were no fresh vegetables or fruits, and fresh meat was to be had only after a hunt. Meals, prepared by men with no cooking experience, were unappetizing; and after the novelty of the trip wore off much of the food seemed barely edible. For the single men, the occasional wagon train community supper was a great event.

There were, lastly, the inevitable deaths, which were poignant experiences indeed. To bury a relative or friend on the borderless plains was a jarring experience. Deaths were frequent since medicine was scarce, gun accidents common, and the toll of death in Indian raids fearful. The immigrant's grief was overwhelming as he moved on, leaving only a few rocks as a marker on the plain, but promises to reclaim the body, though sincerely made, were rarely kept. Even if finances and conditions of transportation permitted return, the grave could never be located. Likely too, animals would have been there first. A terror ran through the wagons with a death on the prairie, and the event created a bond among travelers.

The immigrant of 1864 nonetheless enjoyed some pleasures on the long hard trip. Many of these were rooted in the unchanging elements of the West. There was enjoyment in appreciating the vastness of the land, the spectacular terrain, and the wild life. These were indigenous delights not yet altered by human invasion of the land. Initially, the vastness of the prairies was inspiring; the first view of the mountains and then the plunge from the mountain wilderness into the wildness of Virginia City were exciting events. The strange waters of Great Salt Lake were a source of wonder and curiosity, and prosperous Salt Lake City afforded the immigrants a much needed respite from arduous travel. Such experiences were, however, fewer than the travelers would have liked.

During the long journey they had to devise their own amusements. Fishing with a burlap sack as a sieve was a time-consuming pastime and promised a most uncertain meal. Hunting with a rifle gave the immigrant more certainty of success but, again, results were poor because few of the travelers were marksmen. (Hunting did, however, give them some badly needed rifle practice that helped to prepare them for attacks by the Indians.) They sought out the antelope, buffalo, deer, and prairie chicken. Tantalizing in the distance, the animals were wary of the hunter, and a kill was an event. The fresh meat was savored by everyone, and any left over was "jerked" in the Indian fashion.

Recreations were often unplanned. Spontaneous singing and aimless talking lifted the spirit. Card playing and letter writing in the evenings around the campfires were relaxations to end many a dull day. Undeniably, the greatest enjoyment came from reading and rereading letters from home.

Inevitably, since the trail was peopled by all types of men, tensions developed as the trip wearied on. Lucia Darling Park, who traveled to Montana in 1863, described the need for patience on the part of all members of the train: "Little faults grow to be immense...."[7] Human explosions came as normal results of close living and physical exhaustion but were usually soon forgotten. People showed their mettle, as strengths and frailties were magnified in the struggle for survival. The pressures of travel went on relentlessly, but, in a community where no one was entirely self-sufficient, hardships sometimes welded lifelong friendships.

Sentiments of brotherhood also developed as travelers were exposed to a variety of ethnic and racial groups. Sharing bed and board or trail experiences with Irish, Dutch, Germans and others, the immigrant learned that snap judgments were inaccurate. Firsthand observations of the legendary Indian gave them an opportunity to distinguish the individual from the group. Indians became personalities—human beings; some were lazy, others proud, a few charming. Western travelers taking passage via Panama had similar reactions to the Central-American people: their ways of life—though unacceptable—came to be understood and were remembered. Unconsciously the immigrant was educated in brotherhood.

Stanfield did not follow the route of the usual immigrant

in 1864. Although his objective was the west coast, he looked over the new Montana gold fields on the way, with an eye open for business opportunities. Thus he detoured north from Fort Laramie to Virginia City, in Montana Territory. There he caught a stage south to Salt Lake City; then he proceeded west along the main immigrant road to California.

He left South Bend for Chicago by wagon, traveled from there to Grinnell, Iowa, by rail, and went on to Council Bluffs by wagon. The journey to Chicago was easy—the trip by train was first-rate—but the poor roads in Iowa caused problems; they were impassable on rainy days, and on dry days the ruts were hard as iron.

Leaving Council Bluffs, Stanfield followed the old Mormon route to the Platte and went along its length, following its north branch past Fort Laramie. The trip became increasingly strenuous: Indians were more numerous; fodder was scarce; and the travelers were mentally and physically exhausted.

As the wagons turned northwestward into the Fort Laramie region, into the mountainous Bighorn country, and into Montana, the Nebraska prairies seemed mild in retrospect. Large wagon trains became a necessity. Indians were everywhere, and only large trains gave protection. At night the wagons formed a circular barricade with travelers and animals herded inside and guards posted outside. Stanfield's group joined a large train, formed beyond Fort Laramie, and reached Virginia City under the guidance of John M. Jacobs.[8] Although Jacobs' leadership was deficient, the trip was successful. Finding mountain passes, fording sites, and water and grazing grounds presented difficulties, but to a traveler in the company of a group of travelers facing their problems with some degree of patience and good nature, the hardships were less arduous than they would otherwise have been.

From Virginia City southward to Salt Lake City, and from

INTRODUCTION 9

there to Folsom, Stanfield traveled by stage. The coaches were no improvement over wagons. Even the best were crude; some lacked springs and had unpadded boards for seats. Each mile of their progress was a bumpy—and sometimes heart-stopping—ride; often the drivers, speeding to keep up with schedules or even charging through mountain passes, lost control of their coaches. The trip was routed through a spectacular mountain and lake region, through deserts and grain fields, past mining towns and Mormon villages.

In California Stanfield reached civilization again—railroads and wagons took him to his destination, Indiana Ranch. There his pace of living slowed. A pattern of life resembling that of Indiana took over.

After spending the autumn and winter in and around Indiana Ranch, Stanfield decided to return home. He missed his family and the sights of South Bend. His parting sentiment was probably much the same as that of his South Bend friend and neighbor Schuyler Colfax, also going home from California about this time.[9] The politician phrased these feelings well when he said: "There have been weary hours in all this incessant journeying, but they have been happy and golden hours too; happy, because full freighted with hospitalities and feasts, to the eye and mind; golden, because filled with recollections that will never die, friendships never to be forgotten till this heart ceases to beat."[10] With such thoughts Stanfield booked passage on the steamer *Moses Taylor* to Central America. At Panama he crossed the Isthmus and boarded the *Golden Rule* for New York; from there it was an easy rail trip to South Bend.

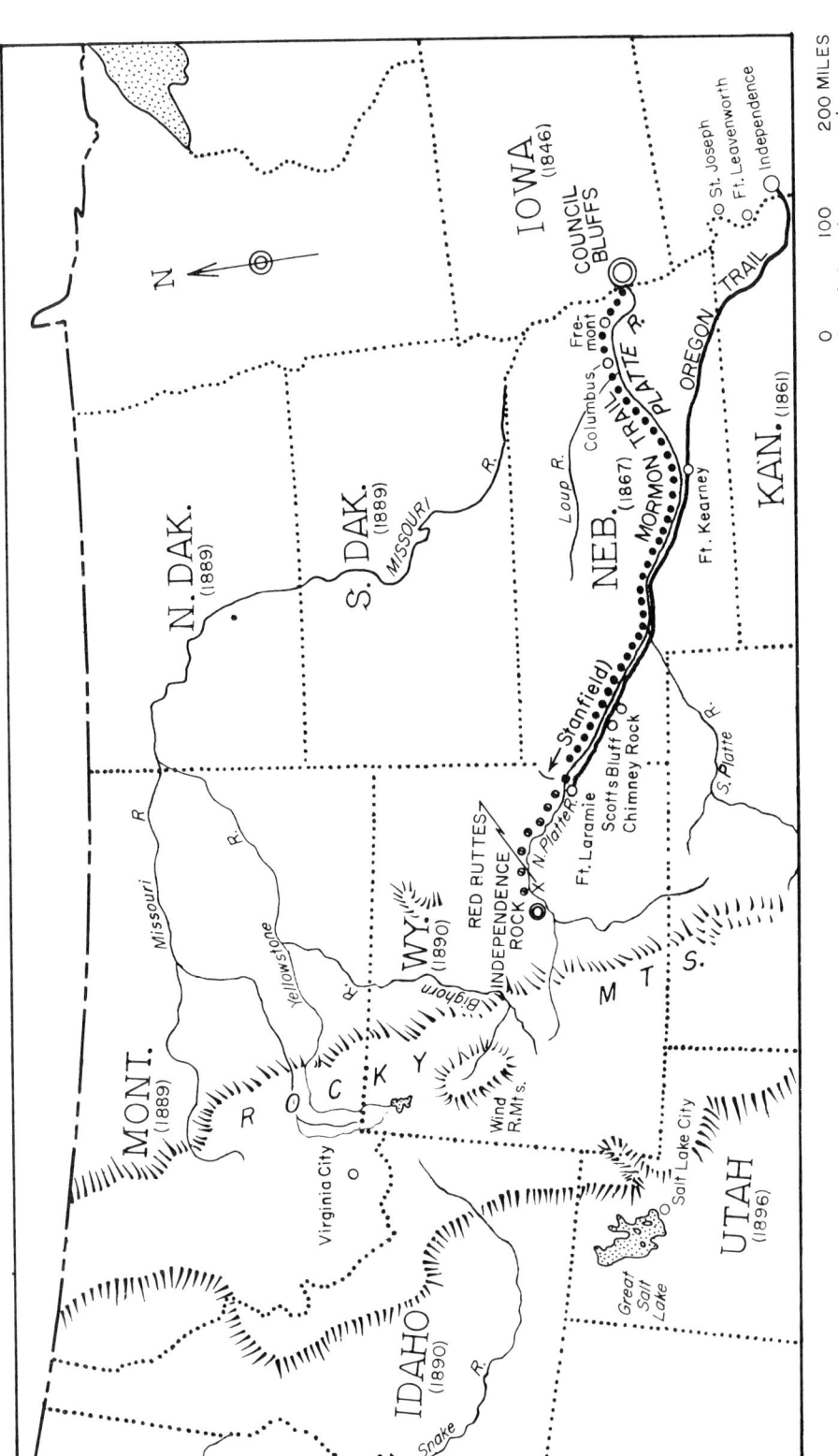

FIRST STAGE OF JOURNEY

Stanfield followed the Mormon Trail from Council Bluffs to Fort Laramie and then continued westward along the north bank of the North Platte to Independence Rock.

ONE | THE TRIP BEGINS

SOUTH BEND in 1864 was feeling the burden of the war. Many of its sons were dying in the Union cause, and since its population was less than 4,000, most of the young men going into the army from South Bend were neighbors. Every casualty was an acquaintance—perhaps a friend. No amount of war prosperity could hide the human cost.[1]

For young Howard Stanfield, who was prevented by illness from joining the army, the war atmosphere presented a personal problem; but his spirits rose as he became absorbed in gathering supplies to go West with his friend William S. Bartlett. The boys collected the staples—corn meal, beans, flour, rice, hominy, crackers, pickles, salt, sugar, lard, coffee, tea, dried fruit, salt pork, and bacon. Tobacco they took along for trading. General equipment included a small stove, cooking utensils, low chests (to serve as beds), blankets, and spare clothing of dark colors to save washing. Flannel shirts, leather vests, buckskin pants (cloth wore out too quickly), boots, buckskin gloves, and a tweed jacket were standard items. The dark felt hat soon had colorful ribbons woven into the brim lifting the immigrant's spirit with a touch of gaiety.

The choice of a covered wagon was easy. The Stanfields and Bartletts were family friends of the Studebakers, whose wagons were especially manufactured in South Bend for the overland trip. The Studebakers advertised that "one of the firm has crossed the plains and consequently knows just how to make them."[2] Advertisements pointed to the sturdy construction, with ample storage and sleeping room. The white cloth stretched over hickory bows gave the wagon the traditional look of the prairie schooner. For locomotion, the boys chose a mule team (rather than horses or oxen), thinking that it would make good time and pull a sizeable load. They bought two draw mules and one saddle animal in South Bend; others they would acquire before reaching rugged terrain.

Ready to leave on his adventure, Stanfield experienced some doubts. Never having been away from South Bend, he had second thoughts about exchanging his comfortable life for the rough wagon trip, the hostile Indians, the hot plains and uncharted mountain paths. Traveling with a friend helped, and his family would be in Chicago for a farewell party, but the thought lingered that he might not see home again.

The beautiful spring day of departure seemed a happy omen for a good summer, and Stanfield shed his homesickness within fifty miles when he met some other South Bend people going west. These new companions provided a sense of security and rekindled his enthusiasm. His determination returned. Everyone talked of sights to be seen and pleasures to come.

Stanfield and Bartlett wanted time to become familiar with their equipment, so they employed a Negro, George Clark, to drive their wagon to Chicago.[3] The good roads of northern Indiana gave little hint of the difficulties to come on the rutted tracks and unbroken trails of the West. They soon discovered, however, that their wagon was overloaded and sent home hundreds of pounds of supplies. Like most travelers, the boys took to walking alongside the wagon, and on the way they learned about animal management. The pattern of wagon travel was beginning to take form.

Almost from the beginning the novice travelers had difficulty securing food, water, and shelter for themselves and their animals. Even in heavily populated northern Indiana accommodations were not always available. Adjustments had to be made daily—sometimes beds were uncomfortable and the food barely edible. Washing with dirty water was a new experience, but even this they wrote off with a laugh. Nothing was burdensome, as yet.

The road from South Bend to Michigan City was well established. Just west of South Bend, at Terre Coupee, it joined the main highway from Detroit to Chicago. This town and neighboring Plainfield were being eclipsed by Carlisle Hill, which lay on the Lake Shore and Michigan Southern Railroad. Carlisle Hill was a town with a future, located on the rich Terre Coupee prairie with excellent east-west rail connections.

The first major stop on the road west was Michigan City, a roaring lake-port town. Although the size of South Bend, Michigan City was a far different community. It was built around a poor harbor (which boasted a new lighthouse inspected by all visitors), but the town had prospered as Indiana's only port and as the terminus of the Michigan road. The town's commercial and industrial life was centered around the harbor, where the roaming sailors from the lake boats gave the place a slightly unsavory air.

After an overnight stop, the wagons moved toward Chicago through the small railroad towns of City West and Tolleston. The landscape was as interesting as anything that the boys were to see in their travels farther west. Shifting white sand dunes served as a curtain, open here and there to a glimpse of the blue waters of Lake Michigan. It seemed impossible that Chicago—with its 100,000 people—lay so close to this wilderness.

Stanfield and Bartlett spent a few days in Chicago. They stayed at the Myrick House, an old inn on the city's south

View of Davenport, Iowa, from across the Mississippi (c. 1854)

side. The surroundings were noisy and rough, but the inn was close to the Rock Island Railroad. Busy as he was loading his wagon on the train, Stanfield nevertheless found time to visit friends and enjoy a farewell dinner with his father and his sister Eva, who had come in from South Bend. The elaborately served meal at the new Sherman House in downtown Chicago (a hotel noted for its marble facade and plush furnishings) was a luxurious send-off.

Railroad accommodations from Chicago to Grinnell, Iowa, were excellent. The Rock Island went as far as Davenport, from which the Mississippi and Missouri line ran on to Grinnell. Stanfield's Pullman berth was a model of comfort. There also was the pleasure of seeing the Mississippi at dawn and marveling at the new railroad bridge at Davenport. The most pleasant part of the journey ended at the city of Davenport, described usually as a fine town.

Now, with the easiest part of his trip behind him, Stanfield knew that he was beginning one of the great adventures of his life.

The Diary

South Bend Ind March 22 1864

This is to be the journal of H. S. Stanfield who is about to start on a journey to Idaho Salt Lake City Oregon and California in quest of health and adventure. Anything in the shape of fun or romance that comes under the notice of the above named individual will be faithfully recorded with dates in these pages. The writer is a young man not quite 18 years of age is five feet six or eight inches in his boots has brown eyes black hair light complexion is accounted tolerably good looking and weighes 120 lbs averdupois

Tavern Seven miles from South Bend[4]

Started from home this afternoon March 23rd 1864 at two oclock with a heavy load traveled about 6 miles when we discovered that we had lost our shot gun My partner Wm S. Bartlett immediately started back to find it and after being gone about an hour returned without it much to our sorrow. We have got along so far very well only having a little trouble with our mules who did not like to pull up hill. We intended to make Plainfield[5] tonight but owing to our heavy load and the time lost in hunting the gun we have only accomplished seven miles

Ross's Barn Laporte County
7 oclock pm 26 miles From South Bend Mar 24 64

We got up this morning at 6½ oclock went out to see our team and found them all right. Went back to the house

DIARY

and washed our hands and faces with hard water and no soap wiped on a dirty rag eat a miserable breakfast which our supper repeated with very little adition. We started from our last night camp at 8 oclock this morning We concluded our load was to heavy for our mules and so left a bushel of corn and $1.25 in the landlords hands to pay for our board and lodging. We also sent 100 lbs tobacco and 40 lbs rice [and] hominy with a team which I accompanied about seven miles to Carlisle Hill from whence we shiped it home.[6] We tugged along through the mud until we came to Portland[7] otherwise called the bootjack where the road forks one branch going to Laporte the other to Michigan City at this place we took our dinner and fed & rested our mules for about an hour when we started up again and in the course of an hour or two drew up at Rolling Prairie Station where we shiped one keg pickles 100 lbs one barrel crackers 100 lbs and other things making an agregate of 380 lbs after which we started on again and drew up at this place where I write sitting on a blanket book on a cracker box by the light of a lantern Good night

Wagon Porter County 14 miles from Michigan City   Mar 25th 64 8 PM

We arose from our couch of straw in Rosses Barn this morning about six oclock fed and watered our mules eat our breakfast and started on our way at 7½ oclock AM. Near the place we stoped last night there was a man aged about sixty took it in to his head to marry and last night the boys took it into their heads to give him a serenade and about 12 oclock at night we heard about as horrible a noise as you can well imagine. boys yelling old cows bell tin pans etc. but upon the whole our first night in a barn went very well. As I said before we got started about 7½ oclock and in about half an hour passed through Springville[8] a little town of

William S. Bartlett was born in South Bend in 1843 and died in Los Angeles in 1914. After completing his journey west, he settled for a time in Oakland, California, and later became a banker of some prominence in Los Angeles. (See also the entry on Bartlett in App. I, pp. 178–79, and the note on Bartlett's family, p. 186.)

about a dozen houses. We jogged along over good and bad road until noon when we drew up at Michigan City[9] 10½ miles from our starting place where we stopped and made our dinner. After which we started again and about 3 oclock P M passed through the flourishing village of City West[10] consisting of two houses. Along the road we continualy hear of Holman and his train as being 2 or 3 hours ahead.[11] We drew up at this place about 5½ oclock having traveled 14½ miles Since dinner 24½ today pleasant dreams ho for our barn

Wagon Lake County Ind
20 miles from Chicago   Mar 25 1864[12]

We spent last night upon a downy bed of hay and for some reason or other we couldn't sleep more than 2 hours out of the whole night first we were to cold the we were in an uncomfortable position, but as all earthly things must have an end So did this night much to my joy. We started from our Dutchmans barn at seven oclock and traveled along without adventure of any kind the forenoon seeming to me the longest one I ever had anything to do with. We stoped at 11 oclock AM and fed our horses and our selves We also tryed our skill at shooting but did not do any thing to brag of. We have traveled today over the worst country I have most ever seen crossing one Rail Road 9 times and 2 other ones once or twice apiece.[13] Both the wagon and Rail Road lay on a little strip of land with water on both sides of them and where it was not wet lowland it was barren sand hills we did not see a house on one streach of land of six miles.[14] We had first stoped and put up our team for over Sunday when Fowler and Crockett[15] came along and after a long talk we decided to drive Sunday as a necessity Bartlett Brownfield and Rose went to Chicago from a station nearby in the car.[16]

Grinnell Iowa March 30th 1864

I have not had any time or place to write in this journal since I left the Dutchman barn place where I spent the night and a miserable one it was to in a wagon for the first time in my life and slept very soundly to the next morning (Sunday) we started on our journey[17] about seven oclock and traveled along without anything of moment occuring except it drizzled a little and a cold mean wind blew direct from the lake [Lake Michigan] which you may imagine was not very agreeable and the country we passed over was not the best I have ever seen well we arrived at Chicago at 3 oclock PM and were met by a number of the South Bend boys to took us to the Myrick House[18] near Camp Douglas[19] which is a very good one of its kind but of a very poor kind. The same afternoon I went down and seen Arnold[20] and took supper with him. The next day about 10 oclock A M we commenced loading our wagons on the cars and at the same time it commenced raining we had to take our wagons all a part and pack them in cars four to a car it took us about two hours and it rained about two hours. We loaded our horses[21] in the afternoon and the train started at 4 oclock P. M. most of the boys going with the train[22] but I staid over to meet my father that night I spent with Arnold and the next morning I walked around the City a while and finally drew up at the Sherman House[23] and staid there about two hours when my father and Eva came in I took dinner with them and seen them off on the cars at 5 40 PM I left at 11½ oclock P. M. took a sleeping car and took the best nap I ever had in the cars. At 7 oclock AM we crossed the Mississippi it being the first time I ever seen the Father of Waters. I had a very good breakfast at Davenport. . . .[24]

TWO | IOWA—A TRANSITION

*T*HE TWO-WEEK trip across Iowa was a fairly gentle transition into immigrant life. Although the travel difficulties were greater than those in northern Indiana, there were no real hardships. Much of Iowa was reminiscent of home, and, for the most part, young Stanfield felt at ease with the people and conditions that he encountered along the way. In Iowa the wagon traveler first learned to sleep in his wagon, to cook tolerably well, to ford streams and ferry rivers.

Of all the things in Iowa that impressed the travelers, the most distressing were the bad roads. They were the "worst in the world," and almost all diarists noted the fact, day after day.[1] The Skunk River bottoms lying across the main routes west consisted of a porous soil, and spring rains turned these lowlands into huge mudholes. The mud-clogged roads improved when they were swept dry by the wind, but at best they were deep ruts. There was little to choose between a dry washboard road and a wet slippery slough, although in hilly areas, where the rain ran off the camber, conditions were a little better.

The bad roads passed by superb Iowa farms—level and fertile, with fat cattle grazing around houses and barns. There was no prairie rawness; yet the region was not overpopulated. The absence of large timber stands, useful on any farm, was the only feature of the landscape that the immigrants criticized. Without trees breaking the horizon, the rural landscape seemed unreal. In all other respects, however, the travelers found that the farms in Iowa compared favorably with those in their homeland.

Most of the immigrants were excited at their first meeting with Indians in Iowa. Encountering Indians was nerve-tingling, just because these were the legendary wild red men. Immigrants usually talked with the "dirty beggars," gave them tobacco and trinkets, observed their splendid ponies, and absorbed the details of each brief contact. The Indians did not fit the expected image: picturesque but not formidable, they were poor people who evoked Christian sympathy.

After arriving in Grinnell, the farthest westward extension of the railroad, the usual immigrant spent a day or so in the town. He reassembled his wagon, bought more mules for the long prairie haul, and looked the place over. It resembled a New England town, and although only ten years old, already had a college. Strong abolitionist sentiment was much in evidence. The Bailey House on Main Street accommodated most visitors and, though not first-rate, was adequate.

Several wagons daily left Grinnell together for Des Moines. Their route lay along the bottoms of the North and South Skunk Rivers and extended to Newton through a region where the roads were poor but passable. Immigrants often paused in this small town that was surrounded by fine corn-producing farms. Like so many towns in Iowa, Newton had a main street bordered by a hotel, tavern, post office, school, small stores, and a blacksmith shop. It is very likely that Stanfield and Bartlett stopped at the hotel for dinner before moving on toward Des Moines over the quagmire roads. Beyond Newton, the road contained some surprises. Discarded household goods littered the route wherever chairs,

A TRANSITION

stoves—in fact, all heavy equipment—had been thrown aside to lighten loads.

The state capital, Des Moines, tied the rich agricultural region together. This political center was becoming a major outfitting site for the mass of immigrants rushing to the Montana gold fields in 1864. In the capital, where a Unionist governor was guiding the city as well as the state, a war atmosphere was evident. Like most towns of 4,000 in Ohio, Indiana, Illinois, and Wisconsin, Des Moines was responding enthusiastically to calls for troops and supplies.

From Des Moines the wagon trail lay southwestward toward Council Bluffs. The farms were good and the roads, as usual, bad. Since frost in the ground hardened the roads and made them a little more passable, immigrants were usually up and moving by seven in the morning. With the exception of the coal mines west of Des Moines, few new sights appeared, and only an occasional town gave variation to the landscape. Adel, located on the Raccoon River and settled in 1846, was one of these communities; like so many western towns, it had been founded as a stage stop. Other settlements of the same kind were encountered as the travelers moved on from Guthrie County into Cass County and to its seat at Lewis, on the East Nishnabotna River. One of these towns looked like all the others; only the inhabitants could tell them apart.

Finally, the wagons reached Council Bluffs, which overlooked the Missouri River. The city had prospered under Mormon control, from 1846 to 1852, as a supply depot for the argonauts of 1849. After the Mormons left, the city declined, but new western mining strikes were bringing a revival in 1864, and the population had grown again to 2,011. The spring immigration of that year had mushroomed. Council Bluffs now was the major departure point for the west. Wagons arrived daily by the dozen, and camped there, poised for the prairie trip. The city offered immigrants their final chance to collect supplies and mend equipment.

These last moments in civilization were filled with anxiety, but uneasy feelings were hidden under the campfire relaxation of singing and fellowship. This companionship helped to make the travelers feel secure and to banish thoughts of the dangers ahead; there would be time enough for them when the journey was resumed. Council Bluffs represented the end of one world and the beginning of another.

The Diary

Grinnell Iowa March 30th 1864[2]

... and arrived here at 1½ oclock P.M. our wagons having arrived at seven oclock the evening before. In coming over the road this morning I saw large prairies for the first but I hope not the last time in my life. We have for sometime thought our team to light and today we purchased two more mules for $175.00. I am now writing in the Bar Room of the Baily House[3] which crowded to over flowing one fellow is fiddling another dancing the rest looking. A man left here this morning for California with 39 splendid horses and 11 mules the emmigration has just commenced and this hotel is more than crowded. We intend starting some time tomorrow.

Newton Jasper County Iowa April 1 64

We started from Grinnell yesterday morning at 10½ oclock[4] Before starting we made a purchase of a second hand harness and I had to wait about half an hour to get it fitted to our new mules. We made seven miles before dinner and I caught up with the team just as they were leaving their noon camp when we hitched on our new mules and had a four mule team which pulled our wagon along nicely Some places on the road we could see for ten miles on either side. The road along which we passed was quite undulating and hilly and in some places very muddy. We saw considerable game along the road and there were some shots fired at them with no effect. This town[5] like Grinnell is very much scatered land being cheap and level people can spread as much as they please this town of 2000 occupies more ground than South Bend. Land about here as rich as Terre Coupee[6] brings from $2.50 to $5.00 an acre around Grinnell it is worth $5 00 to $20 00 for the best. We got here at 7 P.M. yesterday making 20 miles since 10 30 A M on the road we passed a man who had stuck in the mud at the bottom of a hill he wanted us to pull him out but as soon as we passed he pulled himself out

2 miles West Desmoine Iowa
April 2 1864

We stoped at Newton night before last where we had very good table and I slept with John Dunn in his wagon. The next morning we started from Newton at about seven oclock in the morning we went through Newton where we were offered one hundred dollars for our saddle mule which we refused We left the town behind with the expectation of passing some terrible roads especially in the Skunk River bottom but were very much folled and agreeably surprised at finding it so good.[7] The only really bad place being across the above named valley River and part of the way it was splendid Towards evening we inquired at several houses for barn room for our mules and at two of them were recieved almost with contempt but at last we come to the houses of a kind hearted farmer who although he had sickness in the family he allowed us to put our mules in his barn and that night we slept in the hay loft. This morning we started out about seven oclock. Most along we noticed splendid farming country and lots of cattle fine ones at that.
April 1 We saw our first Indians today in Skunk River bottom to papooses aged 11 or 12 galloped on ponies and begged tobacco which one of the boys gave them

Yesterday we traveled 21 miles and today before noon 14 miles and arrived at Desmoines at 12 oclock. DesMoines[8]

seems to be a very enterprising place covers a large tract of ground and is a great place for buisness it is the capital of Iowa the Legislature just adjourned last week and we met the Governor and members of Legislature on their way home at Grinnell. The town has probably about 4 000 inhabitants and is seperated by Desmoine river which has a bridge across it owned by a company who are outrageous in their toll[9] We passed through the City and are going to stay here at a farm house over Sunday. There is any quantity of game all along the road ever since we left Grinnell but it is very hard to get near it. We tryed to sell our extra mule today but it was no go.

April 4th 1864 2½ miles west De Moine[10]

We stoped here Saturday night with the intention of staying over Sunday. We have good stabling for our team and night before last I slept in Fowlers wagon again and slept splendidly. Yesterday morning it commenced raining and blowing four or five of us wrote home and of course they had to be taken to the post office and so Dunn Bartlett Rose & myself set out for town through mud and rain we reached there about ten oclock and stayed to a very good Dinner at the Savery House[11] we started back about three oclock P M Still Raining and as muddy as ever we got here in about an hour and it rained so hard that we all concluded to sleep in the house some in bed some on the floor nine in one room. This morning it still continues windy but has quit raining and the clouds are blowing away the sun coming out I guess we will start this afternoon or in the morning. Yesterday afternoon a company of three or four wagon and twenty or thirty lead horses they begged hard to stop here but there was no room and they had to go on through mud and rain. I thought I would go out hunting to pass away time and so started out and was gone about an hour with very poor success having seen only three pheasant and not getting a shot at them the roads about here are horrible the soil being intermixed with clay is when dry the best kind of road but when it gets a little wet is awful so on account of the roads we concluded to stop here until tomorrow and no person knows what to do with themselves it is read sleep eat talk and smoke all day and the hours drag wearily one Sunday in seven days comes very convenient but two one after another is decidedly a bore but we are making up for last week when we traveled all Sunday in order to reach Chicago in season. As I come along Saturday I noticed coal shafts in the hill sides and learned for the first time that there was coal near Des Moines and find it is almost universely used for fuel[12]

Teusday April 5th 1864 Adel Dallas Co Iowa

We started from our last place this morning at 7 oclock after paying an enormous bill for our board and lodging the morning was beautiful the ground being slightly frozen until about nine by which time it was thawed out and became very muddy and in some places miserable we stoped about 11 30 A M for dinner at a nice little plot of ground near a stream of water. We left our noon camp at 12 30 P M and started along the road which we found worse than ever and in several places we went in up to the hub of the wagons and in one place came very near swamping but we finally come until we reached this place about 5 oclock this evening having traveled 22½ miles today. We passed some beautiful farming country but it has not enough timber to suit me it is quite thinly settled and we seen any quantity of prarie chickens but did not shoot any. As soon as we reached this town we drove to the western home[13] where we are at present. three of Holmans teams got in about 6 this evening. Adel is a small town of about 800[14] inhabitants the county seat of Dallas

County the houses are mostly frame they have a brick Court House but no jail every person being Honest.[15] this day has been Beautiful

Guthrie Co Iowa April 7th 1864

We laid over at Adel all day yesterday on account of Gerrit Crocketts health and while there nothing of interest occured of any interest to this diary. We started from Adel at 8 oclock this morning and traveled over miserable roads made so by a hard rain the night before. We took dinner about eight miles from our starting place where we stoped an hour. When we started again and what praries did we see we forded a river called the middle Coon[16] it was about axle deep to our wagons and had considerable trouble getting our team across. The road this afternoon was better than this morning on account of the influence of the wind and sun. But nevertheless it was nothing to brag on. The day has been beautiful over head and rather warm at least we thought so when we walked and took off our coats. We traveled twenty miles today and when got here prarie chickens were so plenty that I was tempted and took my rifle and killed two which we expect to eat tomorrow. If this is not writen as it should be you must excuse me on my old plea that so many around me are talking I get interested and cannot write strait Pleasant dreams to you

Dalmanutha Iowa Friday April 8th 1864

We left our resting place in Guthrie County this morning about 7:30 and traveled three or four miles over splendid roads prarie chickens as thick as hops so thick indeed that I was tempted to take out my gun having in view the terrible object of destroying the life of a few. but the elements were opposed to such cruelty for just as I had commenced loading my rifle it commenced raining and by the time I had rammed down the bullet it was a right sharp shower and I concluded to get into the wagon It was well that I did for it rained harder and harder and the wind blew a perfect hurricane about this time we were crossing what is called the big prarie and is thirty miles across and I dont know how far it extended on either side but I do know that the wind has full sweep for ten or twenty miles and as the road ran along a ridge we had the full benefit of it and no house where we could put up in sight raining as though for a wager the roads soon became horrible and our cover let the water through I spread my rubber blanket along the top which done some good then John Dunn got in with us and he and Bartlett sang and we had a very good time notwithstanding the weather. We reached this place 14 miles from the starting place at 12 oclock and still raining

Sunday April 10th Cass Co Iowa

We Stayed all day yesterday at Dalmanutha a little place composed of 5 or six houses[17] In the afternoon I took my gun and started out to hunt prarie chickens and I did have to hunt them to I only seen a few but killed none. We concluded we would start out this morning if it was a nice day it being a case of necessity. The sun rose this morning in all its splendor. So after breakfast we started out the roads were terrible with innumerable hills this afternoon we crossed six or eight sloughs where the wagons sunk hub deep in the mud. The weather over head had been quite pleasant today but I am afraid it will not remain so. We have traveled nineteen miles today which is pretty good considering the roads. It does not seem to me much like Sunday yesterday seemed Sunday and this monday. We are about 70 miles from

Council bluffs and want to get there by thursday evening but I am doubtful whether we can or not considering the roads most all of the boys are or have been chicken shooting it seems from the explosion of powder more like the fourth of July than Sunday. I have another item to add since writing the above. I thought I would take our wheel mules down to a pond a quarter mile distant to water so I mounted one and led the other with nothing but halters on one took a notion to hoist his heels I did the same he come down on his feet and I on my back nobody hurt Such is life

Pottawatamie Co Iowa April 11th 1864

We left our last night camp this morning between seven and eight oclock and traveled over about 12 miles stoped at 12 oclock for dinner where stayed over an hour when we pulled out again over very good roads only the Country which has all along been very rolling become quite hilly if the roads had been as bad as yesterday with todays hills we could not have managed it. This day has been a real April one rain and shine about equally divided. About 4 oclock P. M. we passed through the thriving little town of Lewis[18] where we stoped about half an hour and near where we purchased three hundred weight of flour which added to the load we had made pretty hard pulling up the Iowa hills. This afternoon we have traveled 16 miles and reached this place by seven oclock which was very good every thing considered Council Bluffs is continuously drawing nearer and as they are our starting post we are all anxious to reach it and commence our journey over the plains. We are stoping at a farm house 8 miles west of lewis it is now about 8 oclock PM We had a very good supper but what worries us is that our mules have to stand out but they have plenty of hay and the night is clear I guess they will sleep sound they are tired enough

Council Bluffs Iowa Apr 14 64

It has now been nearly two days since I wrote in this journal and during this time we have traveled over 40 miles of Iowa roads the worst in the world At the place where we stoped Monday night we were directed to take the South fork of the road and thereby avoid a great number of long tedious hills and of course we followed directions but when we had got within 15 miles of this City we took the wrong road and instead of having nice going we run into a lot of hills and nearly broke our necks going down them but yesterday afternoon about 3 oclock P. M we arrived at this place and after hunting around for a hour or two found a camping place in the northwest portion of the City.[19] Council Bluffs contain about 3000 inhabitants most all of them living on one street there is an immense amount of business done in this place for one of its size and it is surprising to me that is not larger there are some very nice building in the place and some very poor ones. We have been around today buying we have got a tent and a stove and I dont know what. But John Dunn is waiting for me to go over to Omaha (5 miles distant) with him we are going to enquire for letters from home. Well we have been to Omaha about 6 miles distant and walked all the way I got two letters and a paper it was the first time I was ever in a territory but guess it will not be the last time. I am spending my first night in a tent there are half a dozen tents right around us and the boys are having a fine time fiddling and dancing I am very tired to indulge in anything of the kind I got a letter from home which stated that all were well would walk twenty miles any day for such a one but as I have letters to write and tis after eight oclock P.M. I will stop for the night and give my opinion of Omaha at some future day

DIARY

Council Bluffs Apr 17th 64

It is now three days since I have written in this book and during that time I have been laying idle in Camp therefore nothing has happened worth putting in this book. We have been living in our tent ever since we got it and are very much charmed with the style of living and if our food is not properly cooked we have no one to blame but ourselves. When we first came here this place was a vacant lot with nothing at all upon it but now there are a dozen wagons and seven or eight tents besides five or six team which left for California day before yesterday. We have selected a very nice place for our camp being upon the Missouri bottoms very level just on the edge of town with a creek where we water our stock running beside us. We have had two or three visits from three vagrant Indian who come around miserably dressed and present a paper stating that they are good Indians very deserving asking for money but could not see it and they left about as rich as they come. Where we are we have full benefit of the wind which sweeps over four or five miles of country and trys to blow our tent down but it is no go but for all that it is blowing very hard the hardest we have had since we have been here for by the way we have had pretty fair weather although one night was a winger and froze water for half an inch in depth it is quite a pretty day out only the wind blows hard and a little cold. Bartlett has returned from church hungry wants and I guess I will eat just to keep him company if for no other reason

THREE | ENDLESS PRAIRIES

*B*EFORE beginning the long trek across Nebraska, Bartlett and Stanfield broke up as partners. Bartlett had decided that the team was too small and inadequate for the journey, and though Stanfield felt this might be true, he wanted to continue. He relented, however, when Bartlett insisted, and in Council Bluffs they sold everything—four mules, a tent, the wagon, and harnesses—for a "good price" of $700. Then, without making any mention of what Bartlett did thereafter, Stanfield attached himself to another South Bend group, and at Fort Kearney more travelers from South Bend joined the company to make a twelve-wagon train (Journal, p. 29).

Traveling across Iowa was actually exciting when compared with the journey over the empty plains of Nebraska. The prairie crossing, which took three to four weeks, was sheer monotony. Only a few small towns and an occasional farm dotted the trail from Omaha to Fort Kearney. Fremont, on the Platte River, was typical, and quite similar to the towns on the Iowa prairie. The main street had a hotel, post office, blacksmith shop, and general store. West of town the immigrants crossed Shell Creek and, beginning to feel their isolation, often made arrangements to travel with other wagons. Occasionally they passed a house or two, presumptuously identified as a town; such was "Eldorado," east of Columbus. Larger towns, like Columbus, were important as supply stations and stage stops. At Columbus the tricky Loup River had to be crossed in a rope ferry. A rope held the ferry until it was loaded; then the rope was released, and the ferry floated downstream until it struck the shore or a sand bar. Stanfield later noted in his journal that the ferry took the wagons only across the main channel (which was forty feet wide) and required the wagon owners to negotiate the remaining two or three hundred feet of the river bed. The immigrants denounced the ferry as an "unprincipled monoply."[1]

Reaching Fort Kearney on the Platte was a sort of milestone. Established in 1848, this "Guardian of the Trail" had sheltered thousands of immigrants. War had reduced its troops, but in April, 1864, new units of the Ohio Cavalry were sent in. (The Ohio Cavalry consisted in part of Confederate prisoners who had taken an oath of allegiance to the Union and enlisted in the Union army, on the understanding that they would be assigned duty in the West to fight the Indians.)[2]

The Fort itself was a typical western garrison. Visitors were unimpressed with its four-acre parade ground surrounded by cottonwood trees, rundown barracks, officer quarters, sutler stores, and a hospital. The high-flying American flag offered the only bright contrast to the scene. Two miles away was the adobe town of Kearney, consisting of saloons and dives frequented by soldiers and avoided by most wagons.[3]

At Fort Kearney wagons usually organized into trains, pledging to abide by common rules of travel until they reached their destination. This arrangement was recommended by the army, for the possibility of Pawnee or Sioux attacks increased with each mile westward. Guards were regularly posted at night, since even within sight of the Fort the Indians were thieves if not killers.

The next segment of the trip west covered the plains from

Fort Kearney to the Scottsbluff area.[4] Many travelers followed the south side of the Platte, but Stanfield's group remained on the north, following this shoreline even as they took the River's north branch. The trail was rougher than the roads in Iowa and seemed to be endless. The wide plains, empty except for prickly pear and low sandhills, extended from the river to distant mountains. The short prairie grass growing sparsely along the rivers was seldom sufficient feed for the stock. The men passed their days walking alongside the wagon, daydreaming. At night there was never a farmhouse-inn for rest; never a warm bed or shelter for the animals; never a hot meal prepared by a competent cook.

There was, however, an occasional moment of natural beauty.[5] Prairie fires against the night skies created a fairyland—delightful when the wind kept flames away from camp. The Platte River was a bizarre sight, hardly a river at all— by turns too wide or too shallow, too swift or too sluggish. Equally unreal for the Midwesterner were the prairie grass, sagebrush, prickly pear, and colorful wild flowers rising out of the barren sand. The best sights were the strange natural formations—Castle Rocks, Chimney Rock, and Courthouse Rock. Every traveler looked at them with awe.

Wild animals along the trail also created excitement. Occasionally, to pass the time, immigrants hunted the plentiful buffalo. The buffalo herds were magnificent to behold—the grand lords of the prairie. There were also antelopes and deer, darting at the first sign of danger, moving with frightened swiftness away from the intruders, as did the prairie chickens and jack rabbits—each a good meal if the inexperienced rifleman had luck. Other animals were a danger; wolves and coyotes would attack any animals that were left unguarded in the train.

Travelers in this area were especially nervous about the Indians. Pawnees were the most numerous around Fort Kearney and along the Platte, but their enemies the Sioux had not abandoned the area. Both tribes favored surprise attacks, and immigrants were wary even when everything seemed peaceful. Fort Kearney's commander sought to assure peace by employing the Pawnees, and although the Indians seemed calm in this summer of 1864 the travelers never felt secure. In fact, just a few months after Stanfield passed by, devastating raids took place throughout the area.

All in all, Nebraska Territory offered few compensations for its hardships. Nature's exciting landmarks were few and far between, and her barriers were everywhere.

The Diary

2½ miles east Fremont N. T Apr 24th

It has been just one week since I last wrote in this journal having been so busy part of the time and not having anything to write about But a great change has taken place since I last used this book but as I said before I have had no opportunity to put it down. In the first place Bartlett took it into his head to sell out and sell out we must We finaly hit upon some persons who were going to Idaho who give us a reasonable price for every thing we had except personal property it was friday that they took possession and the same day I made arrangements to go with C.W. Carleton & Co[6] buying out one quarter and with the purchase money with some more we bought another span of mules which we put on for leader a head of the splendid pair he had before so have got according to our notion as good a team as there is on the road. About friday noon Fowler & Co and Crockett and Co pulled up stakes and left for Idaho but we stayed until Saturday noon when we pulled up and left[7] We drove to the ferry where we crossed and entered Omaha the Capital of Nebraska it is a town containing about four or five thousand inhabitants[8] it is very well laid out and very well built for a town of its age being as I understand only about six years settled it is situated on the Missouri river it contain quite a nice capitol built upon an imposing hill which commands a splendid view for miles around Omaha appears when looking at it from Council Bluffs to be only about a mile distant but is actualy six miles off it built upon a nice slope and will in time make a beautiful city every thing in that city like it is in the Bluffs is very high in price. We stoped there about an hour and then started upon our long journey across the plains we only made about six miles from Omaha the first day and camped We got up this morning rather late and did not get started until 8½ oclock A M although it is Sunday we concluded it just as well to travel[9] as to lay bye where we were notwithstanding our late start and although we stoped over an hour at noon we reached this place 28 miles from our starting place about 6½ oclock this evening we passed quite a number of teams some camped over Sunday. We also met 6 or 10 Indians I expect before we get through they well be quite a common sight we hope to overtake Fowler before tomorrow night by traveling early and late. Hurrah for bed

Shell Creek N. T. Apr 25 1864[10]

We started from our last nights camping ground at 7½ oclock this morning and traveled until noon without anything of interest transpiring. We stoped for dinner about 12 miles west of Fremont[11] where we stayed 1½ hours when we continued our journey occasionally meeting a few stray Indians and in one place seen twenty or more Indian ponies grazing near a wigwan made of hay.[12] We struck the Platte about three oclock this afternoon it is a singular kind of a stream being about half a mile wide and full of sand bars so as to render it unnavigable the bottom of it is I understand covered with quick sand I do not know how deep it is but it is very muddy and the banks are but five or six feet high still they say it never overflows it is fed principally by mountain streams and our road follows it for six or seven hundred miles if not more so we will see more of it before we get through I am very much impressed with the country we have passed over today it is generaly very good soil and as level as a floor a better farming country than Iowa. A great many places we saw the ground plowed up and prepared for grain but it had no fence around by which I suppose the cattle not very troublesome in this section for the first 20 or 30 miles out of Omaha it was quite rolling and hilly but is now as smooth as you could wish for every few miles we see a house and in some places little towns but how people could bear to live here isolated from all the rest of the world I can not tell I am sure I would not like it For the last five or six nights we have been almost surrounded by prarie fires presenting a most grand and sublime scene one for a painter and especially tonight it is within a quarter of a mile of us the night is is clear and beutiful a cool south wind blowing and the fire burning grandly.[13] About seven oclock this evening just as we reached our camping place we found Fowler and Crockett had reached here before us and were camped for the night so we have caught them at last and shall endeavor to stay with them throughout our trip they hardly expected us so soon thinking we would not leave the Bluffs until today but they were mistaken as we come along today we met some freight teams returning to Omaha and the drivers were a hard looking set even worse than the Indians themselves sun burned dirty and ragged such is life on the plains the fire is so bright I can read fine print ¼ mile distant but tis 10 oclock I must to bed

3 miles west of Columbus Apr 26th

We pulled up this morning and started at 7½ oclock. What a change sometimes occurs in a few hours yesterday was warm and beautiful with a gentle southern breeze and seemed as though it never could get cold again but last night about ten oclock the wind shifted to the north and come near blowing the beautiful fire I spoke about into our tents it blew harder and harder every minute so that towards morning it became a perfect hurricane[14] it also became very cold the wind freezing you almost to the marrow but the wind could not check us and as I said we started the dust blowing in clouds. We stoped at Eldorado a town consisting of one house post office and store combined we took our noon bite there started forward and reached Columbus a little town on loup fork[15] about 3 oclock in the afternoon ½ mile beyond this place we crossed the fork or rather about twenty feet of it on an old fashioned ferry boat and had to drive 2 or 3 hundred through the water some places up to the hub with quick sand bottom we had to pull or sink they charged us $1 75 for crossing.[16] We traveled 3 miles and put up here having come twenty five miles by 5 oclock We are baking bread for the first time.

Silver Creek N. T. Apr 27th 64[17]

This morning broke cold cloudy dreary we started about 7½ oclock went about a mile stoped sometime to get some horse shoes fixed at a blacksmith shop the wind continued to blow increasing in force every minute and after a while it commenced to rain we traveled until noon when we put up here at a ranch where we obtained stabling and hay for our animals and concluded to stay until tomorrow. As we were coming along this morning about 9 oclock we saw a few steps from the road a grave it was from all appearance that of a child buried miles away from any house it had a head board with the initial J. H. D. It seems so sad to die and be buried away out civilization and be all alone with the Indian and prarie wolves only for companion but I suppose if a person is prepared for it it makes no difference where they die or are buried they will be found on the resurection day as well as those who are buried in magnificent cemetery splendid vaults with the pomp and ceremony of the world and with beautiful monuments to mark their resting place with a pompous epitaph instead of a simple cottonwood board with just the initial it is all the same at the last day

Some place N T April 28 1864

This morning was but a slight improvement upon that of yesterday the only difference being that it was warmer we started out about our usual time it continued the same for an hour or two when it grew colder and after a while became warmer and rained I bet it rained it just poured down in a steady stream this was about eleven oclock an no house in sight in about 2 hours we seen a house at a great distance and it took another hour to reach it by which it was about two oclock we found to our great discomfiture that he had no barn room or any hay but we had to feed our teams and ourselves raining all the time. We were told that we might find cover and hay for our mules about nine miles ahead. We went five miles when we seen a house with a pretty large stable but already full so we come a mile and one half further and arrived at this place 25 miles from our starting point we get stable room but no hay raining all the time it is the first rain in these parts since last harvest it has now stoped but still remains cloudy. A great number of the stable along the road are made of sod and covered with poles brush and hay it make a warm stable. They make them so on account of the scarcity of timber. but I must write home and the page is full

Nebraska May 2d 64

It has been several days since I have writen in this journal during which time we have had some good and more bad weather things have been going on as monotonously as possible until yesterday which was a very disagreeable day being very windy and cold toward evening but I have got a head of my story about noon we came to the Platte opposite Fort Kearney where we came up with some more St Jo boys who had gone ahead from Council Bluffs, we camped near them put up our tent picketted our mules and some of us started to cross the river to the Fort for letters we had to go about three miles down the river to reach the fording place it is the querest river I ever saw I do not believe it has a chanell any place more than seven feet deep and where we crossed there must have been a dozen chanels for it is two miles wide after we crossed two or three of them we we on a large Island which we thought the main shore but discovered to our chagrin that we were not more than quarter way across we finally reached shore and then the fort which is a little hamlet composed of 20 or 30 houses besides five whoping big stables where they keep cavalry horses for the two hundred cavalry man that are stationed there. I went to the post office and got three letters and five papers which were quite acceptable we then returned across the river of many chanells which if it had one deep one would be of immense value to this country instead of being merely a large sewer used for the purpose of draining the Rocky mountains. We returned to our tents and two of our men stood guard the first guard that has been set over our wagon since we started[18] We are now out on the plains there are a dozen wagons in our train and will be about thirty in our camp tonight I expect to have to go out on guard this evening and stand for two hours. We have camped near the only water within ten miles

Platte River May 4 1864

Exciting events have come to pass within the last 36 hours Yesterday morning before we started five of our train and two of our company set out on a Buffalo hunt going to a range of bluffs directly north of us which appeared to be ½ mile distant but was in reality 6 or 8 miles They intended to overtake us at a creek 25 miles from the starting point but for some reason or other we passed the creek and made about 35 miles that day starting at 6½ oclock and traveling until 7½ in the evening in order to find wood and water but succeeded in finding only the later it was the bigest days travel we have yet made having traveled over thirteen hours for we only stoped ¾ hours at noon About 10 oclock in the morning we seen a couple of antelope the first I ever had seen they were coming toward our wagons and got within ¼ miles when the turned and run from us one of the men shot at them which although it missed them served to quicken their speed and soon placed them beyond the range of any gun in our crowd. There was a man who had been traveling with our train who was possessed of from fifteen to twenty mules that he allowed to run loose we camped on the river and he camped up above us on the same stream About an hour after we arrived at camp a wolf got in among his mules and stemped them when a mule once get scared (and it is very easy to scare them) they have even less reason than a frightened horse. They come pell mell like a young thunder storn right toward our camp and frightened some of our stock almost to death three of them running right over one mans tent he barely escaping as it fell to the ground. They did not run far before we caught them and took them back but they had been there but a short time before the started again but were checked before they done any damage after which we made him take them down below us for the always ran the way the come that day after they moved we had no more trouble with them. I did not have to stand guard night before last as I expected but my time come last night from 12½ until 2½ A M and between late traveling stampedeing and guarding I had no sleep until three oclock this morning and got up at five. it was my first watch there were about a dozen wagons and forty or fifty animals that me and my partner had to watch with the wolves howling around one time they come very near stampedeing our horses for they got within ¼ mile and commenced howling all of a sudden which brought the horses to their feet in less than no time but the wolves were scared of by the dogs and we had no more trouble with them. This morning about 8 oclock our buffalo hunters made their appearance having walked near fifty miles yesterday they stayed all night with a party of emigrants who gave them their supper and a place to sleep they walked seven miles that morning to catch up with us this morning and they were just about used up they only seen a few buffalo and could not get near them so they had their walk for nothing but I must help get supper so good night

Platte River May 7th /64

We have been jogging along at our usual rate for the last two or three days before I left home I was told by old Californians that the roads were the nicest in the world that they were perfectly hard and as level as a floor but I have not seen it yet they must be on the south Platte for our roads has been a continuation of sand hills [dry] creeks & sloughs with some level good roads ever since we left Kearney.[19] It has been threatening rain for several days and today about ten oclock we got it and it lasted until two. We arrived at this camp at eleven this morning raining as.hard as it knew how during which storm we pitched our tents unharnessed our mules and picketed them out. We are right beside the road about half mile distant from the river from which place we carry all the water we use for cooking and I tell you it is the farthest I ever carried it for it seemed like a mile before I got back with the water.[20] About noon we saw a great number of Buffalo come down to the river on the opposite side to drink there were to all appearance four or five hundred they are the first we have seen on this trip they lingered on the bluffs on the other side of the river for two or three hours the Platte is near a mile wide at this point but some our boys attempted to ford it in order to ge a shot at the wild bovines we had all spoke for our parts of Buffalo meat and the hunters started out in the rain but the grapes were sour for before they had gone a dozen rods from shore before the water reached their middles and they were afraid of stepping into a hole and losing their guns so the returned without accomplishing their object the buffalo remained grazing in sight on the side of the bluffs as though they wished to aggravate us by seeing but not being able to reach them. We had some miserable sand hills today and the prospect of worse ones tomorrow. We resolved to stop here this afternoon and travel tomorrow but I would rather stop tomorrow to but I cannot do anything against a whole crowd of them. I have not seen a house since I left Kearney last Monday morning but nevertheless can not realize that I am on the plains it is so different from what I expected nothing but hills on both sides

Sand Hill Creek N. T. May 11th 1864

We left the Platte river camp early next morning and traveled all day as usual the roads in some places being good in others miserable we went about 25 miles that day and camped by the side of Goose Creek[21] a miserable little stream of water emptying into the Platte. That evening we took a vote wether or no to stay there the next day and recruit our teams and concluded to do so. Just as we arrived at our camp we seen a couple of deer about 30 rods from our wagons and the boys all rushed out each one determined to have the first shot the result was that they all missed them but one of the boys followed them to an Island in the Platte about three miles distant and so a lot of us made up our minds to have a deer hunt next day so we started for the Island 9 of us (which was a mile long and from ¼ to ½ wide) at 7 oclock next morning some of us crossed to the Island others stayed on the bank to keep them from getting off there were more deer there than I ever saw together in my life some of the boys counted as high as 15 we killed six that we got and do not know how many we lost but do know we got enough to supply the train in venison for more than a week and left some on the ground about 7 oclock that evening and heard the cry of sand storm rushed out of the tent and sure enough here it come in a regular cloud but we got our wagons staked down and so sustained no injury except the tearing of our tent it was only a light one or we might have been hardly used as it was several tents were overturned. We bought a quarter of an antelope of an of an Indian the other day it is as good meat as I ever tasted although he made a miserable job in cleaning it and we had to wash it half a dozen times yesterday morning we struck our tents early and started toward sunset part way the road was very good and hard but in some places the sand was 4 or 5 inches deep and we had some steep pulls through just such sand I have heard considerable about the good roads on the plains about it being just as hard as a floor but have not yet seen them they must be across the river for I am sure they are not on the north side notwithstanding the mean roads we traveled 28 miles and I walked 20 of it the bigest day walk I ever made and Ill bet I was tired that evening when we camped at the foot of a big sand hill that we have been dreading ever since Kearney and I tell you it was a socker[22] We camped last night on Wolf Creek[23] and this morning bright and early put eight mules on a head of our wagon and went over the hill which is the worst on the road We camped this noon on the Platte and across the river was a large camp of Indians and a mile up the river was another from both of which we had visits all of them wanting to swap or begging one of them was the oldest one I ever saw being gray headed and looking one hundred years old and as good natured as you please with hands as soft as a womans. We made twenty miles today and camped on Castle Creek[24] at three oclock where we now are and are going to have supper after a while which is a thing we all relish.

Platte River Montana May 16th 1864[25]

It is about five days since I last touched this book I must be excused for not writing oftener on the plea of urgent business[26] but this evening we had a cold supper and there being no work for me to do I took advantage of the opportunity to use my pen a little. We have had hot sultry weather for several days past and were it not for a breeze most always stirring we would almost suffocate for when it does slacken we can hardly breathe. Within the last few days we have witnessed some grand freaks of nature such as the ancient Rocks resembling the ruins of ancient castles or reminding a person of a city that has been burned the walls of the houses only standing in all sorts of fantastical shapes the continued for about two hours by which time we had passed out of sight. We also had a fine view of Chimney Rock which is one of the greatest curiosities to be seen on the plains. We could see it 1½ days before we arrived opposite it and for a day after we had passed it.[27] Then there was the court house Rock resembling the remains of some old Court House and various other Rocks of curious forms out in one place it looked as though there was a city a few miles off but it was only rocks. The distances here are very deceptive some places seeming only about ½ mile were in fact seven or eight miles distant.[28] I had seen no house for two weeks until today I come upon the Indian agency[29] a log house white washed we have seen any quantity of Indians. This day has been quite windy and very dusty this evening the wind increased to a gale and for 1 or 2 hours blew terrifically blowing gravel like hail and cutting almost like knives but it has subsided and is getting to dark to write

FOUR | INTO THE MOUNTAINS

*L*EAVING Scottsbluff and continuing along the North Platte, the immigrants reached Laramie, "Queen of the Frontier Forts." This Indian camping ground at the confluence of the Laramie and North Platte rivers had become a fur-trading post in 1834 and after 1849 was government-controlled. Even in the war years it was fully garrisoned, since it linked east-west communications. Travelers looked over the Fort while picking up their mail and found it much like Kearney. One diarist—Katherine Dunlap, who made the overland trip in 1864—thought that the soldiers were insolent and noted that they were ". . . no protection to the immigrant at all." Another immigrant, a man, expressed similar doubts—he believed the soldiers had all they could do to take care of themselves.[1] Still, for the majority of travelers, this isolated post was a symbol of security.

For many of the wagoners there now arose the question of whether to head toward California, Oregon, or Montana, and some of them undoubtedly asked themselves which prospect looked brightest. In 1864 many voted for the new gold strikes in Montana.

A decision to go to Montana forced the immigrant to leave the established trails to California and Oregon and to enter a roadless wilderness that was inhabited and dominated by Indians. Indeed, as he attempted to open a new trail, he was

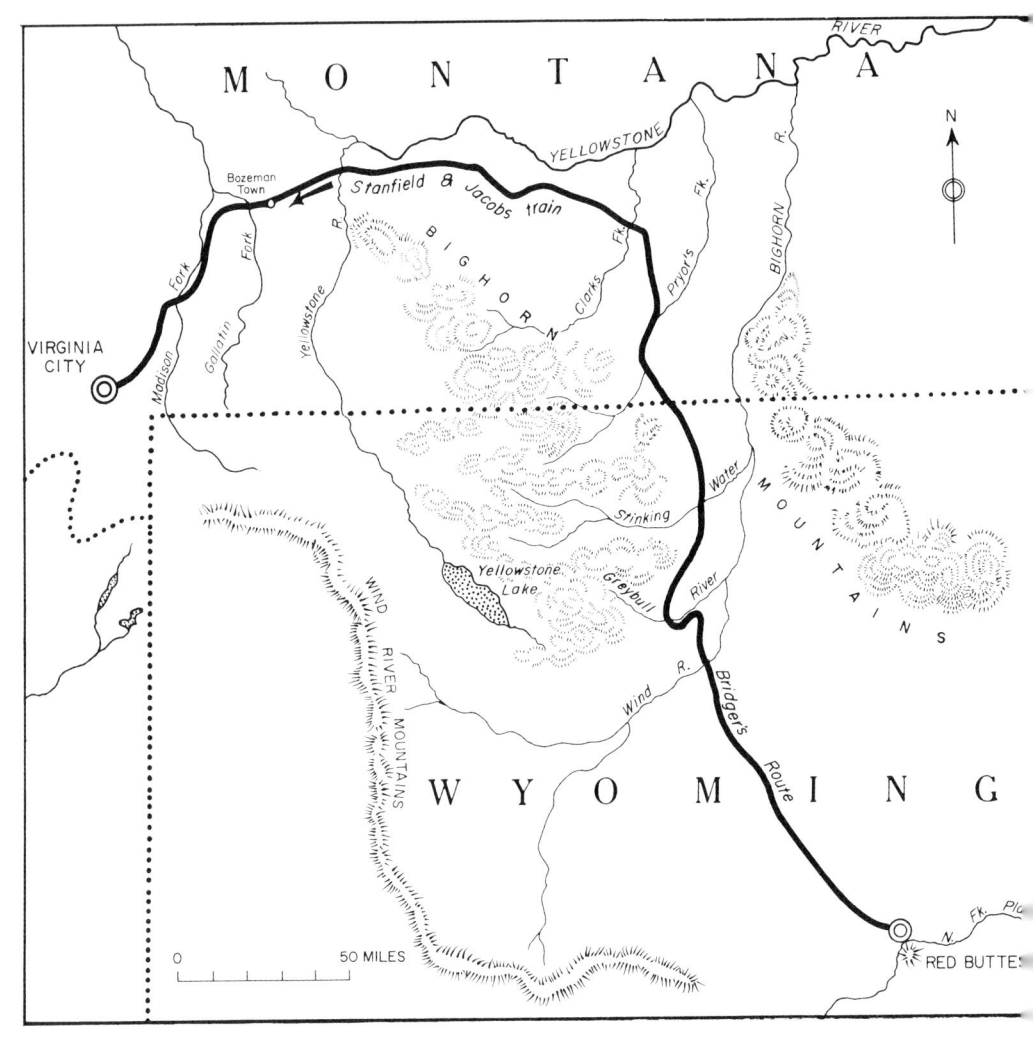

SECOND STAGE OF JOURNEY

Stanfield's route from Virginia City, Nev., to Salt Lake City is not known, but he may have followed the same one that was used stage coaches in 1864. See Notes, pp. 202

confronted by the same difficulties that had faced his predecessors in 1849.

Most travelers stopped briefly at Alder Clump west of Fort Laramie, and moved on to Red Buttes with mounting excitement as plans took shape for the final leg of the trip to the gold fields in Montana. Stanfield and his Hoosier companions decided to attach their twelve wagons to a train of sixty going to Virginia City. They agreed to travel together—partly for protection and partly to pool funds and hire a competent guide.

The man employed was a mountaineer named John M. Jacobs. Jacobs, rather oddly described as a "red-bearded Italian," seemed well suited for the job. In 1862–63, with John M. Bozeman, he had searched for a shorter route to the West and had successfully reached the headwaters of the Missouri River. On this trip Jacobs took his train over the Yellowstone Cut-Off rather than follow the Bozeman Trail, which he had helped blaze.[2] This route offered a chance to prospect in the Bighorn Mountains along the way and also was less exposed to Indian attacks than the Bozeman Trail, which lay east of the mountains. The drawback was that it did not yet exist! Just ten days before, Jim Bridger,[3] the most famous of all western guides, had left the North Platte with a train bound for Virginia City over this route, blazing the path as he traveled. Bridger's trail crossed from the North Platte into the Bighorn Valley, then moved northward, fording or following successively the Greybull, Stinking Water (Shoshone), and Clarks Fork rivers. Turning west he followed the Yellowstone, forded the Gallatin Fork, and reached the Madison.

The wagons in Jacobs' train plodded toward Virginia City, and by the middle of June they had caught up with the slower-moving, trail-breaking company that was being led by Bridger, and thereafter kept pace with it. Gradually, however, Jacobs lost the confidence of his train; he was criticized for just following Bridger (instead of acting as a real guide), for failing to locate good feeding and watering places, for drinking inordinately, and for acting like a dictator. (Later, in his journal, Stanfield noted that the "greeneys" in the company who had hired Jacobs did not realize that the Bridger train was, in effect, laying out the road.) By July 6 most of Jacobs' wagons had attached themselves to Bridger. Two days later, with Virginia City almost in sight, the Bridger train began to break up as many wagons struck out on their own to race to the gold city. Most of the Indiana wagons joined in the dash on July 9, but Stanfield chose to take his time, save his mules, and move at a leisurely pace into the city. He arrived on July 10 and found a rough mining town that had scarcely existed a year before.[4] Gold had been discovered there in May, 1863, and hundreds of prospectors had rushed in. That year the strike yielded over ten million dollars, and much of the easy money went into liquor, gambling, and prostitution. The economy hinged on speculative mining, and since no one knew how long the riches would last, Virginia City lived for the day.

Stanfield noted in his journal that at least one half of Montana's resident population were "sharpers" and "cut throats," and Virginia City seems to have had its share. He says that four large gambling houses and a great number of houses of prostitution were permitted to operate without restriction, and he saw cock fights being held openly on one of the town streets (pp. 67–68). The blatant acceptance of vice made it easy to label the city a "God forsaken place." The physical appearance of the town—and its inhabitants—was equally dismal. High prices, shoddy services, lawlessness, and poor housing were also characteristic.

The more optimistic Montana *Post* (Aug. 27, 1864) reported that visitors to Virginia City were impressed with its size and business activity and noted, rather ambiguously: "That it is a fast place none will doubt" (p. 3).

Nevada City, located a quarter of a mile from Virginia City, Stanfield found equally unpromising. At the Nevada City mines the sight of the miners—who worked standing knee-deep in water—discouraged Stanfield from trying a similar occupation. Though Virginia City had been Stanfield's objective, he decided to move on. Mining was hard and often unrewarding work, and Stanfield felt that the land was unsuitable for cultivation. Other immigrants were also disappointed. Some—like his South Bend friends Fowler and Crockett—went on to California while others headed back home.

Although Indian raids along the trails into Virginia City had been increasing daily, Jacobs' train escaped any such experience. His wagons were regularly approached by Indians asking for gifts, and the immigrants passed out food, tobacco, clothing, and trinkets—glad to keep the peace at so small a price. These contacts gave the immigrants an opportunity to observe the western Indians at first hand. The Flatheads especially seemed to be stable, good-looking, intelligent men, and the immigrants contrasted them with the dirty and lazy Cheyenne and Sioux who begged and loafed about the government agency twenty-five miles east of Fort Laramie on the North Platte. Innocuous as all these Indians appeared to be, the immigrants knew they were not to be trusted. It was always a relief when the Indians moved on.[5]

Large trains gave protection against Indian raids but had serious drawbacks. Early morning starts were impossible and so the best traveling hours were lost, while early evening stops were essential to assure accommodations for the many wagons; noon stops could never be brief; grass for the stock was hard to find; and serious sickness in one wagon brought the whole train to a halt.

Health hazards plagued most travelers, and medicine was scarce.[6] Even a healthy traveler could not adjust to the freezing cold in the mountains, coming so quickly after the heat of the prairies. The problem of adjusting to the weather was intensified by the fatigue resulting from three months of travel, inadequate food, and enormous physical exercise. Hardly any immigrant had ever walked twenty-five miles a day, day after day; and most were unaccustomed to a diet lacking any garden freshness. These conditions produced illness and sometimes death.

Nevertheless, the immigrants were drawn together by their hardships. Among most of the wagon travelers there was a characteristic feeling of collective responsibility, a constant awareness that they all depended on one another for survival.

The Diary

Noon Camp near Platte May 22 64

We are stoping here for an hour or two to let our stock graze and as I will have nothing to do within that time I embrace the opportunity to write in my journal once more. We stayed two miles from Fort Laramie[7] on this side up the river all day Wednesday and John Dunn and my self went across the river to get letters. I got two and he got none We crossed the river on a ferry. We left the camp near Laramie Thursday morning the road has been very rough and hilly ever since in some places very steep almost perpendicular so we have not made very good time we crossed the black hills one of which I ascended from the top of which I had a very fine view of the surrounding country Laramies peak[8] the third highest in the country has been in sight for three or four days and the top is today enveloped in clouds. It has rained every day since we have been in the hills always in the afternoon and clears up by dark the next morning the sun rises beautifully and continues fine until afternoon when it commences to thunder and lightening and then rain I expect we will have it this afternoon again Friday noon we reached Alder Clump a grove near a couple of beautiful little springs about thirty miles from the fort[9] and as it looked very dark and lowering we concluded to stay until next day it rained very hard for about three hours when it slackened and the sun come out about that time we heard that **Wm Fowler** the son of one of our train was dying in his fathers wagon of consumption and in about an hour he was dead he died very easy poor fellow he expected that the trip would cure him but instead of that it killed him We dug a grave on a hill near by at the side of four other graves and in it we buried him and marked his grave so that his father can obtain his remains at some future day which he intends doing. We started this morning about six oclock traveled until after ten and stoped here to let our stock graze on the fine grass which abounds in this spot Larmie looms up in the distance head and shoulders above the rest of the range. I just heard it thunder which confirms any belief that we will have rain this afternoon I have heard that we will have it every day for a month but I hope it will not prove true[10]

Yellow Stone Cut-Off May 30 64

Some time ago some or rather most of our boys took it into their head that they wanted to go by the Yellow Stone Cut-Off so as to pass the big Horn Mountains[11] and stop and prospect they having heard that there was better diggins there than at Virginia City this cut-off is a new route not yet surveyed and scarcely ever traveled in fact we are the second large train that ever passed over it the first numbering 80 wagons started out a week from friday under the guidance of Major Bridges[12] we are part of a train composed of 72 wagons under a man named Jacobs we started this morning we were for some time in doubt as to whether we should take this road or not but finally concluded to go with the crowd

Yuba County Cal Aug 22 1864

There has been considerable lapse of time between the date on the last page and the date of this one and the places have been placed on the geography of our country at a very great distance apart but I will account for my neglecting my journal in this way I could not write while the wagon was in motion and when it stoped for the night I would immediately have to commence unhitching the team or rather help doing it and then there would be the tent to pitch the water and wood to get sometimes carrying them both ½ mile then would come supper and washing the dishes after which I would like to have a social chat during which it would get dark I would be tired and go to bed leaveing the journal untouched in the mornings and at noon I would either have no time or no dispositions to write and so it went and I resolved to give it up but have kept a little journal in my memmorandom book and now having plenty of time and to spare I shall try and complete what I have begun taking the memmorandom book aided by my memory for a guide I see nothing noted in memmorandum book from the time we left the old road until we arrived at the Big Horn river but I find it noted in my memory the first three or four days on the new road feed and water were most fearfully scarce that we crossed what was almost a desert 70 miles in width on which we had a tight pinch to get grass for our stock on the evening of the first day during which we traveled 15 miles five of the teams turned back concluding to take the old road[13] this left our train 67 wagons[14] which we found to be entirely to large to make good times the best sized train is composed of about ten or twelve teams which will generally have sufficient men for guard or in case of trouble there not being so much fear of an attack from the Indians and then there will not be so much much to delay a train of that size as there would be a larger not so much sickness you can get off earlier in the morning need not stop so long at noon travel later in the evening and after all get more feed for the stock. But we were compelled to go in large trains for fear of the Indians who were very few in numbers and a peaceful as kittens. But of course as we were about passing through a new country which had never been traveled before Bridgers train passed over two weeks ahead of us therefore we thought it necessary to be cautios and paid a guide between three and four hundred dollars to pilot us through when we had no earthly neccessity for him save to tell the train when to move and when to stop which he did in an outrageous manner swearing at the men as though he were a pirate and the men his slaves I have frequently wondered why they submited to it and occasionally he did catch a tartar much to the delight of the rest of the train. He was withal and without exception the greatest coward in the train and also the most extravagant lier he would never leave the train half a mile he once lost his pony went back a ways after it come back to camp and said it was so deseased that was not fit to bring along but afterwards a train behind our brought the pony up all right[15] as I said before we had no use for him any man in his place could be selected from the train and small train traveled without molestation over the road all ready laid out by Bridger. Our train saw but very few Indians not over fifty on the whole route and they were as polite and civil as it is possible for the sons of the forest to be in their own native home they were of the flathead tribe they were not like the pawnees or Siouxs for they never asked for a thing nor stole a pennys worths from us but if you would offer them anything they would gladly accept of it. If any party of Indians had had the temerity to attack our train they would have been well recieved for there were near a thousand shots in our train in the hands of several hundred men one night while laying on Clarks fork we had a false alarm which amounted to nothing. We seen nothing of the crows or Snakes the two tribes who inhabit the territory we passed over. But we did see sage brush and prickly pear to our heart content miles and miles of it covering millions of acres of the most miserable soil I had ever seen up to that time. I was very much surprised to see prickly pear which at home is a hot house plant growing in such profusion on such ground.

Big Horn River Wed. June 8th 1864[16]

Crossed the River today with 66 wagons 218 men 250 head of stock in Eleven hours in a ferry boat built by Maj Bridger This is the first entry I find in my memmorandum book since the one that gave notice of our departure from the main or rather what had been up to then the main traveled route. But this is not telling what memory knows of the Big Horn Well hear it comes (but as memory is very treacherous you must not expect much) We arrived on the banks of the above named river on the afternoon of the seventh expecting either to find an established ferry or a boat left by Bridgers train but if neither we were determined to build one for the river was to deep to ford and turn back we would not but fortunately just as we got there a small train calling themselves the Independant consisting of ten wagons which had arrived the day before and had been searching for the boat ever since had found it buried in the sand on the opposite side but were not strong enough to launch to so our arrival was very oppotune and the assisstance of a number of our men who swam the river they soon got it afloat and took the Independents across and the next day come our turn. We commenced early in the morning the smaller and weaker ones being sent out to guard the stock while the larger and stronger ones were detailed in squads to manage the boat I come under the head of stock guard and of course having such a competent person as my self on the list the stock were well guarded except when the guard happened to be playing cards or sleeping which not unfrequently the case. The wagons were first all ferried across which took until late in the afternoon[17] and then we swam the the stock across in small herds every thing was got across in safety for all I and my party come very near haveing one of our mules drowned and just as we had got the last thing across here come three men on horse back from

Bridgers train stating that they were the owners of the boat had authority to establish a ferry and would like to have us fork over three or four dollars apiece but very singularly we could not see probably on of approaching night fall making it quite dark

Friday 10th June 1864 on the Big Horn

This is the next date and now that I think of it I recall to my mind that the next day after crossing the river we shook the dust from our feet and took our departure from the ferry after burying the boat in the sand and leaving notice of its whereabouts for the benefit of the next train the pretended owners of the boat seeing how little they made out of our train had retired in disgust to ponder no doubt upon the stinginess of this world. But I have wondered from my subject I suppose we traveled all day thusday and over some rough roads etc for they abound in that country but although only a supposition yet it is very near correct without any doubt. We started as usual on friday morning but camped at noon on the before mentioned which we had been following since we crossed it and here at noon we camped and remained all that day and the whole of the not moving until Sunday morning on account of the sickness of a child who died on Saturday of scarlet fever. While at this camp I took occasion to perform an operation generaly alloted to the washer woman that of washing clothes for my own dear self it not the first time that I have done this same thing but this time I had something call water a kind of compromise between mud & water but I finally worried it through and got them wet and then dry if not clean.[18] The book says that while at this camp I was over on an Island thinking of home. Well I do remember crossing over to the Island and thinking the folks at home were doing or thinking about while I was hundreds of miles yes a thousand of them away from home out in the Big Horn but then even though I say it I have never once regretted taking this trip nor once wished myself home should have said but once that comes a good while after I had left the Big Horn and all its tributaries and has been all over with for some time

Sunday June 12th 1864

The entries now become more frequent. On the 12 of this month buried the child that I have already mentioned as dying of fever the day before She was a bright interesting little girl probably about four or five years of age and had only been sick for a few days the physcian was of the opinion that she could have been saved if could have had clear pure water to drink for where she drank half mud the medicine could have no effect She was buried just before we started and the train passed on and no more was thought (except by friends) of the little girl we left on the lonely prarie. Where we camped that night may be known by some but I am not of that body for my memordum guide does not speak of it and my memory has failed me. I do not remember Mondays tramp except when the book and my memory both tell me it was on the evening of that when we forded the Gray Bull[19] not a very elegant name but as a faithful historian I must give the name of the places wheter elegant or inelegant. It is a beautiful stream very swift and narrow with a rocky bottom not to deep to ford. We camped on the opposite side that night A herd of buffalo 5 miles lots of hunters some buffalo killed could not bring to camp to far

Gray Bull River June 14th 1864

This day we only made a short drive of 12 miles up the River and camped but the next day Wednesday the 15th come the tug of war and some of them nearly tuged out. 15th

We left our last nights camp this morning about seven oclock hoping to find water in about twelve miles we traveled of terrible dusty road the dust flying in clouds we had one fearful ravine to cross but by useing rope to let the wagons down and applying the whip briskly to the animals in coming up we all managed to get safely across but it was warm work and a very hot day when we had gone the first twelve miles we neither found water nor grass we found a dry creek where there had once been water but that time was then numbered with what was and is not but as for grass is gave no evidence that there ever had been any thing of the kind in the vicinity it about noon but we had no inducement to stop but we did have something to hurry us forwards and that was to find water for ourselves and stock beside something for our animals to eat for we had most all run out of stock feed[20] and relied solely upon grass the to keep our stock in running order so we hurried on giving the poor things no rest and when arrived at the next creek four miles from the last it to was dry and our only hope lay in reaching Stinking Water[21] and so we pushed on some of the stock giving out both men and animals nearly dying for water we had not counted upon such a long drive and consequently we had not made neccessary provision by laying a supply of water as we should have done had we known what was before us. Well a part of us reached Stinking Water about seven in the evening after a long hot dustry thirsty drive of 28 miles and some did not get in until midnight or next day Stinking Water is a slandered River it is about as clear beautiful and nice tasting water as I ever have seen having not the least possible bad smell about it. It generaly supposed by those who are thought to know that the River had been much smaller it would have been drained by man and beast combined fortunately I was not one of the thirsty that day We found no grass that evening the stock had to go hungry

Stinking Water Thursday June 16th 1864

This morning we started at four oclock in search of grass for it not have taken a very wise man to have told that our stock needed after yesterdays drive and nothing last night We had started about two hours when we found some tolerable good but the spears were few and far between it being the best we could find we concluded to we stayed seven hours to let the stock eat all they could find and then we moved on to the river from which we had wandered.

Stinking Water Friday 17th 1864

This morning orders were giving to start for the ford about a mile distant. Where we commenced crossing about 8 oclock the water reached the wagon beds but not go in it was a most miserable place to cross but it was the best in the vicinity it might be on the River therefore we had no alternative except to cross or remain on the same side. The current was very swift and our guide and Captain drank the result was the train lost one ox and a wagon the rest passed over in safety occupying 5 hours in the undertaking and camped on this bank

Stinking Water Saturday June 18th 1864

We are at the same camp we had last night where we have remained all day we are the middle train of three. Bridgers numbering one hundred wagons ½ mile ahead and Allensworth[22] consisting of 88 wagons just crossed the River today so there are a goodly number of white men in this part of the country at the present time more than there ever will be again at any one time. I forgot to state in yesterdays writing that we buried a man from Missouri who died of mountain fever it is the third burial we have had in our train since we have been on the plains. We were very much pleased to see some freinds who caught up with us today they were in the train and are from South Bend. Same camp Sunday 19 Some of our party took it into their heads that they would like to explore the Big Horn mountains probably 50 or a 100 miles distant in hopes of finding gold. And so about 50 of them started this morning with a half breed guide each man with a mule to pack for him.[23] They intend to be gone ten days

Monday June 20th 1864

Monday traveled a short distance today when we come to splendid grass and stoped the rest of the day to let stock graze it was near small creek

Tuesday June 21st 1864

Started on the trail again this morning traveled through a pretty valley in which we stoped at noon and while there we were visited by about thirty friendly FlatHead Indians both men and women they are the first we have seen since we started on the cut-off and I can say this one thing of them they were the most polite Indians we have seen upon the route they do not beg nor steal if you offer them of course they will take it they were some fine looking fellows among them the chief was acquainted with our guide they only stayed a short time and then took their departure[24] This afternoon we entered Pryors gap have been traveling in it all afternoon.[25]

Wednesday 22

We have traaveled in the Gap all day and are now encamped on the banks of Clarks fork[26] which runs through the Gap.

DIARY 65

Game exists here in great abundance Buffalo Elk & antelope roam the praries

Clarks Fork Thursday June 23rd 1864

We moved out this morning at our usual starting about seven oclock and drove one and a half miles to the ford the river was not very wide but had a swift current and was so deep that we were compelled to block up our wagon boxs to keep the water out. We all finaly got across without any accident and drove five miles down the river to good feed where we camped on its bank with the intention of remaining until our prospectors return

Friday 24th[27]

This morning about one half of our train some of them having no prospectors out and others who have being to mean to wait and thinking to get their comrades kept at our expense pulled out determined to reach Virginia City first. Although it is hardly a christian feeling I do not believe there are many men who intend waiting that would feel very bad to hear of the whole train that left this morning being captured by the Indians. A number of us contributed a lot of coffee sacks of which we made a seine that we used in the river with tolerable success catching a fish apiece

Clarks Fork Saturday June 25th 1864

A number of us had made it up between us to start out this morning in quest of antelope which abound in this neighborhood but are very shy game to hunt. Well we got all ready to start (five of us each on a mule) about 7 oclock we knew that it was going to be a very hot and dry day therefore we filled a canteen at camp none of us ever thinking about it until miles away. We had gone about three miles when we discoved a number of antelope about half a mile distant and we all scattered out with the intention of surrounding them if possible but it proved not to be so but while attempting it one of our men become seperated from us and returned to camp leaving us but four in number. When we come together again (none of us having shot anything) we went into a little valley where we picketed our mules resolved to try it afoot. Near us was an immense plain almost covered with antelope that were for some reason unknown to us extremely shy. So we adopted the best plan we could which was to lay down in the hot sun and wait until they took a notion to come our way but few of them seemed so disposed and if we would approach them no difference how cautiously by the time we had gone a few hundred yards they would be out of sight After about eight hours of this unsuccessful sport having tried every method I had ever heard of to approach them or get them to come to me such as tying my red pocket handkerchief to my ramrod and holding it aloft trying to imitate their call or attempting to craul towards them like a snake but it was no go and having become seperated from my companions I returned to where our animals were grazing I was nearly dead with thirst the memory of which I tried to drown in sleep laying in the shade of one of the only two trees within miles of there. But that to was a failure the ants seeming to have nothing else to do that to keep me awake which they did to a T so well in fact that they drove me from under the tree then I tried it under a bush but that was to warm then back to the tree but it was a very short time until the little pests found me this time they drove up into the tree where I fell asleep and nearly fell out. I managed to pass an hour or two as best I could by which time my comrades returned having shot two antelope one being a large buck the largest I ever saw probably weighing over 200 pounds the other was a fawn. The mule we brought along for packing was terribly freightened at the smell of blood and we could not get the least bit to stay on his back on account of his kicking and rearing another one of the mules which we tried became so frightened that it broke away from us the two mules that we had no idea would pack were the only ones that we could carry the meat on and only a little on them we were therefore obliged to leave half of it and it was with no little regret after liveing on bacon so long. We all of us were nearly dead for a drink and made for the river 2 miles distant which was lowered about two inches by the water our men and mules drank. I and another man were each compelled to walk half way home 6 miles having but one mule between us. The other following about 10 yards behind it. I ever wanted to shoot a mule it was that one arrived about dark

Clarks Fork Sunday June 26 1864

This day has seemed to me more like the Sabbath than any we have had since we left the Missouri River it is the first Sunday we have laid over for a month.

Divide Creek[28] Thursday 30th

We are now camped about ten miles from our camp on Clarks Fork which we left on Monday last and moved about two hundred yards and settled down again this move was made to escape the filth which had accumulated in the place we had remained for three days. We stayed in this last camp until Wednesday when we again pulled up stakes and started for this River where we are now encamped Constantly expecting to see our prospectors returning but some of our men became so dreadful anxious to get to Virginia City before it became as large as and so they pulled out this morning our camp is occasionally enlivened by foot races dances etc. Divide Creek is a nice little River with beautiful water as clear as crystal. Near us are the remains of old Indians Huts made of brush and also an old corral which have not been occupied for a long time. About noon today we were all very much pleased to welcome our prospectors back to camp but no more so than they were to get in. The whole crowd mules and all looked as though it was a pretty hard place over in the Big Horn mounts They all (except the mules) had marvelous stories to relate about the terrible times they had passed through without losing a man it almost impresses one we the belief that there was a divine interposition that sheilded them from all harm.[29]

Friday July 1st 1864

This morning we pulled up stakes and started passing every thing on the road We come within in sight of some of the snow caps of the Rocky Mountains this day we have made 27 miles which we consider a pretty good begining for July.

Saturday July 2nd in a Cannon

We were up and going by six this morning for we are anxious to made time for what we lost while waiting for prospectors who I forgot to say discovered nothing but quartz Rock. We made Rose Bud Creek[30] by noon it is a most splendid mountain stream and well desereves the name it has received only it should be called River instead of creek for it is large enough to be called that when some little stream you can step over are designated by the name of River. It has a very swift current is about five rods wide about four feet deep with a hard rocky bottom and beautiful grassy banks. We stop here for noon and had all forded it by 2 oclock P. M towards evening we entered a very long cannon which we thought at the time was but 3 miles in length it is a just wide enough to admit of a wagon road in some places two teams could not pass but it was in some places plenty wide for a camp and in one of these places we stoped for the night all the old Californians say it is the nicest cannon road they ever traveled so smooth and nice

Carson River Sunday July 3rd 1864[31]

This morning we left our cannon camp and traveled the longest three miles I ever have seen notwithstanding we had come a part of it the day before we did not get out of it until 9 or 10 oclock it proved to be 12 instead of 3 miles and one creek which ran through the cannon we crossed by actual count 79 times at 11 oclock A M. we arrived on the banks of the Yellow Stone I think it was the southern bank it might have been the eastern but I scarcely know any thing about the points of the compass and not put it down in the memorandum book have forgotten for we traveled in every direction some time west then north or south at one time directly east and then northeast northwest and most every other direction I am completely mixed up and do not remember the points of the compass well were all of us as glad to see the Yellow Stone as the Hebrews ever were to see the Jordan for we thought ourselves near our journeys end. We took dinner with Mrs. Yellow Stone. Then crossed Carson and and camped for the night a number of miles from the Yellow Stone

Yellow Stone July 4th 1864 Monday

We reached the Yellow Stone about noon today when some of us commenced ferrying and other forded it.[32] It is a beautiful river near a quarter of a mile wide a very strong current clear as crystal very good water to drink and where we forded it about 5 and one half feet deep we crossed over without any serious accident and camped on the evening of the 4th on the banks of the Yellow Stone I most forgot to state that we had a national salute this morning about sunrise.

Tuesday July 5th

This morning we left the Yellow Stone taking it cross lots for Virginia our old train (what was left of it) Split all to pieces some going with Jacobs other with Bridger the Indiana train still held together. There was a snow on the mounts today which made it very cold in the valley overcoats being in recquisition we only made about 20 miles today notwithstanding the fine weather we had for traveling

Wednesday July 6th 1864

Still continues very cold snowing on the mounts it is the first time in my memory that I ever had thick wollen clothess on all buttoned up overcoat and all and then had to walk to keep comfortable on the sixth day of July We caught up with Bridger today our old guide Jacobs concluded that he knew of a shorter & better road than we was taking to our destination and consequently turned off with eleven wagons instead of 66 the number he had up to Clarks fork. I understand that we have a mountain to cross tomorrow our train number from two to three hundred wagons[33]

Cannon Thursday July 7th

Pulled up stakes this morning and started through a cannon terrible rough roads up and down along the side of precipices and then on good roads for a short time then rough again. We are now camped on a level place in the canon train scattered along for miles. Last night was bitter cold I nearly froze and no wonder up here in the mountains with a heavy frost falling boys tried fishing this evening with poor success

DIARY   71

Canon Friday July 8th 1864

We are now about the middle of the train After about two hours traveling over bad roads we emerged from the canon onto the open plain the train is now all broken to peices and it is who can reach Virginia first the plain being covered with small train of two to six wagon it is a most disagreeable day cold dismal rain on the prarie and snow on the mountains. We crossed the Gallatin fork of the Missouri this afternoon.[34]

Hills Saturday July 9th

The panic has at last taken possession of the Hoosier train and they have dissolved some being almost crazy to see Virginia Acting as though their whole fortune depended on getting to that city as soon as possible they may be in the right but I do not see it in that light I am of the portion who would would prefer seeing Virginia 24 hours later and saving my stock just so much six teams of the same opinion have formed a train of our own. I seen a house today the first I have looked upon for six weeks and its an old log shanty We crossed the Madison fork today[35]

Near Virginia City Sunday July 10th

We have at last reached that place in which were centred the hopes of nearly all the men I have conversed with on the road. The country over which we have passed for the last 30 or 60 miles has been very hilly and undulating We have passed but few ranches along the way and they were rather poor quality as (I am told) are all of them around here. The hills are filled with quartz but how it pays I do not know. We got here at 2 oclock P. M. When we immediately pitched our tents unhitched our teams and started for the

City 1½ miles distant. All of us being eager to get letters we had walked about a mile in a sudden turn of the road Virginia City lay before us in all is pristine glory about 100 feet below us it is situated in a gulch consists of three streets besides cross streets is a regular mining town and Sunday is by far the buisiest day. It is built up of frame and log buildings and contains from two to three thousand Inhabitants[36] it is a dreadful dirty place and good water is very scarce. We proceeded to the post office where to my great joy I received four letters the first I have had for seven or 8 weeks I then returned to the Camp some of our boys did not get back until after dark having found friends in town from South Bend

Virginia City Monday July 18th 1864

It is now eight days since I last wrote in this journal the next day after we arrived in this vicinity we started with our teams for town and are now encamped within the City limits We get our water from a spring near a quarter a mile distant and miserable stuff it is to My opinion of the Territory of Montana is rather poor. The gold seems to be confined to a few gulchs and they are not remarkable for quantity nor quality besides they are all taken up long ago it is no country at all for agriculture purposes the alkalie being so strong that it does not alow anything to grow. It is my opinion that Montana is in a great measure a humibug it never will be able to keep on fourth part of the emigration every has to be shiped here from Salt Lake City and enormous prices are charged for every thing needful to keep soul and body together the circulating medium is Gold Dust the emigrants have only greenbacks which are at a great Discount there is not work for one quarter of the emigrant and consequently great numbers are returning home ill pleased with their summers work I see notice to take passengers to the Missouri River for 25 35 & 40 dollars signed by returning emigrants who some times do not remain but a day or two in this god forsaken place I realy believe that there is no place in the United States Territories included where there is less observance of religion than in this hole there are three large Gambling Hells in full operation nightly not the least sign of a church in times more buisness is done on Sunday than any other day Races fights etc all come of on this day. It is my candid opinion that if paying quartz is not discovered in Montana that in two years Virginia City will be one of the places that was and is not. As soon as we brought our teams to town we found a ranch and sent our mules out to grass in hopes that we can get them in saleable order for stock is very cheap here at present and none but the best can find a sale. I have visited the mines and have a rather poor Idea of the way in which the precious metal is obtained I did have some distant notion of trying it myself but that thought is entirely dissapated. Two of the companies from S B not finding this the country they imagined have taken their departure for Nevada Ter. I think I shall follow suit as soon as I dispose of the mules. When we arrived in Virginia City in Idaho Ter we were very much surprised to find that by act of Congress we were not in Idaho but in Montana which has been created out of the eastern half of Idaho since we started from home[37]

Salt Lake City Friday July 29 1864

I remained in Virginia City two weeks when having seen all of that town a dozen times over and having also obtained a good price for our stock we dissolved partnership and last Monday morning I sailed out of that port which I hope never to see again. . . .

FIVE | THE STAGE TO THE CITY OF THE SAINTS

Until late summer of 1864 the Oliver and Conover Company held a monopoly on stage travel from Virginia City to Salt Lake City. The route lay through a wild and colorful region of mountains and rocks, sagebrush and wildflowers, gullies and streams in Montana and Idaho territories. The stage passed through the Snake River Valley, continued south through the Bear River region, and emerged from the wilderness at Ogden, Utah, a Mormon settlement where town and country resembled the Midwest. The small houses and farms, stores and streets had a tended look. The 455-mile trip took four full days and eight hours.

The trip was difficult. Coaches lacked brakes and springs and had hard planks for seats. The drivers were autocrats—rough, hostile men whose word was law. The coaches traveled day and night, and the rest stops, at intervals of sixty miles, were just long enough to allow local Indians to round up a team of fresh horses. The meals served at the coach stations varied in quality, and some travelers—to the annoyance of the other passengers—carried their own food. Occasionally coaches overturned on slopes, although the driver's skill (and luck) usually kept them upright. Trails that were hazardous by daylight could be disastrous at night. Traveling without lights, on a poorly marked or unmarked road, the driver frequently lost his way. Passengers then had to get out and help search for the trail. Some of them must have wondered whether they would ever reach Salt Lake.

Visitors liked the Mormon city when they finally arrived. The mountains of the Wasatch Range and the Jordan River hemmed in the platted town, whose broad streets divided the city into four-acre blocks. Most of the houses in 1864 were two-story brick, placed on large lots surrounded by adobe walls and both ornamental and fruit trees. Gardens grew luxuriously, irrigated with water brought from the mountains and fed to the city by open street gutters.

The modest, rather plain-looking Mormon women seen on the streets tended to belie the Gentile gossip about polygamy and sensuality. Stanfield commented in his journal that he saw few women in the streets ". . . and fewer pretty ones, if they have any of that kind they must keep them pretty close, for I saw very little beauty even in the church" (p. 78). Other travelers through Salt Lake City found the Mormons acceptable. Edward M. Lewis said, "The Mormons seem to be very good people. I do not find them any different from other folks." Mrs. Mary C. Fish, who went west in 1860, wrote in her daily journal: "So far as my observations went I thought the inhabitants were fine people."[1]

Public buildings were large, numerous, and grand. The Civic Theatre was especially impressive, and, although it was not yet completed in 1864, performances were held nightly. They featured nationally known artists supported by local amateurs. The building was designed with a plain attractive facade of stone, brick, and stucco. Inside, the auditorium glittered with gilt and paintings, and a great chandelier, fashioned by Brigham Young, was suspended from the ceiling on a massive gold chain. The Mormon Temple was planned as an architectural wonder—it was so immense that after eleven years of construction only the foundations had been laid. The famous sulphur-spring baths were another municipal attraction, for bathing in the hot fumes was invigorating and healthful. Among the public structures only the dirty hotels detracted from this clean, wholesome city.

Great Salt Lake, located eighteen miles from the city, was another major attraction. Visitors who swam in its buoyant waters discovered that the long ride to its shores had been worth the effort. Floating in the brine at Black Rock was good sport, even if dried salt caked on the skin made for an uncomfortable ride home.

Every visitor had something to say about Brigham Young. As President of the Mormon Church, he was a man of great power and pre-eminence in his time, and no one could deny that he had caused the desert to bloom. He looked impressive in his white summer coat, straw hat, and black trousers; his blue-grey eyes, aquiline nose, firm mouth, and curling auburn whiskers combined to give the impression that "he was someone." In his journal, however, Stanfield describes the Mormon leader as ". . . about the medium hight thick set rather inclined to corpulency, has a sour stern look on his face, how can the poor man help it having so many wives to worry him. . . . He looks very concieted" (p. 73).

While in Salt Lake City, Stanfield attended church and heard Brigham Young preach. The sermon was given in the immense Tabernacle, which was being used as a church until the Temple could be completed. The three thousand men and women attending services were seated separately on long benches facing the platform. The men were without coats and wore open vests, while the women were in patterned and plain dark clothes of silks and calicoes. At the end of the hall opposite the platform was a large organ. Vocalists sat in an orchestra pit in front of the platform.

Young's sermons, which were impromptu, began slowly and picked up in tempo as they went on. Although he was a fluent speaker, gesturing freely to emphasize his message, he usually preached for three hours, with the result that even the uncomfortable seats failed to keep everyone awake as the exhortations swept on. His sermons stressed the moral values (except monogamy) common to most denominations.

The *Deseret News* (Salt Lake City) for August 10, 1864, reported his sermon of July 31, which Stanfield heard. Young spoke to the immigrants in the following terms: ". . . I wish to address strangers as well as the Saints; as I desire, with all my heart, that I may have the words of truth to give them, to each one as he may need, that all may be profited." He pointed out that men everywhere believe their religion is the best, and then he explained why the Mormons considered theirs to be the only path to salvation.

Young's activities were closely supervised by the army troops stationed at Camp Douglas in the hills above the city. General P. E. Conner, the fort commander, had established the fort on a rise overlooking the city, rather than on a site forty miles away chosen by the army. He felt it was necessary to be close to the city, for he was greatly suspicious of the Mormons. Many immigrants reported that the soldiers regarded the Mormons as their natural enemies and even blamed them for inciting the Indians to attack the wagon trains. Hearing the gossip about Mormon antagonism toward outsiders, the Gentiles undoubtedly felt reassured by the presence of the fort.

The Diary

Salt Lake City Friday July 29 1864

I left for this place[2] in company with five others all strangers to me we took what was called a stage but was very inappropriately named it was a miserable old thing not worthy of a description we rode in it about thirty miles where we found a better one which I shall attempt to describe. It was formerly built for a light spring wagon but had lost its original cover (if it ever had one) and instead was substituted a wooden frame covered with white drilling lined with calico of the poorest quality which let in the rain like a seive the seats were plain board instead of cushioned ones. The back piece for the middle seat instead of the the broad strap they have in a decent coach was nothing but a slender strip of board with sharp corner and made fast to the top frame by little peices of string the old wagon had three springs and as brake which later we broke before we had gone twenty miles and one of the spring was broken before we got to this city and that was the best coach we could get on the only stage line from Virginia here. Some places they run there horses for sixty miles with out change we considered ourselves fortunate if did not have to wait ¾ of an hour at the change stateion while an Indian hunted up the horses to take us on. The drivers were insolent and mean at one place the actualy refused to take us farther but we finally prevailed upon him to go this time[3] we had no lights and consequently when we traveled after dark were in danger of upseting or something of the kind for it was as dark as pitch one night the driver fell as sleep and lost the road about midinight we were fortunate enough to find it after a considerable hunt in quest of it and after we had got righted again we concluded to stop on the and wait for morning which we accordingly did and all laid to dawn and took a nap good except the next morning some of our horse that we had unhitched in order that they might graze took into their heads to stray off which they did much to our chagrin while the guard was tending to something else besides watching possibly stealing a nap after several hours hunt we found them and hitching em up started We crossed Snake river toward noon that day.[4] We traveled all that day over terrible rough roads up and down hill over steep places with out any brake nearly oversetting a number of times The drivers seem to think themselves made of India Rubber for they will dash down a steep hill and round a corner without any brake one horse at a full jump and I expecting at every moment to be dashed overboard. That night it was very dark but we all wanted to go on We could scarcely see the road and come within one of turning over two or three times and pitching into bear river[5] 8 or 10 feet deep and if there wasnt some getting out of that coach about that time then Im a diggis We finally got through that night without any broken bones and next morning I went to sleep and lost my hat consequently I had the pleasure of rideing two days without a cover. But we stood all this besides having one passenger accidentally shot by another[6] we arrived in this city at 4 oclock this afternoon[7] having made the trip of 455 miles in four days and eight hours during time we passed over some hard looking country where nothing would grow but grease wood not a spear of grass on some parts. Most of the passengers stoped at the Great Salt Lake House.[8] This evening I took a stroll around the city and had justed reached Brighams place when here comes the old chap himself he is a short stout looking man about my height he was dressed in a white summer coat black pants black gloves and wears a high straw hat he looks as though he was somebody his majesty was just returning from his evening ride he stoped at the door to talk with a man and I had a good opportunity to see him and I improved it to

Great Salt Lake City Thursday Aug 4th[9]

I have now been in the City six days during which time I have improved the opportunity of seeing the City of the Saints I have been all over and through it but it is impossible for me to form any accurate estimate as to the number of its inhabitants for it is built more like a village than a city and has such a preponderance of women an children that it is entirely unlike any other city I ever saw. The City is beautifully laid out[10] with a large squares containing four acres apiece each house having a nice large lot attached to it splendid wide streets nicely shaded they were laid out regularly running at right angles and as strait as an arrow the houses are all built of adobe brick and are generally two storys in hight their fences are almost universally built of this same kind of brick which are made of a kind of mud and dried in the sun they are about as hard as chalk. old Brigham has his palace at the upper end of town it is enclosed by a wall 10 or 12 feet in hight and several in thickness this wall encloses his grounds which probably cover 12 or 15 acres and on them he has a house for his wives a school for his children his palaces stables a printing office etc.[11] I have also seen the grounds laid out for their temple which they have been to work on for eleven years and have only got the foundation laid it is to be of granite which they bring 20 miles The grounds contain a whole square and are surrounded by durable wall about three feet thick[12] last Sunday I went to church (for the first time in four months) and was one of the congregation who listened to a sermon or rather part of a sermon from his lordship Brigham Young The reason I didnt hear it all is because I was so sleepy that it was impossible for me to keep awake having been to the theater the night before So after taking a nap in church I proceeded to the Hotel and had my sleep out. It is very dull in this City at present and I do not see how it can help being so at all times for there is only three squares devoted to buisness[13] in the city every thing is very dear Greenback are currency the natives all seem to try and get as much as possible out of the poor gentiles.[14] All the citizens have garden and raise all their truck instead of gutters beautiful little streams of water flow through the streets brought from the mountains for the purpose of irragation for it is very dry in the summer and all the Mormon territory has to be irragated or nothing could be raised. Salt Lake City is surrounded on three sides by mountains on the fourth by a level barren plain[15] it is not situated as is generally supposed on the shores of the Great Salt lake but is from eighteen to twenty miles distant near the city on the mountain side is situated Camp Douglas[16] which commands it and they could made the City of the Saints no more in a short time if the soldiers felt so disposed. The camp is garrisoned by a regiment of California Cavalry sent there to keep the Saints quite. Brigham has a Theatre which will accomadate two Thousand people in which he has performance once a week on Saturday nights when it is always full to overflowing for the proceeds go to the almighty Brigham it is finely finished on the inside but no yet entirely compleated without.[17] Near the city are three sulphur springs one of them so hot I could not hold my hand in it another at about a temperature of 90 and in it a great many bath night and morning. the spring come right out of the base of a mountain the third one is to inconveenent for bathers to get at.[18] The Kingdom of Brigham is an absolute monarchy the subject paying one tenth their crops tribute to their king.[19] the soldiers and gentiles around here tell hard stories about the Mormons of a few years ago

Friday Aug 5th 1864

I had set this day apart for the especial purpose of useing it for taking a trip to Salt Lake the dead Sea of the Saints. So I made my way to the livery stable very early this morning some time before 7 oclock where I engaged a horse and got started by eight by which time the rays of the sun had become pretty strong for as I found out it was the beginning of a very warm day. Well as I said I left town about Eight oclock and was directed to cross the Jordan[20] and then take the main road I followed directions as far as crossing the river was concerned but there I was puzzled to find the main road and consequently enquired of a couple of boys sitting on the end of the bridge when one of them wanted to know if I seen that little bridge about quarter of a mile ahead I told I did not knowing whether I seen the right on or not there being several small bridges in that vicinity Well says he you go there and then take the left hand road well I went to the bridge and then I was in another quandary for the roads run every which way and ways that were not which so I enquired of a man who put me on the wrong raod which although it lead in the direction of the lake still by it I could not get within ½ mile of the Lake but I did not find that out until I had rode 15 or 20 miles and come to the end of the road where I could see the Lake about half a mile distant but could not reach it one account of the soft swampy nature of the ground between me and the water. But I could see a cliff (which I had been directed as the place where bathers generaly went and where I should have went)[21] from 6 to 10 miles distant off to the left and as I was nearly dying for a drink and imagineing there might be a house over there and if such a well or spring I made for it in about an hours time of nearly swamping my horse I reached a house and to my great joy a spring for I was so dry I could scarcely talk and my lips were so parched that they continued sore for a number of days notwithstanding the spring was so impregnated with salt as to be brackish my horse and myself must have drank some where within in the neighborhood of ½ Barrel more or less. Well after stoping there a short I pushed on to the Lake a mile or two distant where I found a nice place for bathing but as all trees absolutely refuse to grow any where in that vicinity I was compelled to tie my horse to a big stone and then I went down to the water and was very much surprised to see what clear beautiful water it was for being the most salty body of water on the globe (1 barrel of salt to three of water) I naturaly expected to see it very much discolored by the salt as much if not more so than the Atlantic but there it was as clear and fresh looking as the St Joseph River I could scarcely believe it salt until I tasted it or got some in my eyes and then I think I was convinced of it if I ever was of any thing. Now the was to prepare to move in which I accordingly did. The lake at this place about three feet deep with a beautiful white sand bottom which depth extend about one hundred rods when I suppose it becomes deeper for the water there truns from a light green to a blue. I would have went out and explored it for myself but as my horse was very insecurely fastened and having no desire to walk to town 20 miles distant I allowed judgement to get the better of curiosity and stayed within forty or fifty rods of the shore although this is not the first salt water I have ever seen it is the first I ever bathed in and I was very much charmed with it I had heard about the wonders of Salt Lake but did not beleive half of them until I went and seen for myself A person can lie upon the water the same as they could on a board pile with moving a muscle and they will not sink the water being so strong that it keeps a person on the surface it is almost impossible to use the lower limbs while swiming for the feet are sure to fly out of the water at every other stroke it is also very difficult to walk a person being scarcely able to keep their feet on the bottom as all earthly things have an end so did my bath in Salt Lake but what was my surprise and terror when on coming ashore I discovered that my horse was loose and you bet I was on hot coals until I caught him by which time the water on my face had become a crust of salt which had to be washed of with salt water and immidiately wiped dry or I would have been salted well all things being made ready I mounted my gallant steed pointed in head in the direction of the City and giving one last look at the lake started over as desolate looking country as I ever have seen and is saying a good deal country with which the desert of Sahara would compare very favorably for it is so poor that nothing will grow but grease wood which will grow on the rocks a great I forgot to mention the holy Island in the lake[22] better than it does here the ground is dry and cracked baked as hard as a rock the atmostphere is impregnated with salt the sun seemed to have a particular spite at me this day for he just more than poured down his scorching rays on me this day he seemed to know there was no trees in sight to shelter me I only found four or five house on this whole stretch of 18 miles or more and at every one of those I drank something less than a gallon of salty water. The Saints compare this country to the Holy Land they have Salt Lake for the dead sea and from discriptions I have read of the later I think the comparison very good then they have a River Jordan and the City of the Saints is there Jerusalem and I suppose old Brigham to Soloman and the bed bugs at the Hotel to one of the plagues. I arrived at the City about five oclock rode out to the spring and took a bath got to the Hotel in time for the second table that night had a terrible fights with the bed bug they being victorious driving from my bed out on the varandah

Salt Lake City Aug 6th 1864

This day is Saturday and I am as stiff as old condemned stage horse but notwithstanding that I went to the Theatre which was very crowded and very hot and I was very sleepy not having slept more than 2 or 3 hours last night the play was Hamlet and during the play they sung an old prysbyterian hymn which made me feel as though I was back in the church at SB.[23] I have just arrived from the theatre and although I was so sleepy there that I could hardly keep my eyes open am now wide awake which is rather bad for I am to leave in the stage early in the morning and must go to bed if is only to try and sleep they only allow two inches of candle and does not last much longer than it takes to burn bugs and disrobe therefore I will say good night and turn in

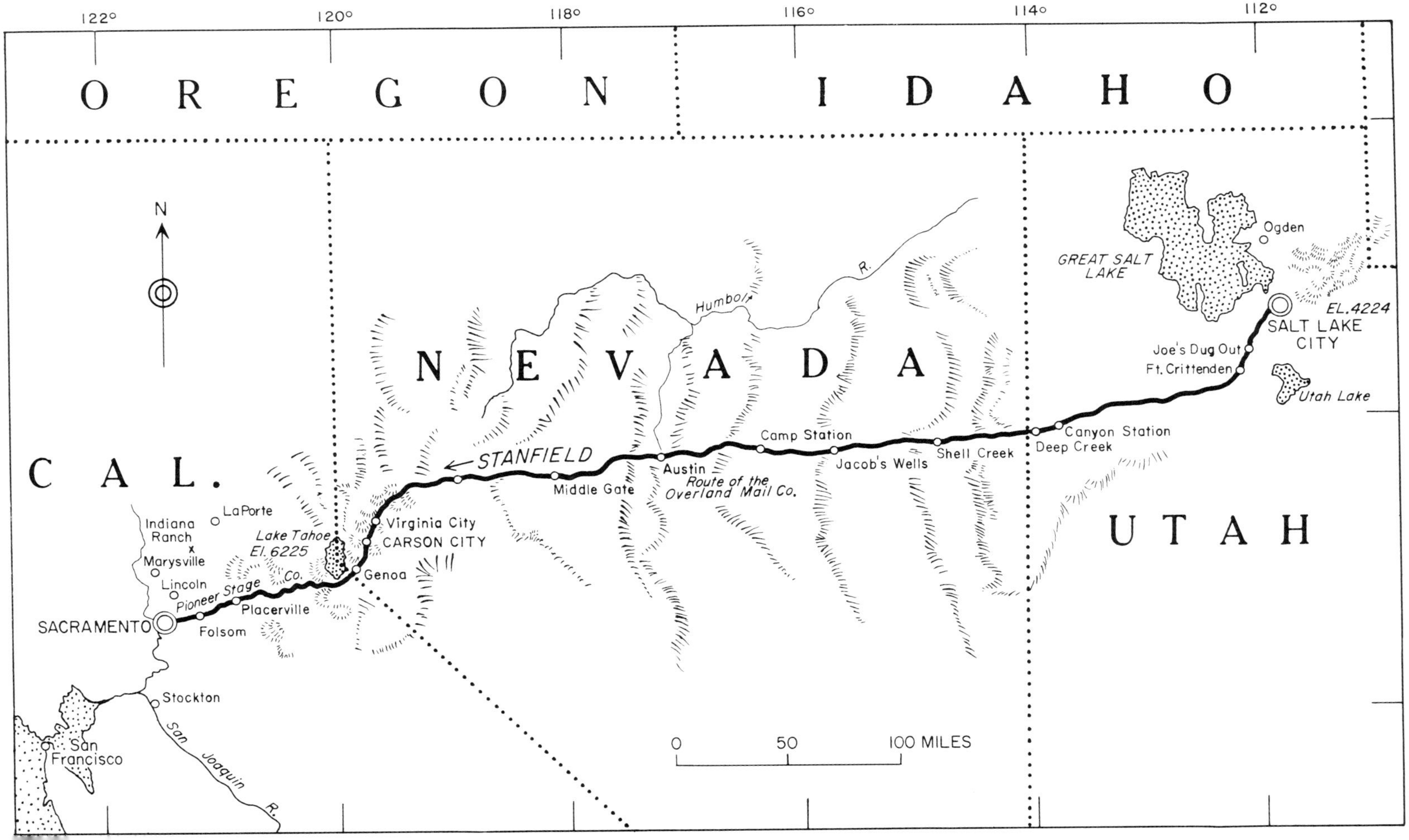
122°
120°
118°
116°
114°
112°
OREGON
IDAHO
NEVADA
UTAH
CAL.
N
Humbolt R.
GREAT SALT LAKE
Ogden
SALT LAKE CITY
EL. 4224
Joe's Dug Out
Ft. Crittenden
Utah Lake
Canyon Station
Deep Creek
Shell Creek
Jacob's Wells
Camp Station
Austin
Route of the Overland Mail Co.
Middle Gate
STANFIELD
Virginia City
CARSON CITY
Genoa
Lake Tahoe
El. 6225
Pioneer Stage Co.
Placerville
Folsom
SACRAMENTO
Lincoln
Marysville
Indiana Ranch
LaPorte
Stockton
San Joaquin R.
San Francisco
0
50
100 MILES

SIX | JOURNEY'S END

Having looked over Salt Lake City, the traveler from South Bend boarded a stage for Virginia City, Nevada. Frequently the coach animals faltered in the gullies or on the hills, and passengers had to get out and walk. Ladies complained of the inconvenience, but men found the exercise a relief from the ride. Dull-gray sagebrush and greasewood covered the alkaline soil, but the late summer wild flowers gave an air almost of gaiety to the countryside. The route crossed the desolate Great Salt Lake Desert to Ruby Valley, then continued southwest over the Diamond Mountains into Austin.[1] This silver-mining center, the only sizeable town on the way to Virginia City, was in the steep Toiyabe Canyon. Coaches stopped there only long enough to change horses and allow the passengers to stretch their legs in a walk around town. The freight wagons lining the streets told of the town's prosperity. Substantial houses—over four hundred—gave further evidence of Austin's thriving economy.

The next major settlement was the long-awaited Virginia City. Visitors in the summer of 1864 faced financial trouble. All transactions were in gold and silver, with greenbacks heavily discounted, if accepted at all. Eastern bank drafts were not honored. Hundreds of travelers were stranded, and few jobs were available. To obtain gold and silver, they had to sell their possessions at great loss. Guns, watches, clothing, and blankets glutted the market. Virginia City, perched on the eastern slope of Sun Mountain, was nonetheless an interesting place. Lining the main street were churches and saloons, little cemeteries and hospitals, hotels and houses, newspapers and mines. The largest business was the Gould and Curry Mine, a tunnel that extended under the town, throughout its length. The mine's Comstock Lode in 1864 yielded fifteen and a half million dollars in ore, but the town had already passed the zenith of its prosperity. Its population of the previous summer, twenty thousand, had dwindled perhaps to half, and land prices had fallen correspondingly.

Going west from Virginia City, the Pioneer Stage crossed the Sierra Nevadas and entered Folsom, eastern terminus of the California railroads. For twenty miles the route paralleled Lake Tahoe, whose blue water glimmered through the pines bordering its shores. The Sierra Nevadas were awesome mountain scenery at its best. Hour after hour new grandeurs towered above the traveler. Another, and very different sight, was the view of the freight trains, hauling supplies east to Nevada. Thousands of these eight-mule and ten-mule teams moved over the narrow paths during 1864, their greatest year, and often terrorized coach passengers, who feared collisions on curves and high ledges.

In Folsom passengers caught trains to Sacramento and Lincoln, then transferred to coaches for Marysville and the surrounding mining camps. Stanfield followed this route and on August 20 reached Indiana Ranch, his journey's end.

Stanfield had a pleasant time in California. He did a little placer mining, moved about in Yuba County as he pleased, made friends, and generally enjoyed life. This relaxed existence continued from August, 1864, to April, 1865. Unfortunately, the climate was a disappointment—snow drifted as high as in Indiana, or higher. No very attractive business opportunities came his way, and as we have seen, he considered mining to be a disagreeable way of earning a living.

He often thought of his family in South Bend, of his little sisters, of his brother just returned from the war. He found himself "sighing for the prairies of Indiana." One year to the month after leaving South Bend, Stanfield set out for San Francisco on the first leg of his journey home. He took a wagon from Indiana Ranch to Marysville and went from there by river boat to Sacramento. Like most travelers he preferred Sacramento to Marysville,[2] which seemed a rough mining community. Marysville's business was slowing down as the gold mines dwindled; Sacramento, as the state capital, was booming with the growing state. He booked passage from Sacramento to San Francisco on a luxurious river steamer the *Chrysopolis*.

San Francisco was an interesting town, worth more than the few days Stanfield could spend there. He toured its historic landmarks; saw the Cliff House with its splendors of service, food, and scenery; passed along brightly lighted Montgomery Street; attended the Bush Street Presbyterian Church with its good preaching; spent an evening at Maguire's Opera House; and toured Oakland's shaded streets. From the seals on the rocks to the people on the streets, everything in this city pleased him, but nothing could shake his determination to get home.

The Diary

Virginia City Nevada Aug 12th 1864

I arrived here last night about 12 oclock and just as I got in the natives had a big fire which I suppose was gotten up to celebrate my entry into the City. I put up that night at one of the Hotels very much troubled in mind as to the state of my purse which was very low. But I have got a little ahead of my story so going bed I will go to sleep and go back apiece to when I left Salt Lake City bright and early which was about eight oclock Sunday morning[3] and traveled all day most of the time over terrible desolate looking country where nothing could possible be induced to grow the stage was so full that could not get to lay down consequently when night come I had to do my sleeping setting up or not at all (and before I got through to this City I had become quite an adept at sleeping in most any position) and passed a miserable night. The next day the 8th was pretty much the same for riding in a stage over a desolate country is terribly monotonous. On the 9th we had tolerable good roads and did not have to get out and walk up hills across gully etc as the day preceeding we also passed over diamond mountains and through Ruby Valley[4] about dark it is a beautiful place. Towards the morning of the 10th it grew very cold and my blanketts proved to be very convenient. Along in the afternoon of the 10th which was yesterday we passed through Austin quite a large and flourishing mining town which contains 10 or 12 large quartz mills it is built right among the mountains where the quartz abound.[5] After dark we passed through new gap a natural pass in the mountains two miles long. And in the dark we

VIRGINIA CITY, NEVADA (1877)

Courtesy of the Nevada Historical Society

were all suddenly startled by a collision with another coach but fortunately there was no damage done to either concern or passengers but we arrived safely at our destination about midnight[6] and went to rest as I have before said This morning I arose took my breakfast[7] and went to every bank in town trying to sell a draft on New York and make a raise but nobody seemed to want to have any thing to do with this modern Gotham and would not even look at my draft[8] I had also been looking for some friends whom I thought were in the city but could hear nothing of them so I come back to the Hotel[9] and a brilliant idea struck me to sell my Revolver watch and some surplus clothing which I had.[10] So I took them down town and almost give them away for I am very anxious to get enough to get to Sacramento for I am sure of finding friends there through whose influence I can draw on New York

Virginia City 12 Aug 1864

This morning I succeeded in selling or rather giving away for a slight remuneration a little more of my personal property but still did not have enough to carry me through and I was becoming very nearly discouraged and thinking which was the easiest way to die hanging shooting poisoning or cutting my throat and who I should make my heirs when I happened to pick up the only book in the room hoping it would give me some information of the subject and upon opening it it proved to be a directory of the city I naturaly turned to the Bs and there was W S Bender Telegraph office[11] that was sufficient Suicide was no where I took a bee line of the Telegraph office and there he was just the fellow I wanted to see. I took supper with him this evening and am now stoping at his fathers house

DIARY

Virginia City Aug 14th 1864

I am now in considerable better spirits than when I arrived within the suburbs of this City and will now make an attempt to say something about it.[12] it is built right in the mountains on the the mountains and between the mountains it has some splendid store houses and contains a population of about ten thousand and is a very lively place but nothing to what it was last summer when it had twice its present population and fortunes made in a day but the fever subsided the mines depreciated and the people fled so the City has in a great measure gone down but it is still lively. Yesterday a friend and myself obtained a pass into the largest mine around the City it is called Gould & Curry We were furnished with a guide and a candle apiece We went in a tunnel which entered the side of a hill 2500 feet right in under the City surface of the earth being 420 feet above us We were shown all through the various tunnell where the men were at work digging out the quartz we were in under the ground about two hours and I was very much pleased with my trip in the hole. I went to church today it being the first gentile church I have attended for four months.[13] I was shown a piece of quartz today that yeilded $20,000 to the tons. This evening I went over to the Hospital and cemetery about a mile distant they have a very nice Hospital filed up in the best comfort for the patients[14] The drug department is in the charge of an old South Bender

Sacremento Aug 16th 1864 Tuesday

I left Virginia City yesterday morning at 6 oclock coming very near being left behind I came on the Pioneer Route[15] past Lake Bigler[16] which has the name of being one of the most beautiful Lake on the globe even rivaling in beauty the celebrated Lake something in Switzerland and I think it well deserves its praise for it is a most magnificent sheet of water as clear as crystal situated right in the Sierra Nevada mountains and surrounded by the most splendid scenery I have ever had the pleasure of looking upon to which the white mountains of New Hampshire are nowhere This lake in the common parlance has no bottom (and I expect it runs through and forms the Peking River in China) for in some place they have searched in vain for it It is a great watering place the Saratoga of the western slope. There were several small sized schooners on it. We rode along the shore 15 or 20 miles and consequently had a a good chance to see it. During the ride from Virginia to Folsom where we took the cars I was treated to such scenery as I have scarcely ever imagined and it was not only on a small part of the road but all through the mountains in which was most all the Road lay After the sun went down we had splendid moonlight scenes tall noble pines rearing their lofty head on every side and the moon shining so modestly and beautifully through their wild rugged tops but I have not words to describe it. The road was lines with eight & ten horse or mule freight teams and a person has no Idea of a wagon until they see a California freighter.[17] I really think it must have averaged a wagon to every ten rods on the whole route some places we had mighty tight squeezing to pass every one of these teams no difference how many animals are driven or rather guided by one line and notwithstanding the immense number of teams I saw. The citizens of Virginia say there are not half as many as there were last year The stage arrived at Folsom at 5 oclock this morning we remained there two hours when I took the cars[18] (the first I have seen since I left Grinnell Iowa) and arrived in this city at 8 this morning it seemed like old times and civilization to ride once more in the cars

Sacremento Thursday Aug 18th 1864

I have now been in this city three days and have seen about all there is to be seen it is a beautiful place containing about 15000 inhabitants situated on the Sacremento River and is the capital of California.[19] Within in its limits are a great number of handsome residences surrounded by beautiful yards and gardens the run at right angles being laid out regularly and in order are well shaded though rather narrow but still wide enough to answer all business purposes. The City is rather low and is subject to flood from the River which is not very pleasant for the citizens although they can take boat ride in the streets. I have found South Bend friends in abundance since come to this city. I am going to leave the city in the morning for Marysville.

Indiana Ranch Saturday Aug 20 Cal[20]

I left Sacremento yesterday morning in the cars at 9 oclock went as far as a place called Lincoln[21] where I took the stage for Marysville[22] and after passing over some terrible desolate looking country arrived at the latter place about 2 oclock P M. I took supper with Rench Sample an old South Bender[23] and left for this place in morning and having got here about 30 miles from Marysville where I have found relatives intend staying awhile here or in this vicinity in fact I think I shall remain in this part of the country all winter and will consequenlty have very little to write in this journal until I start for home. it maybe that I will not write anything in it at all for I may not find anything of interest to put down. I will therefore bid goodbye to this journal for a time at least but I hope not a long one

*Foot Hills Dec 6th 1864**

Dear Mother

No doubt you are wondering where the Foot Hills are well Indiana Ranch is in them and I am at Indiana Ranch have not been away from here but twice in two months once over on the Sacramento gone about four days and the other time over in the Hills gone about six hours So you I am getting kind of used to this part of the country but awful tired of it tomorrow I am going down to Marysville and I will probably stay down there some time do not know for how long. I was going up to Laporte[24] or Rabbit Creek as tis called here, but it commenced Raining and has rained for two weeks but rain or no rain I am going down to town tomorrow It is raining hard and is so dark I can hardly write strait. Up at Rabbit Creek 30 miles above here I do not mean that high in the air but pretty near for it is on top of the mountains up hill all the way Well up there the snow is five feet deep or was day before yesterday and is probably deeper now for when it rains here it snows there and dear knows it it is and has been raining hard enough here. I receive your letters you might say regularly one or two a week sometimes ten days apart and some times two or three at a time We get the mail every other day last Tuesday I got one from you and two of Eds and Thursday I got one from Pa he seems to still think his oil diggins will make him a pile and I hope it will if it does not he will be sorry that he did not sell for $10,000 but so the world goes if you want to make a fortune you must run some risks I see by the papers that oil has been found in southern Ohio & Northern Kentucky I am in hopes they made a mistake and meant southern Indiana. I was sorry to hear that Ed slipt up in his calculations and is in the army

---

* While in California Stanfield wrote the above letter to his mother in South Bend.

again his will[25] and if I was his place and had to stay in the army I would accept of the shoulder straps which sport the leaves. I have no doubt but Eva is anxious to keep up a correspondence with me from the number of letters I receive from her. I do not think she cares much for letters from me for if she did she would ask for them oftener than she does The only way for her to get will be for her to write to me. in one of your letters you talk about making her write I would not do that for if she cares for them she will answer em with out compulsion but if she would rather play with her dolls why let her have her own way any thing is news to me how many chickens you get are there any pigeons around the stable about the cow the Horses the girls and the adjutant majors captains and with whom she became acquainted at Louisville let her fill out her letter with that and recollect it is only to How. I am writing this on the darkest day in the year in this part of the country it is next to impossible to follow the lines and think of something to write at one and the same time so as all good writers say please excuse miserable scraul when I know it is as good as I ever write I do not doubt but what Mammie is the greatest child of the age for I never seen one yet but its mother said it had not an equal in the world they have one here who is destined to be president by its mother but would not stake much on it. Kiss Mammie for me and tell How will come home some of these days and see and kiss her myself sometimes I get dreadful homesick such days as this when a person can not go out of the house then again I am in no hurry to go at all. Your last letter was dated Oct 25 and Pa s 28th. Every time I write I forget to give or send my respects to all the ladies you speak about as enquiring for me Mrs. Rogers Mrs Hammond Mrs Crews and all the rest whose names I do not remember

                                          Your afect Son

                                          H. S. Stanfield

Preface*

The following is a sketch of my trip from California to New York City. It is written merely as an amusement to occuppy my leisure hours for a few days and is entirely a private document but if it should by any mischance fall into the hands of a stranger, I hope he or she as the case may be, will have the kindness to overlook any ingramatacism *(as Artemus Ward would say) misspelling or want of punctuation that may meet their eye. The foundation of this sketch is taken from a journal kept in a memorandum the property of the writer who wrote a little in it every day*

Sunday April 2d The morning which I had had selected for my departure from the hills of California where I had spent eight long and weary months sighing for the praries of Indiana broke bright and beautiful as any April morning can be in this [manuscript torn] 1d[26] The sun rose in all his majestic splendor throwing his rays of gold over the magnificent green foliage of the mountain and beaming down with a kindly look on the little hamlet of Indiana Ranch, which I was now about to leave, perhaps forever, but I can not truthfully say (not wishing to speak disrespectfully of the place at all far from it) that I felt any peculiar twangs like the snapping of heart strings or anything of that kind on the other hand I doubt if there was a happier person in that part of the country. True I had kind friends in this little settlement whom I felt very sad upon parting with but I thought like the wanderer in the song that there was no place like home. It may seem strange why I selected the Sabbath as the day on which to begin a journey and so it would be in and old

---

* Stanfield resumed his diary as he began his journey home from California on April 2, 1865.

settled and civilized country like this [manuscript torn] mining countries I have

[Three pages of manuscript missing here]

poison sold at that bar and it took no eagle eye to discern that Sam had as much as was good for him I very respectfully declined he honor and rode off. A little farther on and I came to the house of Mr C——— who with his wife and children three in number stood ready at the gate to bid me farwell. As both he and her were formerly from South Bend they felt very much interested in me and did all that was in their power to make my stay in their settlement pleasant for which I am a thousand times obligat to them. After leaving the Ranch I pursued my mountain road to the Oregon house[27] the post office of the Ranch where I was to change my horse for a wagon and two horses. After spending about a half an hour at this place which is as its name indicates a public house, and post office for that part of the country we took a drink of something (that biteth like a serpent and stingeth like an adder) lighted a cigar and were off for Marysville twenty eight miles distant. The roads being in none of the best condition and our team not being the best or fastest on the coast we made but very indifferent time. The scenery along the road was of the ordinary mountain character at some points being charming at others the very reverse. We frequently meet those immense freight teams which carry ten to twelve tons and are drawn by from eight to twelve lusty mules driven by one man who sits on the near wheel mule and manages his team with one line. Between eleven and twelve a. m. we stop at the Yuba County house[28] (eleven miles from our starting point) for dinner. it has the reputation which I think it entitled to of setting the best table on the road. We remained here about one and one half hours when we again took to the road which now began to be more level and even for we were now in the Yuba Valley which is not at all noted for the beauty of its scenery The Yuba being a restless and unreliable river is given to frequently falling out of bed and carrying sand dirt and drift wood for miles out into the valley. by this means distroying rich and valuable lands and making the highway a mere sand bank The wind which commenced blowing gently when we left the Ranch was now become a perfect hurricane filling our eyes, mouths and hair with this abomnible sand. But finally as all things earthly have a termination so did this ride, for we arrived in Marysville about dark when we immediatly drove to a hotel the United States[29] where a warm supper and good cigar soon put us to rights Thus ended the first day of my journey towards home

Monday April 3rd

Monday April 3rd This day I spent in visiting my friends and looking around Marysville generally. This city was among the first built when the mining excitement broke out in forty nine. and on account of its being at the head of navigation on the Yuba and the proximity of rich mines it was intended by its founders no doubt to become second only to San Francisco but they calculated without their host most of the rich farming lands by which it was once surrounded have been destroyed by the floods of the Yuba Most of the rich mines in this vicinity have been worked out and the tailings or sand from which the gold was washed has been carried by little streams down into the Yuba is rapidly filling up her channel and if it keeps on as it has for the last ten years, ten years more will see the Yuba more effectually blockaded than ever Charleston harbor was. It is with these same tailings that the Yuba ruines the surrounding country The streets of Marysville are laid out regularly and joining or rather crossing at right angles the run the cardinal point of the compass They are broad and nicely shaded by trees planted along the outside of broad brick paved sidewalks Most of the houses are built of brick, in blocks or separately but close together with scarcely no yard in front or in the rear. It has the appearance of a city of considerable size but it population only numbers about seven thousand. Tis said to be the third city in the State. In almost any part of the town can be seen notices of houses to let which does not look well for a city alas the glory of Marysville has departed its business is no comparison to be in years gone by. Another feature in California towns is the large number of hotels which each one maintains. Now there are six or eight large ones in this place any two of which would be sufficient for a place of equal size on the other side of the mountains. A few years ago these hotels were not capable of accomodating near all of the traveling community. There are also a large number of stables for the accomodation of freight wagons and teams of mules The city also contains a number of churches of different denominations[30] and in cities of this size I am pleased to say the Sabbath is generally observed in a Christian manner as it should be by people calling themselves civilized

Tuesday April 4th

This morning I took leave of the last of my relatives My uncle who had accompanied me down from the mountains This took his departure for home and now it seems to me as if my journey was really begun. This evening we received the joyful news of the capture and occupation of Richmond by the federal forces. We had heard this very same report so often only to hear it contradicted in the next dispatch that we were at first rather loth to believe but it came from such authentic sources (as it always had before) and we were so loyal that we done our utmost to believe it and finally succeeded to the extent of getting the fire engines and cannon out drawing the former all around town and firing the latter as fast as it could be loaded firing guns pistol crackers etc on private account ringing all the bells and hanging flags from every house. After dark most every loyal man in town thought it his duty to the government to see how much liquor he could get on the outside of. That was a jollynight in Marysville it will a long time ere I forget it. Not a copperhead was to be seen on the streets they had evidently crawled into their holes and pulled the holes in after them[31] I only wish Uncle Cap had remained in town to night for I know he would have enjoyed it

Wednesday April 5th

This mornings despatch confirmed the glorius news of last night The Confederate capital is at last in our hands and the so called president and his cabinet fleeing for their lives like common murderers. This news seems to good to be true although we have been anticipating and hoping for it for months yes for years. And now of course the war is virtually closed. To be sure there be little fights and perhaps a moderate sized battle but this cruel war is about over for Mr. Robert Lee Esq is in pretty close quarter according to telegraph and U. S. Grant is supposed to understand his business which is fighting. The people of Marysville seem to think they cannot make noise enough or in any way show how joyous and happy they feel. This evening about dusk the brass band started out to toot patriotic pieces around through the streets and about three hundred men and boys not wishing to be outdone or out tooted by any one on this glorius occasion, but whose education musically speaking had been greviously neglected procured tin horns sleigh bells old tin pans kettles etc. in fact every thing that would make an unearthly noise and followed the bad around the streets until near midnight. It was the worst racket I ever had the pleasure of hearing.

Friday April 7th

This morning at six oclock I took my final leave from Marysville. On the good boat Gov Dana a little steamer that navigates the Yuba and Sacramento rivers.[32] The fare to Sacramento City was four dollars I have forgotten the distance but it took us five hours to make it arriving at the capitol at eleven oclock a. m. I put up at the Golden Eagle a hotel situate on the corner of 7th & R Streets a very nice place to put up at.[33] In the afternoon I sauntered around looking at the city and finding acquaintainces The City of Sacramento is said to contain fifteen thousand inhabitant and I guess it has got that many. It is a beautiful town although the streets are a little narrow as are the sidewalks which are nicely shaded by beautiful trees. The city is quite level and contain a large number of beautiful residences and substantial buisness houses. It has nicely bouldered streets with brick and plank sidewalk and like Maryville is lighted with gas. It has like every other California town its China town where the almond eyed celestial resided and offers to do washing and ironing *belly goot and cheappee*.[34] The city is quite low and has until within the last years been subject to flood from the river which used frequently in the spring time to deluge the city with water in some places two or three feet deep but now the river is so well dyked and banked up that the citizens no long fear it The state house or capitol is quite a large plain looking building built on the Grecian style and is a little out of the center of town

Saturday April 8th

San Francisco the metropolis of the Pacific coast. I left Sacramento. This afternoon about two oclock in the magnificent river stream Chrysopolis[35] the finest in California it was furnished in superb style it plys between the two cities every day going up one day and returning the next. I believe these two cities are one hundred and sixty miles apart and connected by the noble Sacramento.[36] We arrived in this city at nine in the evening the fare down including supper was five dollars which means gold ones for every thing in this state is coin greenbacks are unknown thousands of persons never having seen one. I know while I was up in the mountains a fellow begged a five cent stamp that I happened to have in my possession: to give to his girl as a curiosity. The scenery along the river was quite plain and commonplace. Immediately upon my arrival here I put up at the American exchange on Sansom Street[37] The next street to and running paralel with Montgomery the broadway of San Francisco[38]

Sunday April 9th Both morning and evening I attended church at the Calvary[39] on Bush between Montgomery and Sansome Streets It was of the presbyterian denomination and they had a magnificent choir with a good organ we also listened to a good sermon both times. This is the second time I have attended church since I was in Salt Lake City and heard Brigham Young deliver a sermon. My reason for not attending church was not because I had no inclination, but because I had no opportunity. This afternoon I took a trip out to Lone Mountain the cemetery of the city.[40] I had frequently while in this state heard of the marvelous beauty of this city of the dead. But upon going to view it I was very much disappointed perhaps I had anticipated to much. I am certain of one thing that no person who hears my description of it will expect to see much. I made the trip by horse cars

Monday April 10th

This morning I wandered around the city awhile gazing upon its wonders and wondering what to gaze upon. It is a well built town and contains one hundred and twenty thousand inhabitants a great many of them Chinamen The buildings are principally composed of brick and stone the walk on the principal streets are of flag stone on others of brick and plank. Montgomery is a splendid street and for miles it has stores that no city need be ashamed of after night it presents a beautiful appearance brilliantly lighted up and crowed with gaily dressed men and women. Since coming to this place I have heard a great deal of the cliff house[41] and as I wished to see all that I could I went out there this afternoon part of the way by street car and the rest in an omnibus. The cliff house is situated six miles from the city. It is built on a cliff about two hundred feet above the water hence its name and commands an extensive view of the grand old Pacific. Here I obtained my first sight of the largest and calmest ocean. We could look out upon the water as far as the eye would permit. Directly in front of the cliff house and about a quarter of a mile distance are two immense rocks called seal rocks for they are constantly with these animals. It is interesting to sit on the piazza of the Hotel and watch the movements of these unwieldly beasts some of them said to weigh as much as one thousand pounds and when they sing as the Irishman said they bellow like a bull. Cliff house is quite a fashionable resort of the young bloods from the city and from their prices I should judge it was only the wealthy one who came often, for feeling a little hungry I ordered some thing to eat They furnished me with a cold lunch for which they charged the moderate bill of two dollars. Then I though I would smoke they handed me a cigar for which I paid twenty cents. It was not near so good as the ten cent ones in the city Towards evening I returned to town and completed my second days stay in the city with a stroll on Montgomery Street.

Tuesday 11th

This afternoon I made arrangements and went over to Oakland[42] which is six miles from the city and right across the bay. It is the fashionable place of residence for the wealthy of the city. Part of the way we went in the steamer and part by rail. It is a beautiful little place shaded by magnificent live oak trees from whence it derives its name. Notwithstanding it is the home of the aristocrat I did not see any residences that I considered palatial This evening about sundown I was standing on the steps of the hotel picking my teeth for I had just finished my supper. When who should I see among the passers but two old acquantances from South Bend Men with whom I had crossed the plains last summer. I was not a great while in showing myself to them for there is nothing like meeting a friend when one is away from home. They were just as delighted to see me as I was them and was informed that they and three others boys with whom I had left home were in town intending to return in the same ship I was to take. This pleased me muchly. After dark I went to Maguires Opera house[43] where a band of minstrels were performing. Among them was one Jacobs the finest violinist on the coast and the best I ever heard.

SEVEN | THE PACIFIC VOYAGE

*S*TANFIELD made arrangements in San Francisco for steamship passage via Nicaragua to New York City. He delayed buying his ticket until the last moment, when, he was told, prices would be reduced. With two ships sailing, he did not expect to have any difficulty in getting a reservation, but he had not anticipated that the lagging economy of California would result in an exodus of disillusioned immigrants. The demand for space was such that Stanfield was obliged to settle for steerage on the *Moses Taylor*,[1] and he had to wait hours while the Provost Marshal prepared a passport which, in Stanfield's account, turned out to be a meaningless form. Nevertheless, he was able to thrust aside his annoyance and enjoy the excitement of a steamship departure: porters hurrying about, shippers checking their merchandise, crews swearing, the kissing and hugging of goodbyes. Out of such confusion came an on-time departure on April 13, 1865.

Passengers leaving San Francisco for New York in 1865 profited from the competition between two rival steamship companies—the Pacific Mail Steamship Company and the People's Opposition Steamship Line (also known as the Central American Transit Company). For years the Pacific Mail Company had held a monopoly on transportation between California and New York (via Panama), but in August, 1864, the People's Opposition Line succeeded in reopening the Nicaraguan Route. Soon the companies were engaged in fierce price competition. In December of the same year rates aboard the *Moses Taylor* had been reduced to: first-class cabin, $187; second-class cabin, $135; and steerage, $48. By April of 1865, when Stanfield bought his ticket, prices had been further reduced. Stanfield paid only $35 for steerage; a second-class cabin cost $65 and a first-class cabin $100. These prices included transportation across Nicaragua, food, and a "conductor" (or guide) who remained with the group all the way to New York.[2] The Pacific Mail Company ship, the *Sacramento*, which left on the same day for Panama, charged $170 for a first-class cabin (outside), $120 for an inside first-class cabin, $70 for second-class, and $40 for steerage.

The People's Opposition Line advertised that the Nicaraguan route necessitated 650 fewer miles of sea travel than the Panama route.[3] Still, the company was criticized for not promoting its route more vigorously. An editorial in the San Francisco *Evening Bulletin* (April 12, 1865) blasted the company for not providing more competition for the Pacific Mail Company; and the latter, which owned and operated the *Sacramento*, was accused of "shameful abuses" and "niggardliness."

Steerage on the *Moses Taylor* was cramped and unventilated—tolerable only because it was temporary. Lucky passengers had berths, but many were assigned hammock beds so short that the occupants' feet hung out at one end. The hammocks were slung across aisles and taken down at four o'clock in the morning. The crowding and heat were nearly unbearable, and the best solution was to abandon the quarters in steerage and find refuge on the open deck.

Food was inevitably another source of dissatisfaction. The watery soup had so few solids that counting the beans became a pastime; hardtack was so hard that it could literally break a man's tooth; the salt pork was rotten; drinking water (condensed from the steam of greasy machinery) was unpalatable. The passengers' indignation over the food was increased by the way it was served. Sometimes only the most aggressive got enough food, and the Irish waiters were always disagreeable. They regarded the steerage passengers contemptuously and were pleasant only when bribed. No amount of money could buy decent coffee or tea, and not even first-class accommodations provided immunity to seasickness.

Some of the familiar experiences of seagoing—riding out a storm, sighting a whale, crossing the equator, watching the porpoises—were enjoyable, but all the passengers looked forward to disembarking in Nicaragua. In the port of San Juan del Sur, the tourists observed, compared, and criticized everything. The squalid natives won sympathy but in general the attitudes of the Americans were tinged with contempt. The Nicaraguans seemed inferior in morals, ambition, and physique. The natural resources, however, were invariably admired. Although the luxuriant and strange vegetation seemed unreal, tree-ripened oranges and bananas, everyone conceded, were infinitely superior to the same fruit at home. Seeing the ruins of the home of William Walker, American filibuster and adventurer, some of the tourists were stirred to patriotic sentiments about the enormous power of their government which could reach into so remote a region.

The Americans' stay in Nicaragua ended with the discovery that no transportation across the country was available. The passengers had to reboard the *Moses Taylor* in order to make their way to Panama. By now, however, they were becoming adjusted to life aboard ship, and their routine was quickly re-established: sitting idly, talking, listening, smoking, playing cards, watching the shore go by.

The Diary

Wednesday 12th

This day I have had a lively time of it certainly I had postponed buying my ticket home until this morning for I was told that tickets were to be obtained cheaper just before the ship sailed. But next time I think it doubtful if I put off procuring that little document as long as I did this time. As two steamer each capable of carrying six or eight hundred passengers were going to sail on the same day for the same point I thought that there would of course be plenty of passages and to spare but there is where I missed it. For what was my surprise when upon applying for a cabin passage I was informed that they were all sold and if I went at all on that steamer it would be as a steerage passenger and as a friend of men had told me while at Marysville that I had better go to h——l At once and every body else had told me dreadful stories about the steerage I hesitated for some time as to the course I should persue. finally I concluded to try the other steamer but after an hours unsuccessful search for the office of the other line I gave it up in despair and returned to the opposition office where I sealed my doom by purchasing a ticket as steerage passenger in Moses Taylor or as the passengers had it the rolling Moses. After procuring my ticket for which I paid the moderate sum of thirty five dollars, I was informed that it would be necessary to procure a passport from the provost Marshal a system just inaugerated.[4] After a great deal of enquiring I finally found myself in the neighborhood of his office but I was not the only one their or the first one far from it every man and woman for the female sex had to get passports also had to await their turn so placing myself in the line at ten oclock I waited for my turn which come at half past one and then the passport was nothing but a blank form with my name written in it saying that I was a citizen of United States residing in California and going to New York on the Moses Taylor ant that was all there is no description of my pass an neither was I required to give my age or take an oath as to the truth of my being a native. Therefore I see no more use in it than in a blank piece of paper

Thursday 13th

Out on the ocean Yes we are afloat at last.[5] This morning there was quite a little bustle of excitement at the hotel for quite a number of the guests were bound for New York on one of an other of the steamer which sailed today. About eight oclock I embarked in a coach for the [Mission Street] wharf which we reached in a short time where were congregated more excited people than it had ever been my lot to see in one crowd before. There was the inevitable porter and coachman bringing luggage and passengers drays bringing freight and express matter. Men loading provision and fuel. Men women and children going aboard friend-relatives biding them farwell perhaps forever, kissing hugging and weeping going on on all sides but no one offered to kiss or hug me I guess they thought I wouldnt like it but if they had only tried it once they would no longer have been in doubt in regard to that subject. Captain and mates swearing at the men and the men swearing at each other. The deck covered with passengers baggage and freight At ten and one half oclock amid the parting cheers of the multitude we swung off into the stream and were off for New York on the opposition line via Nicaragua after passing innumerable vessels anchored along the harbor we finally made the open ocean. about twelve oclock we saw steaming up in our rear the Sacramento the steamer belonging to the regular mail line via Panama[6] this ship left it dock half an hour after we did but here she is right behind then abreast of us and finally with loud cheers from her passengers with which her deck is crowded she passes us and by three oclock nothing is to be seen of her but her smokestack at four she is entirely out of sight. But I have gone ahead of my story as soon as I got aboard I met my companions of the plains all five of them having tickets for the steerage They told me that I had better secure my bunk for if I put it off I might have some difficulty in getting. accordingly I went to a hole in the deck. I believe it is called the hatchway where I desended a ladder to the main deck and then I went to another hole and down another ladder into the steerage A large square room about six feet six inches in hight filled with bunks several hundred in number with two passage ways among them. between the floor and cealing of this interesting apartment were three of these shelves. I hunted long and faithfully for the shelf bearing the number my ticket called for. I had finally come to the conclusion that it was not to be found when some kindly disposed individual remarked that possibly it was not yet put up. Upon my requesting an explanation he told me that it was customary when the ship was crowded as it is now to to erect bunks in the passage ways at night and take them down in the morning. I finally concluded that mine must be one of that kind. So I went upon the Hurricane deck again deter mined to see what was to be seen. The sea was and continues to be very smooth consequently very few are sea sick. At noon the call to dinner came and so numerous and hungry were the passengers were that it was the second or third table before I could get anything to eat or near the table. We have to eat on the deck on a plain board hung by iron rods from the lower timbers of the hurricane deck each person is allowed a tin plate sometimes a knife & fork sometimes neither the victuals are brought on the table in large dishes and the strongest man gets the most.[7] For dinner we had soup with a few beans in it hard bread and salt junk which only persons with strong molars could possibly masticate. For supper we had a repatition of the dinner bill of fare *barrin* the soup. The ship is very full and crowded having about eleven hundred souls aboard when by law it is only allowed to carry about six hundred for the ship is quite small only measuring fifteen hundred times [illegible]

Friday April 14

Last night was to me a most miserable one for not having any blankets of my own and as the ship provided none it being quite a cold night I nearly froze. I woke up this morning with a raging sore throat by which to remember my first night at sea. The place where I slept was more like pandemonium than any I have saw this many a day. There were men cursing and swearing while endeavoring to find their bunks women scolding babies crying etc. Some of the passengers were singing Others laughing and all were talking.[8] I think it will sometime before I entirely forget that night. We have as yet had very little sea sickness for the water has been so remarkably calm that it seems more as if we were on solid earth. This day has found us a little more settled for it is like a man moving from one house to another bag and baggage it takes some time to get settled.

Sunday April 16

This day has passed like any other one, but I am so much accustomed to it that it seems natural that it should. Nothing of importance has occured since we came aboard it is the same old monotonous thing day after day. The sea is very calm with a little swell from land ward which tends to make some of my fellow passengers wish they were again on the shores of California the peninsula of which is in sight. I have not as yet been sea sick in the least and do not want to be. Friday night I thought I would profit by my first nights experience and as my bunk which was merely a bit of canvass streched between two poles eighteen inches apart and the canvass being six inches shorter than I was besides being placed directly in range of an air hole of which the steerage [illegible] five inches in diameter so as to let the steerage have plenty of air. I accepted an invitation of a couple of friends to sleep between them in their bunk which is a double one in the lower tier next the floor and near the hatchway They having several blankets assured me I would keep warm and faithfully was their promise fulfilled for I never was or ever want to be while in the state of health warmer than I was that night. It was perfectly awful so many hundred living human beings sleeping in that little room notwithstanding I was almost under the hatch I was nearly suffocated seeming as if every breath would be the last I could possibly take. I endured this living death as long as it was possible but when I could stand it no longer I crawled out and went on deck where I could get the fresh air of heaven exceeding grateful that my bunk was not on the lower tier for the cold I endured the night before was a pleasure to this awful heat If there is any change in the quality of our food it is worse than when we came aboard for at times it is actually rotten I mean that the salt junk is. If I had a dog that would eat such trash I would shoot him and here I have to do it or starve. They pretend to give us tea & coffee but there is no more in common between the slop they give us and the names they designate them by than there is between a digger indian[9] and the prince of Wales. The impudence and meanness of the waiters who are Irish is unparalelled. About noon today a school of porpoises came jumping and playing around the ship they are quite a large fish some of them would perhaps weigh six or eight hundred pounds. They come swimming around the ship and jump five or six feet right up in the air and then fall back into the water again sometimes head first Sometimes tail then again broadside They kept with the vessel about half an hour creating a great deal of amusement for the passengers who have nothing to do but watch them finally they took a different course from the ship and the last we saw of them they were still jumping. They a curios way aboard this vessel of getting some of the passenger up in time to see the sun rise. I happen to be one of the favored few that are routed up at four oclock regularly every morning. As my bunk is put up in the passage way between rows of regular stationary bunks. They are put up late and in order to allow the regular bunk men room to crawl out of their holes are taken down very early each morning and if a passenger refuses to get up he is taken down with his bed so in order to avoid a severe fall of five feet on hard plank I usually make it a point to get up as soon as I hear the ship hands coming. I then immediately go up on the hurricane deck where I can obtain a magnificent view of the suns rising at sea But just about the time it gets fairly up some thing else comes up in the form of the ships crews who begin washing the deck and of course they drive us below to the main deck when the finish the hurricane they commence opporations on the main after finishing that they wash the steerage then the physican comes and inspects things and scatters lime and other disinfectants throughout the vessel.[10] While they are engaged in washing the steerage which is about six oclock we get our breakfast of *coffee* hard tack and salt junk After breakfast we hang around deck talking sleeping or playing cards occasionally some public spirited individual will get up and make us a speech on some question or other or get up a discussion on some worn out subject which has been discussed by every country school in the land a dozen times over but then it serves to relieve the monotony of every day ship life[11] At twelve oclock or 8 bells we get our dinner so called which comprises the same bill of fare that we had the first day out. At six p. m. or four bells we get our supper which is breakast repeated save a different quality of dish water called Tea We generally go into our holes about nine or ten oclock P. M. and thus are our days on the ocean waves passed. My bunk is now one of the most comfortable on board steerage as far as air is concerned for as we have been going directly south for a number of days the atmosphere is much warmer and I can stand it to sleep without blanket. But I am afraid if we would go south unto the ends of the earth that my bunk would never grow longer and my neck would continue to hang over the end while I used my boots for a pillow which I do in order that they shall not be stolen for thieves do abound and have not the fear of the law before their eyes. Besides the hold into which we are packed being filled to overflowing every night. The hurricane deck is so covered with sleepers that at night it is almost impossible for the officers to get around and in order to do so the have to make pathways and allow the men to sleep on both sides of it. Some men in order to keep their place on deck which is deemed a more desireable place to spend the night, sit or lay on the spot almost all the time leaving it only (and then in charge of a companion) when obliged to.

Monday April 17

This day I am nineteen years old It is the first anniversary of my birthday of that I ever spent on the sea and if I have to live as we are now living I hope it may be the last although our feed is slightly improved for the salt junk is not quite so much decayed as it was last week and then for two shillings or as they have it for two bits the waiters will bring a person what we term a square meal which consists of soft bread fresh potatoes and meat besides other little things who has money need not starve.

DIARY 117

Tuesday April 18

Today about noon a large whale had the kindness to come within fifteen or twenty rods of the ship and then as if proud of his bulk displayed the whole of his body head and tail to the admiring gaze of the passengers two thirds of whom were spectators and then as if afraid of over doing the thing he dived down into the water and was seen no more. That was the principal vent of this day. We frequently every day see whales spouting up water in the distance and some times see a head or a tail but this is the first one that has come so near the vessel and showed his enormous self Last night the alarm of fire that cry which appals the stoutest heart and makes the swarthy cheek of the daring mariner pale was given and light wreaths of smoke seen curling up out of the Hatchway leading to the steerage The Captain with his mates and the crew immediatly repaired to the spot and it was extinguished before three quarters of the passengers knew ought of it. I believe it originated near the machinery of the boat but as it was thought best by the officers not to allow the passengers to believe any report regarding the fire that might reach tem They said it was a false alarm and quieted the fears of the fearful

Wednesday April 19

After having been out of sight of land for three day with nothing to look out upon but a dreary waste of water we this day were once more permitted to see our nature element and this morning we passed cape St. Lucas[12] biding farewell to California We crossed the Gulf[13] or rather are engaged today in crossing that body of water but I guess from what the mate says it will take us all day tomorrow to get in sight of

Maximilians so called Empire. As we were sailing along the coast this morning we saw some men on shore which a number of miles distant so we could not tell whether they were native or white people This evening we can see the lights of some ship out out at sea.

Thursday April 20

We are still on the waters of the Gulf but thank fortune we are nearly across it. This day has been by far the warmest we have had since coming aboard for notwithstanding we have each afternoon a heavy breeze afternoons and night and also a heavy dew it is most awful hot The sun coming right straight down on our heads and in order to protect us from sun stroke they stretch awning over the hurricane deck which makes it far the most comfortable part of the ship.

Friday 21st

We are once more in sight of land for having crossed the Gulf of California we are now coasting along Mexicos shores.[14] About three oclock this afternoon we passed we passed the wreck of the Golden Gate lying high and dry on the rocks.[15] We also saw today a sail the first since we left San Francisco The water is very smoothe and we have a fine breeze but it is intensely warm. To night we can see fires on the shore built I suppose by the natives.

Sunday April 23.

We have been running along the coast most of the last two days during which time we have had awful hot weather the water has been extremely smoothe and still for there was scarcely a breath of air astir. A great many fish came sporting around the ship throwing themselves out of the water and having a fine time generally. The foliage along the coast seems very luxuriant and dense every evening we see fires along the beach I do not know what they mean but suppose they are the camp fires of the Natives Yesterday we saw a sail away off to the starboard and having nothing else to do we all watched it and speculated as to its destination where it was from and under what color it sailed until it was out of sight in the dim distance This morning or I should say about noon we left the coast and started across the Gulf of Tehuanapec[16] as soon as we entered the Gulf the wind begin to rise and blew brisker and brisker until toward evening the ship is rolling terribly and every minute the wind seems increasing. Most of the passengers are sick and do not care a straw whether the ship sinks or not but a few who are strong of stomach though weak of heart are fearful that each movement will be their last. Thank my stars that I am of neither of the former parties for I am as well as I ever was on dry land and have perfect confidence in the skill of the officers and crew of the vessel for our Capt and first mate have the name of being the best on the American Pacific[17] so I sit down and take easy as possible while I laugh at the other passenger who are vomiting all over the deck to the no small amusement of the sailors. The ship is small and well deserves the name of rolling Moses for I never saw anything toss about like it does. it is next to impossible for me to walk across the deck the only way to keep in one place is to hold fast to something stationary. Sailors always expect a storm when they cross the Gulf at this season which is the begining of the raining season. I alway thought that I would like to see a good old fashioned storm at sea and now that we have it I must say that I enjoy hugely but I and a few others are exceptions Now as it gets dark we can see what we are informed are volcanoes in process of eruption and also see lights on shore.

Monday 24th Last night about ten oclock as the wind was quite cool and the spray dashed rather uncomfortably over the deck wetting a person to skin I thought it about time to seek my bunk below and as it was near one of the port holes I had my face nicely washed with salt water several times and about an hour after I had gone to roost one old grand father wave a regular old veteran came at the ship and washed her from stem to stern completely deluging the Hurricane deck and pouring my port hole. A number of fellows who had made their beds up on deck came down into the steerage soaking wet and cursing old Neptune soundly towards midnight the wind increased power until it seemed as if it would blow the ship to pieces but along towards daylight it began to abate for we were then nearly across the Gulf and some of the sick ones began to feel better but still the waves run high and the vessel rolls very much. We are now coasting along Gualtimala and it is very warm.

Tuesday April 25

We are still of the coast of Gualtimala the weather continues very oppressive. The country has become more mountainous than it was when we first struck it. This morning we were pointed out the noted water volcano which has several times destroyed the city of Gualtimala it is a large bleak looking mountain with a great hole in its top from whence it throws out immense bodies of water deluging the country for miles around. At two oclock this afternoon we passed the sun which now shines on the north instead of the south side of us.

Wednesday 26.

It has been blowing quite hard for several days and to day we have the wind dead ahead which considerably impedes the speed of our boat. This evening we can see a volcano throwing up moulten lava which we see running down the sides of the mountain, though it is one hundred miles away it looks quite plain[18] We are now off the coast of Nicaragua and expect to arrive at San Juan del Sur tonight or in the morning at this port we leave the old tub Moses Taylor by name and hope to never again have the honor of taking steerage passage within her wooden walls but then I dont know why we should abuse the poor old boat for she has certainly done her part nobly carrying us thousands of miles safly and through one storm. No it is the owners and officers of the ship that deserve our censure long live the rolling Moses.

Thursday 27

in the port of San Juan del Sur.[19] There is I believe and old law to the effect that if the fates are against a man it is of no use for him to attempt to dispute than for man proposes and God disposes. Here we are arrived at last at the port of San Juan that harbor to which we have been looking forward for two weeks fourteen long and weary days where we expected to be freed from the miserable quarters on board this ship and the impudence of the low lived Irish waiters but alas to what do mans plans amount to when even the elements are combined against him as Petroleum V Naseby[20] would say one long doubled barreled nail would now be appropate and in order. for when we arrived here according to statement last night at midnight expecting a delightful journey across the country to the Atlantic the Captain and those of the passengers astir at that hour were informed by a pilot boat which came along side that the vessel which was to transport us across lake Nicaragua[21] was sunk in the water of this beautiful lake and that the last boat load one month ago occupied just eight days in crossing the country on account of the low stage of the water in the river. When they ought have made the trip in three days at most and that the water in the river was now much lower than a month ago and taking all things into consideration it would be an impossiblity to take us across that we would either have to wait until the rain descended in sufficient quantities to raise the river and that we would also have to wait until the steamer in the lake could be raised and repaired or return to San Francisco or go on to Panama and cross the isthmus on the cars of the three alternatives I believe our captain in his great wisdom chose the latter but being out of some of the neccessary of life for we had been drinking condensed steam for several days and it tasted so much of smoke and grease that it almost sickened a person. It was therefore decided to remain in port a couple of days during which time the passengers who desired could go ashore in the boats of the natives for two bittee. being tired of the monotony of every day life on ship board I was among the first to avail myself of that privelege in a short time at least half or three quarters of the passengers were ashore roaming on the country. The port of San Juan is a nice little cove well sheltered and I think it would be a good harbor in a storm as for the town and inhabitant I will do my utmost to give a description of them. The ship was anchored about a quarter of a mile distant from the shore, and the boats of the natives who were conveying us ashore were filled to their greatest capacity sinking them to their gunwales the passengers almost fighting to get at seat in them and if they had not pushed them off as soon as they did we would have been swamped by the number of passengers When we arrived at the wharf and got a foot hold on dry land again it seemed like old times although but two weeks had elapsed since our embarkation it seemed like half a life time. The town is a straggling street with huts on each side of it and a few back of and off the street. They are generally made of bark pieces of wood etc with straw roofs there is perhaps thirty or forty of them altogether. There is also several large frame building in a state of decay which look as if they had at on time been used for hotels but what they would want of such large hotels in this miserable place save during the stay of the passengers which is never more than a day perhaps two days in a months is a mystery to me upon a hill a short distance from the town is a frame of a little house said to have been built by the grey eyed man of destiny Gen Walker[22] as a look out. but I guess he neglected the useing of the structure for certain it is he did not keep a sharp enough look out to evade the United States authority. Leading up from town and running past this look out station is a nice well made carriage way or more properly speaking a fine wagon road flanked by a telegraph line both of which are said to lead to the lake twelve miles distant. A number of us steerage fellow having no money wherwith to procure a conveyance with wheels took natures mode of locomotion and pursued the devious windings of this road for about a mile into the densest woods I ever saw with parrots monkeys parroquets and other tropical birds and animals singing and gabbering on every side of us. It was very pleasant and beautiful in those woods while the telegraph poles and towers looked so natural and home like though it seemed like a great piece of extravagance to use mahogany for poles. The country immediately around San Juan is very hilly and broken consequently the view of the country is obstructed. Almost the first move I made when once more I stood up on the solid earth was for the beach where I was informed we could obtain a good bath and not be arrested by the authorities for indecency. Upon arriving on the spot designated I proceeded to take my first sea bath (but not my first in salt water for I swam in Great Salt last summer), and was much delighted therewith so much so indeed that I took two separate swims one in the morning and tother in the afternoon. We dare not venture far from the shore for fear of sharks which abound in these water for as a friend remarked I wanted to take a whole person home not a boy with one leg or perhaps minus an arm. We found a great abundance of tropical fruit pineapples cocoa nuts orange figs etc which were all obtainable for almost nothing and a person in the more northern latitude can have no idea of the superiority of flavor of these fruits when allowed to ripen on the trees I had frequently read of deliciousness of the fruits in their native climate but had no conception of the reality until I tasted of them. I suppose they are even more acceptable to my palate after the miserable feed to which I have been accustomed during the last two weeks. Some of the passengers have eaten so much of it that I expect they will be sick so much fruit on one stomach after such a long and total abstance from anything of the kind is not considered good and I am afraid that I have eaten to heartaly of it, but being in good health and having a healthy stomach I hope to escape any serious results from my indescretion. The natives at this port like all the rest of the world eager to acquire money and gain wealth for they offer their services in most every possible way in the first place they brought us ashore then they sold us fruit monkeys birds of all description and wanted to show us around the country for a consideration. and through some channel they had descovered that we were unclean perhaps they remembered the condition of other ship loads of passengers and shrewdly judged all mankind liable to become otherwise then clean during a passage of two weeks on a liner therefore the eagerly solicited they job of become lord of the bath and sponging us off some of them obtained what they sought but for my part I would rather not have so much to do with them for they are a miserable dirty set that live by plundering the passengers and stealing what ever they can lay their hands upon. They are quite a small people as are all nations of the tropics few of them measuring over five feet in height or weighing over one hundred pounds. They are of a dusky color something similar to a mulato or a North American indian with a sharp cunning eye which remind one of a cats They is not at all uniform but the prevailing style at present seems to consist of the cast of clothing of the passengers who have passed through the country and consequently very few of them have what would be considered by a broadway dandy an exquisite fit. The women who are nearly as large as the men wear a single frock without hoops which are not fashionable in this section. The children are as generally clothed in the garb assigned them by (nature) although occasionally an aspireing youth may be seen struting around in his first tail coat which was in all probability manufactured in New York for a six footer. When there is no ship in port I am told that they the men and women lay away their clothes and are as innocent of covering as were Adam and Eve in the Garden of Eden before the fall. Their are a few American residing at this place who are in the employ of the company I would think they would terribly lonesome when there is no ship in port. it would take a liberal salary to keep me in this place a year for I think I should have the blues three quarters of the time. Not knowing authoritively how long we to remain here or how soon the ship may take its departure not exactly desiring to be left behind I thought it policy to come aboard at sun down, though I would have liked very much to have slept on shore. The captain promised to fire a gun as a signal of departure but having roamed about and walked a great ways during the day in the hot sun I know I would sleep sound the gun might not awake me and if it did I would stand a poor chance of getting aboard after night for who would ever miss a steerage passenger although I am confident that this same steerage passenger would miss the vessel very much. and now I have stated my reason for not spending the night ashore. It is a good thing to be cautious but I think one of my friends a little to much so for he will not venture ashore when two thirds of the passenger are there for he has a great horror of being left in this country even with a crowd

Friday April 28

Out on the ocean all boundless we ride. Yes we are once again afloat and it seems quite natural to. The ship did not weigh anchor until this evening about five oclock so I had another little recess of six hours on shore but during this time I was careful not to wander out of hearing of the ship gun. Two vessels came into port today on an English brig and the other the famous U. S. Gunboat Wateree[23] whose whereabouts has for some time been a matter of conjecture for where she was no one except those aboard knew. There it was then we arrived a ship in port which had brought coal there for the packets and one other ship making five in all. The largest number of vessels I suppose that have been in that port at one time for a long time perhaps ever making it appear quite lively

Sunday April 30th.

This the third Sabbath I have spent on board this old tub and it will in all human probability be the last for tomorrow morning we cast anchor in Panama When we leave this boat I hope for ever but who knows for that luck had been against us it may continue to and we may have to double the horn yet. The last two day have been the of same old monotonous kind as before we made San Juan del Sur. The weather has been exceeding hot and were it not for an accomodating sea breeze we would in all probability been nicely roasted and ready for the sandwich islanders as they were during Capt Cooks time Ever since we came aboard at San Francisco we have had to obtain our miserable drinking water out of a tank on the main deck it was always filthy and during the week preceeding our arrival at San Juan having run out of water we were compelled to drink condensed steam which was so oderiforous of greasey machinery that we would have to hold our noses while we drank our miserable allowance for a guard was placed over the tank and no person allowed to take but little at a dose. it seemed and was more like an emetic than a stimulant to revive drooping nature for it was generally about as warm as one would want their coffee. When we left San Juan they of course had laid in a new supply of water so called who proper name should be diahoera provocative for it was undoubtedly Cholera right bower and the wonder is that it has not caused death it certainly has sickness for quite a number of the passengers are sick though the ship physican says it is from eating to much ripe fruit after so long an abstanance perhaps it is but I am rather sceptical. Our water is a kind of a compromise between food and drink it composed of three parts water two parts sand or dirt and one part what at home we called wiggle tails and in order to get water as pure as possible under existing circumstance it is necessary to strain it between our teeth and spit out the animal part. I suppose this could truly be called living waters though I doubt if it be the kind to which David refers in his psalms for he would not have sang so sweetly of it.[24] How it is possible for any man woman or child to drink of such filth and live is a mystery to me. Thank the Lord it endureth not for ever One thing I have heretofore omitted though unintentionally to notice. It is something that is to be seen every night and early in the morning. It is the sparkling of the water I have frequently stood on the bow of the boat after dark and leaning over gaze for an hour at a time at the ship plowing through the waves and dashing the spray fifteen or twenty feet in the air which would glisten an sparkle like a lace curtain covered with diamonds I never have learned the cause of its sparkling but have frequently admired the effect. It is something I have never noticed on fresh water and therefore conclude that it is indigenous to salt. The steerage passengers have to wash in salt water pumped out of the sea and as I am one of the early risers on this vessel I have an opportunity of seeing these beautiful water diamonds each morning when we wash our face we always keep our eyes tight shut Experience has taught us wisdom and go feeling around for something to wipe the brine away with and if we are not immediately successful in our search we have to return and wash away the salt with which our face is covered. I think this would be a good country for pork packers. The ship is not only filled with passengers, filth and vermin, but has also a goodly supply of monkey parrots and paroquets that the passengers bought on shore for a trifle and are now endeavoring to take home for pets but they find them a deal of trouble and the butcher is making a fortune keeping and feeding the nuisances if I had one I think I would be tempted to commit to the tender mercies of the deep. The sea life on ship board evidently does not agree with monkeys in generally they were never made for sailors for the begin to look peaked as though they longed for their native wilds and one of them this morning curled up and went to his long home peace to his ashes. Last night we had quite a number of refreshing showers driving us all below and crowding the hold about as much or little than we pleasant for it was almost impossible to breath so close was the atmosphere and so many to breath it. This morning it was hot and clear and has remained so all day. Ever since we left San Juan we have been favored with the presence of flying fish and I must I was very much disappointed in them for from pictures I had seen of them I had concluded that they were from three to four feet in length and had wings some like those of a bird.[25] but they are not more than as many inches in length and their wings are something like those of a humming bird We will see them shoot out of the water and sail along thirty or forty rods and then dive into the water again. it seems that after their wings become dry they can no longer sustain themselves in mid air between the heavens and water. We are also visited by a great many birds who come sweshing out from the shore which is not far off. They whirl around the ship a few times and are off. One of them I do not know what kind of a bird it was was captured on the riggings of the ship to day. Some of the boys tell me that they frequently see serpents of a green color floating in the water both yesterday and today that they are slender and four or five feet long.[26] I never saw any myself though I have watched for them until my eyes ached. Sea serpents always were of rather an eccentric turn of mind showing their gigantic proportions to some while to others they always turn the cold shoulder and are never at home

EIGHT | HOMEWARD BOUND

*O*N PANAMA the visitors were hard put to distinguish the natives from those of Nicaragua. A mixture of Spanish, Indian, and Negro, they resembled the Nicaraguans and followed a similar way of life. Wearing clothes given them by tourists, they were ragged and dirty. They were also beggars, prying small change from the ship's passengers and peddling trinkets, shells, parrots, parakeets, monkeys, pineapples, and oranges. Their offers of valet service tempted the class-conscious Americans, but their personal filth was repelling.

Just as in Nicaragua, the tourists tried to see everything during their brief stay in Panama City. The old city wall—actually a building—was falling down in more places than it was upright and served as a barracks for the unkempt Colombian troops. The soldiers spent their time marching aimlessly, showing little military dignity. Of the churches the most impressive was the cathedral facing the central public square. In a state of disintegration beyond repair and overgrown with vines, the building was nevertheless a magnificent structure that evoked memories of a great past. The Spanish influence was evident in many ways, but especially in the architecture. The adobe houses, which had red-tiled roofs, crowded one upon another, and their second-floor verandahs overhung the narrow streets, which were really flagstone paths wide enough only for single-file traffic.

The passengers from the *Moses Taylor* went by train from Panama City to the Atlantic port of Aspinwall (now Colón). Surprisingly, the forty-nine-mile trip was very comfortable. The American owners of the railroad were competent businessmen who demanded efficiency from their employees. The four-hour ride passed quickly for the passengers, fascinated by the natives and by their huts scattered about in the great mahogany forests. Wild fruit trees, naked children, and strange animals produced an exotic picture.

In Aspinwall, steamship schedules did not permit much sightseeing, and passport clearance took what time remained. The town, with its native huts, half-breed peddlers, junk shops, and dockside freight depots, was similar to San Juan del Sur and Panama City. Most of the travelers wanted to board ship immediately but before doing so, they were required by the American Consul to have their passports validated. Although an aura of corruption hung over the procedure, the travelers paid the fee, protesting loudly and vowing to report this illegal charge at another time. Momentarily they would tolerate anything to get on their way.

At last they boarded the steamer *Golden Rule* for New York City. This finely outfitted ship was twice the size of the *Moses Taylor* and had other advantages: the steerage bunks were comfortable; there were fewer passengers, and they could sleep as long as they liked; the ventilation was good; and the food and water were satisfactory. Even between-meal lunches (hardtack from the ship's unguarded stores and fresh fruit from peddlers) were possible. Neither headwinds nor high seas off Cape Hatteras slowed the *Golden Rule,* and in rapid order the landmarks passed by: The Turks and Caicos Islands, Cuba, Hatteras, Cape Henlopen. Finally, on May 11, 1865, the ship reached New York City.

For a "world traveler" home at last, the rail trip from New York to South Bend was dull. Eastern and Midwestern

America was civilized, tame territory, unworthy of diary keeping; the great adventure was ending.

Back in South Bend, Stanfield settled into a businessman's life, married, and joined the proper clubs. While California and a summer house on Cape Cod might again draw him away on vacation, he would never leave South Bend for a long time. He often spoke of his western trip, but without much nostalgia. For Stanfield, there was "no place like home."

The Diary

Monday May 1st

We arrived in the harbor of Panama New Granada South America[1] this morning early and anchored four miles from the city where the natives boats soon found us out and were swarming around offering to take us ashore in a better boat and cheaper than any one else could do. As the ship is to remain here the harbor being to shallow to approach nearer the shore[2] and as the ships boats which is to take us ashore will not be on hand until tomorrow I with quite a number of the passenger wishing to have as square meal ashore and time to look around the city concluded about eight oclock this morning to give the boatmen a job and leave the old Moses forever So for the sum of one doller in silver we were conveyed to within about three rods of shore. The natives then refused to go nearer saying it was so shallow that their boats would swamp about a dozen natives of a kindly disposition though evidently in league with the boatmen rushed out and offered to carry us ashore for the small sum of one dollar. (They believe in making hay while the sun shines.) Almost forcing us on their shoulders several of the pasenger allowed themselves to be grilled in that manner but the rest of us ordered the boatmen to fetch their boat up to shore when we sprang out many of us reaching the shores of Granada for the first time The first thing I went for was fruit and I found it in a great plenty delicious oranges four or five cents splendid large pine apples fifteen cents to two shillings apiece bananas for almost nothing while cocoa nuts and limes were a drug on the market After having satisfied our appetite for fruit we started for the Hotel so as to be in good season for dinner.

133

While traveling in among the narrow streets which are more like alleys not being more than twenty feet in width sidewalk included we met an institution which satisfied us that we were in a civilized land an omnibus oh how like home it did look fortunatly for it It is the only wheeled vehicle drawn by horses in city for should two such vihicles meet it would be impossible for them to pass each other in these narrow streets on the bus was in American letters the words Aspinwall House.[3] We followed the bus and finally arrived at said house which was kept on American plan. After waiting an hour or so we obtained a first rate dinner for one silver dollar. The house was well patronized today and no doubt did a thriving business with liberal profits after having eaten the best meal for over two weeks and satisfied the wants of the inner man we started to examine the ruins of this renouned city. It is almost entirely built of adobe sun dried brick and are generally three stories high The stories are low. The streets are laid out intersecting at right angle and are about twenty feet wide they are all of them paved with flag stone the side walks are paved with the same material and border the street which properly speaking is but twelve feet wide the walks on both sides occuppy four feet of space each so it would be impossible for the natives to use wagons and horses to only way of transporting merchandise fruits wood or other articles is on their heads or mule back. The houses all have verandas projecting from the second stories a third of the way across the streets and almost meeting midway. The city also contains a number of public squares which are used for market places and for public meetings etc. They are generally immediatly in front of some old cathedral which abound in Panama. Their must be eight or ten in the city all of them built of brick with two towers on the two front corners sometimes these towers have bells in them but others have lost theirs or never had any in the place designed for them We went down to the outskirts of the city where we saw what once was a formatable wall but now it is most of it in ruins though part of it is in a pretty good state of preservation. it is twenty to twenty five feet in width and perhaps twenty feet high. It is not a solid walls for on the inside is the barracks for the soldiers a company of which were kind enough to come out on duty and march up town for our especial benefit at least we took it so. The were all natives and about thirty in number the natives here are a facsimile in color size and general appearance of those we saw in Nicaragua consequently the soldiery are not gigantic in stature Mounted on the this wall was an old fashioned canon eight or ten feet long smooth bore which would hold perhaps a ten pound shot it was mounted on an old carriage the wheels of which we saw out ruin and decay are everywhere apparent.[4] The natives all endeavor to turn an honest penny by selling fruit and little trifles now is their harvest for when no ship is in port trade they say is very dull. The price of all kinds of fruit has risen wonderfully since morning. Oranges such as sold four for five cents this morning now are scarce at three for a shilling or bit as they have it. It was on the arrival of the train from Aspinwall this afternoon that we heard news that made the blood curdle in our veins news that draped the whole country in morning The assassination of Lincoln which occured over two weeks ago[5] but which we just have learned. Every one of the passengers seemed as though the had lost a relative or some dear friend. To night we sleep in the depot where about one hundred of us intend spending our first night ashore for over two weeks. We dare not venture out in this place after dark unless there be quite a number together for the native would as leave kill as look at a person if they thought there was any money to be made by it. This evening we took supper at an Italian restaurant for which we paid one dollar got one dines worth and no more.

Tuesday May 2d   On board the Golden Rule[6]

This morning I was up bright and early and started out to find something to eat after breakfast I visited an old cathedral which was in a very dilapadiated condition but the best in the city. When I came out of this church I met a beggar at the door who was very worthy and very poor who would be very much obliged to Americanos for half a dollar but finally concluded to take a dime. Out on the public square immediately in front of the cathedral I noticed quite a crowd of fellow passenger upon approaching them I discovered that they were talking with the American consul a gentleman from Kentucky[7] He proposed a meeting on the square this afternoon in order to express our great sorrow and affliction upon the murder of the President. We all agreed with him and intendeded assembling immediatly after dinner, but about this time we noticed a commotion on board the Moses Taylor where we perceived that they were landing the rest of the passengers who were taken directly to the depot and shiped to Aspinwall. So our plans for a meeting we knocked in the head and by nine oclock in the morning we were all of us on our way to the Atlantic having bidden farewell to the poor old city of Panama It took two very large trains to hold us all and four hours to cross the distance being forty nine miles over the most crooked road I have ever seen[8] our train which was the head one looked like a snake as it wraggle its slimy form over the ground. The cars were clean and nice with cane bottomed seats steerage and cabin passengers we to be found in each car. We were all equal for once. The country through which we passed are very thinly settled with two or three small stations at which the train stoped. About half way was a fine large house built on the American style I believe it was owned and occupied by an American here we stoped for some time to wood and water. Occasionally we would pass a few na-

DIARY

tive huts made of reeds and branches of trees placed perpendicularly in the ground. With straw roofs and a lot of little natives as naked as when they were born playing around in the sun which was hot enough to roast a white man. Along the road the underbrush is very dense it looks almost impossible for a snake to penetrate it. Mahogany which is so prized at home here grows wild the company using it for fuel for their engines. All kinds of tropical fruits grow wild almost within our reach immense bunches of luscious banana trees filled with ripe yellow oranges patches of pine applies which grow like cabbages and limes by the million are to be seen along this route The first half of the way was through passes in the mountains and hills for the country was very broken but about half way across one struck the river Chagres when the country became smoother and more level we followed this river which is a sluggish looking stream nearly the size of the St. Jo. Most of the way to Aspinwall. The road is very well built though I am told thousand of man lost their lives in laying it in some go so far as to say there is a man buried for every tie laid. Aspinwall is a landing place for the old line of California steamer it has a few large building for freight and a hotel.[9] A few store and native huts complete the buildings of the town I should have said they have a very good depot. I am inclined to think buisness very poor in this place except when a steamer comes When the shop keeper fleece the passenger selling articles at four times their value in New York. At this place our passengers we subjected to most an outrageous swindle. The examination of our passports for which they charged one silver dollar. It was a mere farce all that they done was to past a bit of printed paper on the back of the passport saying that it had been looked at in the port of Aspinwall any one that would give the consul a dollar no difference if he be the greatest rebel in America could have the same thing done for him as a loyal man. Some of the passengers protested at being swindled in such a manner and declared they would not submit to it. When the commander of a U. S. gun boat then in port who was evidently in league with the consul[10] declared that the ship should not sail until every man had shown his passport and paid a dollar for it. So we had to give in but promised them that they should hear from it again. We came aboard upon a signal gun being fired at five oclock this evening At seven we weighed anchor and are now once more out on an ocean sailing.

Wednesday May 3rd

We have returned to same old regime of life on a steamer at sea but as we are now on the home side of the isthmus we all feel much better save those who are subject to sea sickness and they feel miserable for it has been rough all day with a strong head wind which makes it much more pleasant for us that are well We are now on the Carribean Sea and have seen innumerable flying fish today. The Golden Rule is among the largest of ocean steamer her tonnage being thirty five hundred tons. More than twice that of the Moses Taylor. She has an engine of thirty two hundred horse power so the head winds do not discommode her to any great extent. As a natural consequence she is large and roomy. The steerage is not crowded consequently I have a nice large bunk and can lay abed as long as I please mornings. There are half a dozen barrels of hard tack within reach of our berths. Some of the boys broke in the head of one of the barrels so we can take a lunch whenever we choose. The ship has no hurricane deck but has plenty of room on the main deck. I should have said the hurricane deck is only on the back half of the ship not extending forward for the steerage passengers. Every thing is far cleaner than on the other side. The waiters are all darkeys who know their place and do their duty. Then the food is far superior to anything we have had heretofore though it is now hardly what an epicure would crave or pro-

DIARY   139

nounce excellent. We also have ice water to drink. There is a boy peddling oranges bananas etc on board so who so ever hungers for such luxuries if he have the specie can partake.

Thursday Headwind and rough sea all day as we are churning the Carribean Sea we are out of sight of land.

Friday wind and wave remain about the same O ye of the weak stomach how I do pity you. Toward evening we passed what I was informed was round island but for what it is renound if for anything deponent saith not. There must be a little town or something of the kind on it for we saw a ship in a harbor of the island We also saw a vessel out at sea sailing In less than one week we hope to be in New York

Saturday This morning [manuscript missing] break we came in sight of Cu [manuscript missing] along the eastern side of it and in few hours we had left it behind us. We did not approach near enough to see much of anything as much as I want to get to our journeys end I would very much like to stop in Havana a few days but of course it is impossible. Towards evening we passed Turks island[11] a noted salt deposit. There is quite a settlement on the island and were several vessels in its harbor. After dark I guess it was about nine oclock we saw away ahead what looked like a railroad passenger car after night with its lamps all lighted rapidly approaching us then we shortly saw into they proved to be the Pacific Mail Steamer Areil under the escort of a U. S. war steamer.[12] When she got directly opposite us they burned the light and fired a rocket we did likewise the manner in which steamer salute one another after night at sea. They shot past us the [manuscript missing] with her lamps and [manuscript missing] in the dim distance [manuscript missing] South for she was outward bound. When we were coasting along the shores of California I longed to the coast of Mexico so as to be off a forign shore but now I am just as anxious to see the shore of the now United States. I have concluded with the poet that there is no place like my own native land.

Sunday May 7 We have saw no land today save to very small island this morning The wind has died away it is quite cloudy over head the weather is very comfortable. This is the fourth Sunday I have had the pleasure of spending on the briny deep. I think at least I hope it may be the last for some time to come

Monday Have had clear sailing all day saw no land and are probably off the coast of South Carolina have had scarcely no wind and at sun set it was quite calm but cloudy and look like rain. A little after dark The winds rose and rains descended the folk with weak stomach looked sad for it has become quite rough as we are now approaching Hatteras[13] were mariners most always look out for rough weather

Tuesday Weather quite rough raining and cold wind blowing makes it quite disagreeable to be on deck we are now off Hatteras We saw one sail this evening and passed the cape at dark

Wednesday Now that we are north of hatteras every body feels as if the were [manuscript missing] at home and are consequently quite gay notwithstanding the sea is rough and a strong wind renders it cold and disagreeable on deck but the wind is in our favor Some expected to get into New York tonight but were disappointed but we will certainly see the land of promise tomorrow

New York City Thursday May 11th 1865

On[ce] more I am on dry land for good and [in]tend remaining there for some time to come about nine oclock last night we passed Cape Henlope.[14] This morning at day break we

DIARY 141

left long branch in our rear then the pilot boat began to swarm around us like bee around an empty sugar barrel four or five of them making directly for us one of them making the best speed got the job of bringing us into port. We ought to have been landed at eight oclock this morning but a vessel of war was [manuscript missing] Our wharf and it took her several hours [manuscript missing] up steam and leave so we did not [manuscript missing] until near eleven just four weeks [manuscript missing] most to the hour from the time we embarked at San Francisco. My last night aboard was a repetition of my first. A number of men wishing to speculate bought up all the blankets they could among which was the blanket under which I had slept for two weeks. Consequently I nearly froze cought cold and have a sore [throa]t. Thus ended my sea voyage home.

H. S. STANFIELD

Bibliographical Notes

These bibliographical notes are divided into two main sections. All sources are briefly described in the following bibliographical essay, and those that are particularly relevant to this study are also listed in conventional bibliographical form (see Bibliography, pp. 166–73).

In the preparation of this book the resources of libraries and historical societies throughout the country were heavily drawn upon. The collections of the institutions listed below were particularly valuable: Bancroft Library (University of Cal., Berkeley); Beinecke Rare Book and Manuscript Library (Yale University); California Society of Pioneers Library (San Francisco); California State Historical Society Library (San Francisco); California State Library (Sacramento); California State Sutro Library (San Francisco); Chicago Historical Society Library; Chicago Public Library; Church of the Latter Day Saints Library (Salt Lake City); Columbus, Nebraska, Public Library; Guthrie Center, Iowa, Public Library; Henry Huntington Library (San Marino, Cal.); Idaho Historical Society (Boisie); Iowa State Department of History and Archives (Des Moines); Lilly Library (Indiana University, Bloomington); Marysville Public Library; Mishawaka Public Library; Montana Historical Society Library (Helena); Nevada Historical Society Library (Reno); Newberry Library (Chicago); Northern Indiana Historical Society Library (South Bend); Notre Dame University Library (South Bend); Park County Free Library (Cody, Wyoming); Sacramento Public Library; Salt Lake City Public Library; South Bend Public Library; Stewart Library (Grinnell, Iowa); Utah Historical Society Library (Salt Lake City); Wyoming State Archives and Historical Department (Cheyenne).

Interviews with persons having some knowledge of Stanfield and his friend Bartlett were also helpful. Mrs. Thomas Stanfield, widow of Stanfield's nephew, remembered much family lore; and Judge William E. Miller, Stanfield's friend, retained memories of the man. Bartlett's grandniece, Mrs. Philip Stafford, holds manuscripts, newspaper clippings and memories of value. Their contributions added interesting details about Stanfield and Bartlett.

Overland Diaries (MSS, 1863)

The scarce manuscript diaries of 1863 overland crossings are scattered in libraries across the country. The Bancroft Library holds two: the diary of Ellen Tompkins Adams, who traveled by wagon from Council Bluffs to Carson City; and a photocopy of William L. Fulkerth's diary of his trip from Iowa to California, also by wagon. Mrs. Adams, wife of a physician, carefully records the name of each overnight stop, adding descriptive material which gives a clue to problems and pleasures of the trail. Accounts of the discouragements of the traveler and routine requirements for trail life fill the Fulkerth document. The Huntington Library holds A. Howard Cutting's "Journal of a Trip Overland to California" from Illinois. Internal evidence indicates the diary was written some time after events. It contains extensive descriptions of trail life and describes the emotions of immigrants facing new situations. Also in the Huntington collection is a typed copy of Silas L. Hopper's diary which follows his wagon route from Nebraska to California. It contains short comments about water and wood conditions; the Nevada towns are exceptionally well described. J. T. Redman's short diary (Huntington) tells of his boyhood employment as a wagon driver from Missouri to California. His youthful wonderment fills the writing as he first viewed Indians, buffaloes, and other new sights. The Beinecke Rare Book and Manuscript Library of Yale University contains the diary of M. C. Purviance, who traveled from Illinois to California by wagon. He describes the immigrant's mixed first reactions to Indians and the wilderness. His descriptions of Virginia City, Nevada, are outstanding. The Montana Historical Society Library holds a typed copy of the first-rate diary of Lucia Darling Park, who traveled by wagon from Omaha to Bannack, Montana. Mrs. Park excels in descriptions of Indians and of tensions on the trail, and provides a good example of a woman's mixed reaction to the hardships of western travel.

Published Overland Diaries (1863)

Published materials giving first-hand descriptions of western travel in 1863 include the following items: Flora Isabelle Bender, "Notes by the Way, Memoranda of a Journey Across the Plains, from Bull Creek, Washington County, Neb., to Virginia City, Nev. Terr., May 7 to August 4, 1863," ed. William C. Miller, *Nevada Historical Society Quarterly*, I (July, 1958), pp. 144–74. Her account is of interest to this study, for the Bender family, originally from South Bend, entertained and assisted Stanfield when he reached Virginia City. Fitz-Hugh Ludlow's article "Among the Mormons" in *Atlantic Monthly* (April, 1864), records extensive observations on Salt Lake City, its physical and human resources. Maurice O. Morris' *Rambles in the Rocky Mountains* (London, 1864) presents with clarity insights into western conditions; and "Across the Plains in 1863: The Diary of Peter Winne" in *Iowa Journal of History* (July, 1951), is a well-known account of the prairie crossing.

Overland Diaries (MSS, 1864); Midwest to California

Those 1864 manuscripts which describe wagon travel from the Midwest directly to California include Hiram Allton's diary record of his trip from St. Louis to California (Beinecke). Allton confuses places and dates but gives useful evidence of the quick disillusionment of the wagon traveler. Henry Ballard's journal (typed copy at Utah State Historical Society Library) of his trip from Nebraska to Salt Lake City is largely a record of place names along the route between Fort Kearney and Salt Lake City. George Harter followed the north bank of the Platte on his wagon trip from Michigan to California. Harter discusses the Indian agency near Fort Laramie and government troops stationed along the trail; his description of Salt Lake City is far above average. A mimeographed copy of the diary (transcribed by Doris Harter Chase, Sacramento, 1957) is held by the California State Library. Mary Eliza Warner (Maloon), who made the trip from Illinois to California as a fifteen-year-old, gives a list of camp sites (MS at California State Historical Society Library).

Fanny Tomlinson traveled by stage from Kansas to California. She describes with thoroughness her experience as a passenger and the food, clothing, and sleeping accommodations of travelers on the stage. Her description of Fort Kearney is excellent. (Bancroft Library holds a microfilm copy of the journal.)

Published Overland Diaries (1864);
Midwest to California

Published diaries describing wagon travel to the coast in 1864 include the following: E. Allene Taylor (Dunham)—*Across the Plains in a Covered Wagon* ([Milton?], Iowa, 192-)—describes the trip from Iowa to California, and the return via Nicaragua from San Francisco to New York; Thomas J. Lomas, *Recollections of a Busy Life* (n.p., n.d.), recalls the trip from Wisconsin to California by wagon and horseback. Samuel Sharwell's *Old Recollections of an Old Boy* (New York, 1923) traces the wagon trail from Missouri to California. Sharwell describes the buffalo herds, the Indians, and the routine of trail life.

Overland Diaries (MSS, 1864); Midwest
to Virginia City, Montana

Stanfield turned northwestward from the North Platte into the Montana country. Others who took this wagon route and whose diaries supplement Stanfield's account include T. J. Brundage's (typed copy at Montana Historical Society Library), which covers his trip from Ohio to Virginia City and provides information about guides, the election of train captains, and the administration of justice. Katherine Dunlap's journal of her trip from Council Bluffs to Bannack, Montana (Bancroft, microfilm of typed copy) gives detailed descriptions of Council Bluffs, Fort Laramie, and other major settlements. She presents the crisis atmosphere as wagons broke down and is strong in her nature portraits. Richard Owen, who traveled from Omaha to Virginia City, frequently calls attention to the heavier traffic on the south side of the Platte, as he notes daily the places passed by on the north bank (MS at Montana Historical Society Library). John T. Smith's "The Bozeman Trail 1864" (Montana Historical Society Library, typed copy) is essentially a catalogue of places passed along that route.

Of special importance is the diary of Cornelius Hedges (Montana State Historical Society Library), who traveled by wagon from Iowa to Virginia City in 1864. His diary records the progress of Allensworth's train, which followed the Jacobs train from Red Buttes to Virginia City. The document contains many references to Jacobs' train, confirming dates and trail experiences recorded by Stanfield.

Published Overland Diaries (1864);
Midwest to Virginia City, Montana

The diaries of several immigrants who traveled by wagon to Virginia City, Montana, in 1864 have been published. They include Albert J. Dickson's *Covered Wagon Days* (Cleveland, 1929), edited by Arthur J. Dickson. The trip from Wisconsin to Virginia City is described with youthful enthusiasm by a fourteen-year-old boy. An account of Benjamin W. Ryan's trip is given in "The Bozeman Trail to Virginia City, Montana, in 1864; A Diary by Benjamin W. Ryan 1826–1898," *Annals of Wyoming,* XIX (Jan. 1947), pp. 77–104. Ryan details the cost of provisions and other prices in Virginia City. James Knox Polk Miller's diary (Illinois to Salt Lake City and on to Virginia City, Montana Territory) was published as *The Road to Virginia City: The Diary of James Polk Miller,* ed. Andrew F. Rolle (Norman, Oklahoma, 1960). (The original MS is at Bancroft Library.) The diary is strong on information about recreation, fights, food, and injuries on a wagon-train journey. Substantial information is contained in this diary showing the stability of life in Virginia City.

Published Stage-Travel Diaries (1864)

Published diaries of passengers on western stages in 1864 cover portions of the route taken by Stanfield. They include the anonymous "A Trip Through Silverland [Nevada]," published in the Sacramento *Bee,* September 28, 1864, p. 2. This observer gives attention to wealthy ranches along the Reese River and business activity (chiefly mining) from California to Salt Lake City. Archie Argyle's *Cupid's Album* (New York, 1866) describes the stage trip from Nebraska to California, and the return (to New York City) via Panama. Her interest centers on the landscape, but her descriptions of cities are also detailed. Henry A. Boller's *Among the Indians Eight Years in the Far West 1858–1866,* ed. Milo M. Quaife (Chicago, 1959), presents details about contemporary Salt Lake City and stage travel from Salt Lake City to California. William H. Brewer's *Up and Down California in 1860–1864: The Journal of William H. Brewer* (New Haven, Conn., 1931), edited by Francis P. Farquhar, is a detailed record of travel and business in Nevada and California. Brewer also describes his sea voyage from San Francisco to New York via Nicaragua. Both horseback and stage transportation were used by George Thomas Marye, Jr., who commented on the coaches, the scenery, and the towns in Nevada and California in *From '49 to '83 in California and Nevada* (San Francisco, 1923).

Sea Travel Diary (1864)

James M. Spence's 1864 diary (Huntington) tells of shipboard routine from San Francisco to Panama and to New York. He describes the menu and gives sketches of harbors visited by the steamer.

Minor Western Diaries (1864)

Other manuscript and published materials relating to the 1864 overland trip include: Gilbert Benedict, northern route to Montana by wagon (Montana Historical Society Library); Richard Brownlee, ed., "Description of Train Leaving Fulton, Missouri, April 22, 1864" (notes on a wagon train leaving for a trip across the plains), *Missouri Historical Review*, LVIII (October, 1963), 131–32; Gottlieb Ence, to Utah in 1860, and life in the Great Salt Lake area in 1864 (Utah State Historical Society Library); Andrew Jackson Fisk, northern route to Montana, government troops (Montana Historical Society Library); James Fisk, northern route to Montana, government troops (Montana Historical Society Library); John W. Grannis, life in Virginia City, Montana (Montana Historical Society Library); William L. Larned, northern route to Montana by wagon (Newberry Library); Theophilus Muffly, life in Virginia City, Montana (Bancroft).

Overland Diaries (MSS, 1865); Midwest to California

Several 1865 manuscript diaries describe the overland wagon trip from the Midwest to California. These include the H. D. Barton diary (California State Library, typed) from Iowa to California; the Lawrence D. Chillson diary (Huntington) from Iowa to Nevada; the Mary Hall Jatta diary (Bancroft, typed) from Nebraska to California; and the Edward M. Lewis journal (California State Historical Society Library) from New York to California by railroad and wagon. Barton's entries are brief notations of places passed and things seen; these jottings are too terse to be of much value. Chillson gives unusual information on stage fares and meal costs, and notes the variety of wagons and animals that made up a train. Jatta confuses dates but gives exact details about vegetation in the Salt Lake area. Lewis dwells on daily problems—clothing, cooking, hunting, terrain—and carefully describes the major settlements.

*Published Overland Diaries (1865);
Midwest to California*

There are several published diaries of 1865 trips from the Midwest to California. Among the best are Bond's *Foot Travels Across the Plains* (Richmond, Indiana, 1868), the account of a wagon trip from Indiana to Salt Lake City which gives a complimentary view of the Mormons; the readable and observant *Across the Continent* (Springfield, Mass., 1865), written by the editor, Samuel Bowles, describes a stagecoach trip from Nebraska to California and the steamer passage from San Francisco to New York via Panama; Mrs. Sarah Raymond Herndon's *Days on the Road; Crossing the Plains in 1865* (New York, 1902) Iowa to Virginia City, Montana Territory, by wagon, relates typical immigrant experiences from the woman's point of view. Sixteen-year-old J. Allen Hosner describes travel in Montana Territory in his *Trip to the States in 1865,* ed. Edith M. Duncan (Missoula, Montana, 1932); and R. D. Inman, *Crossing the Plains in 1865* ([Portland?] 1915), records his trip from Iowa to Oregon by wagon and gives critical comments on the Indians and soldiers. Colonel Henry McCormick, *Across the Continent in 1865* ... (Harrisburg, Pennsylvania, 1937), traces the stage route from Kansas to California and the voyage from San Francisco to New York via Panama. This is a well-written, incident-filled narrative journal. Francis M. Watkins, *Story of the Crow Emigrant Train of 1865 written by Ralph L. Milliken from conversations with Francis M. Watkins* (Livingston, California, 1935), describes a trip by wagon from Iowa to California, giving many details about preparation for the trip and the immigrants' fears as they entered Indian country. Albert D. Richardson, *Beyond the Mississippi* (Hartford, Conn., 1867), traveled by stage to the coast with Bowles and House of Representatives Speaker Schuyler Colfax, and returned via Panama. His literary style and factual reporting are comparable to Bowles', as both diarists sought to evaluate the resources and potential of the west.

Western Travel Bibliographies
(1849, 1850's and 60's)

Overland diaries by the forty-niners and the immigrants of the 1850's are numerous. An excellent bibliography of these sources, published and unpublished, is Irene Padden's *The Wake of the Prairie Schooner* (New York, 1943). American periodical literature of the West for the period from 1811 to 1957 was thoroughly combed by Oscar O. Winther for references to the trans-Mississippi West, and these have been published as *A Classified Bibliography of the Periodical Literature of the Trans-Mississippi West 1811–1957* (Bloomington, Ind., 1961). Subjects covered include travel, territories, buffalo, forts, Indians, and Indian agents.

Western Travel Accounts Supplementary to Stanfield's
(1849, 1850's and 60's)

Selected diaries and travel accounts of these years useful to supplement Stanfield's record include the following—all manuscripts: T. J. Ables, Missouri to California in 1857 by wagon (Newberry Library); George H. Baker, travel in the Indiana Ranch area in the 1850's (Society of California Pioneers Library); Eugene Bandel, across the plains through Kansas in 1857 (California State Library); James A. Blood, Illinois to California by wagon in 1850 (Newberry Library); John Heath Bonner, Iowa to California by wagon in 1861 (Bancroft Library); Lafayette Fish, Iowa to California by wagon in 1860 (Bancroft Library); Mary C. Fish, Iowa to California by wagon in 1860 (Bancroft Library); Mrs. Nicholas Harrison Karchner, Ohio to California by wagon in 1862 (California State Library); Marie Nash, Michigan to California by wagon in 1861 (California State Library); Silas Newcomb, Wisconsin to California by stage and wagon in 1850 (Newberry Library); I. M. Smith, Missouri to California by wagon in 1859 (Newberry Library); Jane Augusta

Gould Tourtillot, Iowa to California by wagon in 1862 (Bancroft Library); J. A. Wilkinson, Michigan to California by wagon in 1859 (Newberry Library); Mrs. S. Wisner, Missouri to Oregon by wagon in 1866 (Newberry Library); Joseph Warren Wood, Wisconsin to California by wagon in 1849 (Huntington Library).

Published materials include: J. Ross Brown, *Adventures in the Apache Country; a tour through Arizona and Sonora, with Notes on the Silver Regions of Nevada* (New York, 1869), travel in Nevada; Richard F. Burton, *City of the Saints* (London, 1862), travel in the west in 1860; Major Howard Egan, *Pioneering the West 1846–1878* (Richmond, Utah, 1917), overland mail information for 1855; Horace Greeley, *An Overland Journey from New York to San Francisco in the Summer 1859* (New York, 1860), descriptions and evaluations of land and economy; Leroy Hafen, ed., *Overland Routes to the Gold Fields 1859 from Contemporary Diaries* (Glendale, 1942); William G. Johnson, *Overland to California* (Oakland, 1948), 1849 trip to California; David R. Leeper, *The Argonauts of 'Forty-Nine* (South Bend, 1894), Indiana to California by wagon in 1849; A. P. McConahay, *Incidents as I Remember Them Closing 1865* (Van Wert, Ohio, 1927), Ohio to California by wagon in early 1860's and the return to New York via Panama; John Olmsted, *Trip to California in 1868* (New York, 1880), New York to San Francisco via Panama, California to Nevada by stage; James A. Pritchard, *The Overland Diary of James A. Pritchard from Kentucky to California in 1849* (San Francisco, 1949), ed. Dale Morgan, Kentucky to California by wagon; Jules Remy and Julius Brenchley, *A Journey to Great Salt Lake City*, 2 vols. (London, 1861), San Francisco to Salt Lake City by wagon and stage in 1865; Captain James Stuart,"The Yellowstone Expedition of 1863 from the Journal of Capt. James Stuart," in *Contributions to the Historical Society of Montana*, I (Helena, 1876), 149–233; John Udell, *Incidents of Travel to California Across the Great Plains together with the Return Trips through Central America and Jamica to which are added sketches of the Author's Life* (Jefferson, Ohio, 1856).

BIBLIOGRAPHICAL NOTES 153

Among diaries and travel accounts of 1849 and the 1850's and 1860's relating to the voyage from San Francisco to New York are: August S. Bixby, Diary, 1855–64 (California State Library); Joseph Crackbon, Narrative of a voyage from New York to California via Panama 1849 (California State Library); and Charles T. Bidwell, *The Isthmus of Panama* (London, 1865), travel in Panama in the 1860's.

Newspapers

Newspapers provide local color and document events which affected contemporary western travel. Obituary notices give biographical data. Newspapers of value to this study include: *Alta California* (San Francisco), 1864, 1865; *Daily Dramatic Chronicle* (San Francisco), 1865; *Daily Union Vedette* (Camp Douglas, Utah Territory), 1864; *The Deseret News* (Salt Lake City), 1864; Los Angeles *Evening Herald and Express,* 1934; Marysville *Daily Appeal,* 1864, 1865; Mishawaka *Enterprise,* 1864, 1865; Montana *Post,* (Virginia City), 1864; Sacramento *Daily Bee,* 1864, 1865; Salt Lake *Telegraph,* 1864; San Francisco *Daily Bulletin,* 1865; South Bend *Tribune,* 1922, 1923; and Virginia *Daily Union* (Virginia City, Nevada Territory), 1864.

Directories

City and territorial directories are also primary sources. They contain business advertisements, descriptions of community institutions, and lists of residents. Contributing to this study were *Halpin & Bailey's Chicago City Directory for the Year 1862–63* (Chicago, 1862); the *Chicago Directory* [for 1866] (Chicago, 1866); *The Salt Lake City Directory and Business Guide for 1869,* compiled and arranged by E. L. Sloan (Salt Lake City, 1869); *Second Directory of Nevada Territory* [1863] (San Francisco, 1863), by J. Wells Kelly; *The Nevada Directory for 1868–69* (San Francisco, 1868), by William R. Gillis; *Amy's Marysville Directory for the Year Commencing June 1858* (Marysville, 1858), compiled by Mix Smith and G. Amy; *Brown's Marysville Direc-*

tory for the Year Commencing March 1861 (Marysville, 1861); and *San Francisco Directory for the Year Commencing October 1864* (San Francisco, 1864), compiled by Henry G. Langley.

Maps

Many publications contain maps showing the wagon routes west. The principal roads to California and Virginia City, Montana, are in Oscar O. Winther's excellent *The Transportation Frontier Trans-Mississippi West 1865–1890* (New York, 1964). Maps of main routes can also be found in *1540–1861 Mapping the Trans-Mississippi West* (San Francisco, 1963), by Carl I. Wheat, and A. B. Hulbert, *Crown Collection of American Maps* (Colorado Springs, 1925).

Since the wagon trail blazed by Jim Bridger and followed by John M. Jacobs from the North Platte into Virginia City, Montana Territory, did not become the established road, few maps show its direction. An exception is the 1864 map of W. W. deLacy, commissioned by the First Montana Legislature, which appears as a fold-out map at the front of Volume I of the *Society of Montana Pioneers Publications,* ed. James U. Sanders (Helena, 1899). The papers of Cornelius Hedges (Montana Historical Society Library) contain a map labeled "Jacobs map of his and Bridgers routes to Virginia City." Hedges was a member of Allensworth's train, which followed the Jacobs train into Virginia City.

Several good maps show the stage route from Salt Lake City to California. The best are in Frank A. Root and William E. Connelley, *The Overland Stage to California* (Columbus, Ohio, 1950; originally printed in Topeka, 1901), which lists all stage stations west of Salt Lake City to California; and Roscoe P. Conkling and Margaret B. Conkling, *The Butterfield Overland Mail 1857–1869,* III (Glendale, Cal., 1947).

Early stage routes from Virginia City, Montana, through Idaho to Salt Lake City are nowhere clear. The southern part of the route is in "Early History of Malad Valley [Idaho]," by Glade F. Howell (master's thesis, Brigham Young University, 1960). Helpful in tracing the road is the letter of "Governor" E.

M. Pollinger to J. E. Calloway, 28 May 1904, at the Montana Historical Society Library. Pollinger was an early agent in Montana for the Oliver and Conover Stage Company.

National Archives

The National Archives and Records Service of the General Service Administration, Washington, D. C., contain records concerning western travel—records of army activities at western posts, the Indians, the immigrants passing by. Reports of the Indian agents give insight into the deterioration of the Indians, as well as records of their lives and those of the passing immigrants. The Archives also contain information about the American consul at Aspinwall and his authority.

SECONDARY SOURCES
Guide Books

Of value for quick identification of places and simple historical briefs are the Federal Works Projects Administration books published in the 1930's and 40's: *Indiana: A Guide to the Hoosier State* (New York, 1941); *Iowa: A Guide to the Hawkeye State* (New York, 1938); *Nebraska: A Guide to the Cornhusker State* (New York, 1947); *Montana: A State Guide Book* (New York, 1939); *Nevada* (Portland, Oregon, 1940); and *California: A Guide to the Golden State* (New York, 1939).

Histories (Indiana)

Indiana travelers passed through several northern Indiana communities which have by now disappeared. Some appear in *A History of St. Joseph County, Indiana*, 2 vols. (Chicago, 1907), by Timothy E. Howard; and in *Counties of Porter and Lake, Indiana* (Chicago, 1882), ed. Weston A. Goodspeed and Charles Blanchard. Other places mentioned by Stanfield in Porter and Lake counties, Indiana, were identified through the unpublished research of Mr. Norman Coambs of Chesterton, Indiana.

Histories (Chicago)

Stanfield's brief stop in Chicago enabled him to see some of the sights in that city. These places appear in A. T. Andreas, *History of Chicago*, 3 vols. (Chicago, 1884–86); and Bessie L. Pierce, *History of Chicago*, 2 vols. (New York, 1940).

Histories (Iowa)

Secondary references for Iowa are plentiful. General histories are Benjamin F. Gue's *History of Iowa* (New York, 1903), and Edgar R. Harlan's *People of Iowa* (Washington, 1931). County histories provide more detail: *History of Poweshiek County, Iowa*, I (Chicago, 1911), by L. F. Parker; *Past and Present of Jasper County, Iowa*, I (Indianapolis, 1912), by General James B. Weaver; and *Des Moines Together with the History of Polk County, Iowa* (Chicago, 1911), by Johnson Brigham. Brigham gives specific information about the Civil War era. *Josiah Bushness Grinnell* (Iowa City, 1938), by Charles E. Payne, is a study of the city of Grinnell, as well as a biography of its founder.

Histories (Nebraska)

Immigrants usually followed the Platte River through Nebraska, and information about the area is readily available. Best of the standard state histories is *History of Nebraska* (Lincoln, 1955), by James C. Olson. Older works are Morton J. Sterling's *Illustrated History of Nebraska* (Lincoln, 1911); and Morton J. Sterling's and Albert Watkins' *History of Nebraska* (Lincoln, 1918), edited and revised by Augustus O. Thomas, James A. Beattie, and Arthur C. Wakeley.

Histories (Wyoming)

Histories of Wyoming containing references to the early trails include two older works: C. G. Countant's *History of Wyoming*

(Laramie, 1899), and I. S. Bartlett's *History of Wyoming* (Chicago, 1918).

Histories (Montana)

Basic secondary works on early Montana contribute to a knowledge of the area as it was in 1864. The standard Montana history is M. A. Leeson's *History of Montana 1739–1885* (Chicago, 1885). Also helpful is *The Montana Frontier* (Helena, 1942), by Merrill G. Burlingame, dean of present Montana historians.

In addition to diaries, several contemporary accounts of activities in Montana give color and detail. The best are Granville Stuart, *1834–1918 Diary and Sketch Book of a Journey to America in 1866 and return trip up the Missouri River to Fort Benton, Montana,* Introd. by Carl S. Dentzel (Los Angeles, 1963); and *Forty Years on the Frontier as seen in the Journals and Reminiscences of Granville Stuart,* ed. Paul L. Phillips, 2 vols. (Cleveland, 1925). Originally published in 1865, *The Vigilantes of Montana* (Virginia City, 1921), by Thomas J. Dimsdale, shows how law and order came to Virginia City.

Histories (Idaho)

General histories of Idaho describe early mining and travel conditions. Basic are C. J. Brosman, *History of the State of Idaho* (New York, 1918); John Hailey, *History of Idaho* (Boise, 1910); and James H. Hawley, ed., *History of Idaho,* 3 vols. (Chicago, 1920). Frank C. Robertson's *Fort Hall Gateway to the Oregon Country* (New York, 1963) traces the importance and development of that historic spot. Glade Howell's master's thesis (Brigham Young University, 1960), "Early History of Malad Valley," gives the early history of a good part of the Idaho area crossed by the Virginia City-Salt Lake City stage in 1864.

Histories (Utah)

Information about Salt Lake City and Utah in 1864 is available in many sources. Richard F. Burton's *City of the Saints and*

Across the Rocky Mountains to California (London, 1862) is a thorough treatment, by an intelligent observer, of the city, its people, the surrounding countryside, and travel conditions. General histories of Utah (which include information about Salt Lake City, its founders, and their religion) are: J. Cecil Alter's *Utah the Storied Domain: A Documentary History of Utah's Eventful Career,* 3 vols. (Chicago, 1932); and the older Hubert H. Bancroft's *History of Utah 1540–1886* (San Francisco, 1889). Other general histories: *Salt Lake City Past and Present* (Salt Lake City, 1908), by E. V. Fohlen; *History of Utah,* 4 vols. (Salt Lake City, 1892), by O. F. Whitney; *Founding of Utah* (New York, 1924), by L. E. Young; *Life of Brigham Young, or Utah and her Founders* (New York, 1877), by Edward W. Tullidge; and *Utah, Her Cities, Towns and Resources* (Chicago, 1891–92), ed. Manly and Litteral. *Hiram Rumfield's Letters of an Overland Mail Agent in Utah* (Worcester, Massachusetts, 1929), edited by Archer B. Hulbert, gives a personalized glimpse of the city at the time of Stanfield's visit. Information about the troops stationed at Camp Douglas in 1864 is in *Records of California Men in the War of the Rebellion 1861 to 1867* (Sacramento, 1890), compiled by Brigadier General Richard H. Orton.

Histories (Nevada)

For Nevada history see J. Ross Brown, the primary contemporary chronicler of the silver country in his *Adventures in the Apache Country: a tour through Arizona and Sonora with notes on the Silver Regions of Nevada* (New York, 1869); and his *Crusoe's Island: A Ramble in the footsteps of Alexander Selkirk, with Sketches of Adventures in California and Washoe* (New York, 1867). These books are crammed with first-rate descriptions of people and places. Other useful histories are Hubert H. Bancroft's *History of Nevada, Colorado, and Wyoming 1540–1888* (San Francisco, 1890); *The History of Nevada,* ed. Sam P. Davis, 2 vols. (Reno, 1913); and Effie M. Mack's *Nevada and History of the State from the Earliest Times through the Civil War* (Glendale, 1936). The standard reference is *Reproduction of Thompson and West's History of Nevada 1881 with Illustra-*

tions and Biographical Sketches of its Prominent Men and Pioneers with introduction by David F. Myrick (Berkeley, 1958; originally published in Oakland, 1881). A book far broader than its title indicates is George and Bliss Hinkle's *Sierra-Nevada Lakes* (Indianapolis, 1949) which presents a history of the Lake Tahoe area, including important information concerning early stage routes. George D. Lyman has documented his *Virginia City: The Saga of Comstock Lode* (New York, 1946). The same scene, depicting his life in Virginia City, was handled earlier by Samuel Langhorne Clemens (Mark Twain) in his contemporary *Roughing It* (Chicago, 1872). Effie M. Mack digs into this period and place in her excellent *Mark Twain in Nevada* (New York, 1947).

Histories (California)

California histories are numerous and contain contemporary and modern descriptions of the period, towns, and institutions. Charles L. Brace gives contemporary views in *The New West, or California in 1867–68* (New York, 1869); better yet are the writings of Samuel Bowles and Albert Richardson, already cited. As experienced journalists they noted pertinent details and were able to give accurate descriptions of their experiences. H. H. Bancroft's *History of California,* 7 vols. (San Francisco, 1886–90), is standard.

Useful to identify California place names are *The Directory of California Land Names* (Los Angeles, 1951); Erwin G. Gudde's *California Place Names a Geographical Dictionary* (Los Angeles, 1949); and *Historical Spots in California* (Stanford, 1948), by Mildred B. Hoover and H. E. and E. G. Reusch.

Studies relating to areas, organizations, and people in California are important for gathering information about Stanfield's experiences. Among these works are county and regional histories: Peter J. Delay's *History of Yuba and Sutter Counties, California with Biographical Sketches . . .* (Los Angeles, 1924); *Thompson and West's History of Yuba County, California* (Oakland, Cal., 1879); and the typed, unsigned copy of "History of Camptonville: Its People and Community" (Marysville Public

Library). Others are *The Centennial Year Book of Alameda County, California* (Oakland, 1876), by William Halley; and *The Memorial and Biographical History of Northern California* (Chicago, 1891). Information concerning the Sacramento area is in W. J. Davis' *An Illustrated History of Sacramento County, California* (Chicago, 1890); and *The Sacramento: River of Gold* (New York, 1939), by Julian Dana.

San Francisco's history, its people, institutions, and attractions are described in many sources, among these Louis F. Byington and Oscar Lewis, *The History of San Francisco*, 3 vols. (Chicago, 1931); *Historical Sketch of Calvary Presbyterian Church* (San Francisco, 1869); *A History of the City of San Francisco and incidentally of the state of California* (San Francisco, 1878), by John S. Huttell; *San Francisco As It Was As it Is and How to See It* (San Francisco, 1912), by Helen T. Purdy; *Industries of San Francisco* (San Francisco, 1889), by J. D. Samson; and John P. Young, *San Francisco A History of the Pacific Coast Metropolis*, 2 vols. (San Francisco, n. d.). Emphasis on the people of San Francisco is in Julia Cooley Altrocchi's *The Spectacular San Franciscans* (New York, 1949); and in Miriam A. deFord's *They were San Franciscans* (Caldwell, Idaho, 1941). The San Francisco theatre is treated in Thomas A. Brown's *History of American Stage* (New York, 1870); John H. McCabe's "Theatrical Journals 1849–1882," 4 vols. (Sutro Library, typed); and "Tom Maguire, Napoleon of the Stage" in *California Historical Society Quarterly Reprints* (San Francisco), Volume 20, number 4; Volume 21, numbers 1, 2, 3.

Central America

Works relating to travel experiences in Central America—in addition to those already cited—include the following: Atlantic and Pacific steamship companies, their ships and schedules are discussed in *Gold Rush Steamers of the Pacific* (San Francisco, 1938), by Ernest A. Wiltsee. The Guatemala shoreline observed by Stanfield is described in *Four Keys to Guatemala* (New York, 1961), by Vera Kelsey and Lilly Osborne, and in *Guatemala: The Land and the People* (New Haven, Conn., 1961), by Nathan L.

Whetten. Stanfield's observations on Nicaragua are confirmed in *The Key of the Pacific: The Nicaraguan Canal* (Westminster, 1895), by Archibald R. Colquhoun and *Nicaragua Past, Present and Future* (Philadelphia, 1859), by Peter F. Stout. William Walker's role in Nicaraguan history is explained by Albert Z. Carr in *The World and William Walker* (New York, 1963); *The Filibuster The Career of William Walker* (Indianapolis, 1937), by Laurence Green; *The Story of the Filibusters* (New York, 1891), by James J. Roche; *Filibusters and Financiers* (New York, 1916), by William O. Scroggs.

Stanfield's experiences in Panama are rounded out with background on the history, land, culture, and people in *Panama and the Canal* (New York, 1914), by Willis J. Albert; *The Isthmus of Panama* (London, 1865), by Charles T. Bidwell; *Panama* (New York, 1912), by Albert Edwards; *California and Oregon; or, Sights in the Gold Region, and Scenes by the Way* (Philadelphia, 1851), by Theodore T. Johnson; *The Chagres* (New York, 1948), by John E. Minter; and *South America and the Pacific ...*, 2 vols. (London, 1838), by P. Campbell Scarlett.

Wagon, Stage Travel

Western wagon and stage travel is the subject of many secondary works, but several are noteworthy: *The Wake of the Prairie Schooner* (New York, 1943), by Irene Padden, follows the overland trails to the west and describes the problems and pleasures of the wagon immigrants; W. Turrentine Jackson's *Wagon Roads West* (Berkeley, 1952) carefully traces routes taken by western immigrants; and, for a full view of western transportation during the era following the Civil War, the authoritative work is Oscar O. Winther's *The Transportation Frontier Trans-Mississippi West 1865–1890* (New York, 1964).

Wagons

Although most western travel books contain incidental information about the covered wagons, monographs are useful. These include H. C. Frey, *Historical Papers and Addresses of the*

Lancaster County Historical Society, XXXIV (Lancaster, Pa., 1930); and *The World on Wheels* (New York, 1878), by Ezra M. Stratton. Oscar O. Winther has concisely given the origin, the characteristics, and the use of the Conestoga wagon in his pamphlet *The Story of the Conestoga* (South Bend, 1954).

Wells Fargo, Holladay Lines

The Wells Fargo and Holladay stage lines are discussed in many studies. Among the best are *U. S. West: The Saga of Wells Fargo* (New York, 1949), by Lucius Beebe and Charles Clegg; *Wells Fargo Advancing the American Frontier* (New York, 1949), by Edward Hungerford; W. Turrentine Jackson, "A New Look at Wells Fargo, Stagecoaches and the Pony Express" in *California Historical Society Quarterly,* XLV (December, 1966), 291–324; and *The Early History of the Wells Fargo Express* (Berkeley, 1922), by John G. Schaffer. Describing the Holladay stage empire is the well-documented *Ben Holladay: The Stagecoach King* (Glendale, 1940), by J. V. Frederick. *The Butterfield Overland Mail 1857–1869,* 3 vols. (Glendale, Cal., 1947), by Roscoe P. Conkling and Margaret B. Conkling, documents the history of that early stage line and its dissolution and absorption by other lines.

Stage Travel

Broad studies covering many facets of overland stage history include Leroy Hafen's *The Overland Mail 1849–1869* (Cleveland, 1926); Oscar O. Winther's *Express and Stagecoach Days in California* (Palo Alto, 1935) and his *Via Western Express and Stagecoach* (Palo Alto, 1945). These are basic modern works, but also useful is the older Frank A. Root and William E. Connelley's *The Overland Stage to California* (Columbus, 1950; originally published Topeka, 1901).

Wagon Freighting

Wagon-freight commerce is described in many of the above references, but Byron G. Pugh's University of California (Berkeley) master's thesis, "History of the Utah-California Wagon Freighting" (1949), is the most complete.

Forts

Although almost all materials relating to western travel make some references to forts along the trail, several books and articles specialize on that subject. Those dealing with forts seen by Stanfield include "The United States Overlooks Camp Douglas 1862–1965" (*Utah Historical Quarterly*, XXXIII [Fall, 1965], 326–50), by Leonard J. Arrington and Thomas G. Alexander; *Old Forts of the Northwest* (Seattle, 1963), by Major Herbert M. Hart; *Fort Laramie and the Pageant of the West 1834–1889* (Glendale, Cal., 1938), by Leroy R. Hafen and Francis M. Young; and "The Establishment and Early History of Fort Laramie," by Francis W. Smith (University of Wyoming master's thesis, 1917). Each gives added insight—from a point of view other than Stanfield's—into experiences that Stanfield might have had.

Indians

Similarly, all western travel accounts refer to the Indians and many special works describe the tribes encountered by Stanfield. Monographs include the informative *Pawnee Hero Stories and Folk Tales* (New York, 1889), by George Grinnell; and John B. Dunbar, "The Pawnee Indians" in *Magazine of American History* (November, 1880), pp. 321–45. *Pawnee, Blackfoot and Cheyenne* (New York, 1961), by George Bird Grinnell, with introduction by Dee Brown, broadly treats the background and activities of several western tribes, as does *Relations with the Indians of the Plains 1857–1861* (Glendale, Cal., 1959), ed. Leroy Hafen and Ann Hafen. The Flathead Indians, greatly admired by Stanfield, are described in *Historical Sketch of the Flathead Indian Nation from the year 1813 to 1890* (Helena, 1890), by Peter Roman; and in Harry Turney-Hugh, "The Flathead Indian of Montana," *Memoirs of the American Anthropological Association*, No. 48 (Menasha, Wisconsin, 1937). Indian wars of the year of Stanfield's trip are documented in E. F. Ware's *Indian Wars of 1864* (Topeka, 1911).

John M. Jacobs

As diaries such as Stanfield's come to light, increasing emphasis falls on the role of John M. Jacobs in western trail blazing. This matter is the major concern of the paper, "John M. Jacobs and the Bozeman Trail," by John G. Brown (Montana Historical Society Library). References to Jacobs dot the writings of his contemporaries—examples include Peter Koch, "Historical Sketch," in *Contributions to the Historical Society of Montana*, II (Helena, 1896), 126–39; and "Affairs at Fort Benton from 1831 to 1869 from Lieutenant Bradley's Journal" in *Contributions to the Historical Society of Montana*, IV (Helena, 1903), 140–228.

Jim Bridger

Jacobs led his train over the trail being opened by Jim Bridger into Virginia City, Montana Territory. The Bridger story has been told many times. The best work is *Jim Bridger* (Norman, Oklahoma, 1962), by J. Cecil Alter. Others of value are William S. Brackett, "Bonneville and Bridger" in *Contributions to the Historical Society of Montana*, III (Helena, 1900), 175–200; and *Jim Bridger Mountain Man, a Biography* (New York, 1946), by Stanley Vestal.

John M. Bozeman

Jacobs is best known for his trail-blazing work with John Bozeman. Bozeman's career is traced most completely by Merrill G. Burlingame in "John M. Bozeman, Montana Trailmaker," *Mississippi Valley Historical Review*, XXVII (March, 1941), 321–45. This article notes the possibility that Jacobs was still working with Bozeman as he trailed Bridger into Virginia City. Bozeman's activities are further described in *The Bozeman Trail*, 2 vols. (Cleveland, 1922), by Grace Hebard and E. A. Brininstool, with an introduction by General Charles King; and James Kirkpatrick, "A Reminiscence of John Bozeman," *The Frontier,* IX (May, 1929), 354–58.

People Mentioned by Stanfield

A variety of sources are drawn on for information about persons mentioned in Stanfield's diary. Already cited newspapers, diaries, and secondary works turned up fragmentary clues. The Federal *Census Reports* for 1840, 1850, and 1860 contain the only known references to many of the people listed by Stanfield. The Minutes of the Marysville Common Council were consulted but included, of interest to this subject, only the name of Rench Sample. The Yuba County Recorder's and Clerk's records contained traces of Stanfield's relatives in California.

Other information about Stanfield, Bartlett, and their travel companions, not already cited, was obtained from *An Illustrated History of San Joaquin County, California* (Chicago, 1890); *South Bend and the Men who Have Made it* (South Bend, 1901), compiled by Anderson and Cooley; *Greater Los Angeles and Southern California* (Chicago, 1910), ed. Robert J. Burdette; *History of San Joaquin County* (Oakland, 1879), by Col. F. T. Gilbert; and *Historical Biographical Record of Los Angeles and Vicinity* (Chicago, 1901), by J. M. Guinn. Stage personalities mentioned by Stanfield were traced in George C. D. Odell, *Annals of the New York Stage,* VII, VIII (New York, 1931).

Bibliography

Ables, T. J. Missouri to California by wagon in 1857. Original MS at Newberry Library, Chicago.

Adams, Ellen Tompkins. Diary record of the wagon trip from Council Bluffs to Carson City, Nevada, in 1863. Original MS at Bancroft Library, Univ. of Calif., Berkeley.

"Affairs at Fort Benton from 1831 to 1869 from Lieutenant Bradley's Journal," *Contributions to the Historical Society of Montana*. Vol. 4. Helena, 1903.

Allton, Hiram. Diary record of a wagon trip from St. Louis to California, in 1864. Original MS in Beinecke Rare Book and Manuscript Library, Yale University.

Alta California (San Francisco), 1864, 1865.

Alter, Cecil J. *Jim Bridger,* Norman, Oklahoma, 1962.

Amy's Marysville Directory for the Year Commencing June 1858, compiled by Mix Smith and G. Amy, Marysville, Cal., 1858.

Argyle, Archie. *Cupid's Album.* New York, 1866.

Baker, George H. Travel diary describing the area of Indiana Ranch in the 1850's. Original MS at Society of California Pioneers Library, San Francisco.

Ballard, Henry. Journal of a trip from Nebraska to Salt Lake City in 1864. Typed copy at Utah State Historical Society Library, Salt Lake City.

Bandel, Eugene. Across the plains through Kansas in 1857. Original MS at California State Library, Sacramento.

Barton, H. D. Diary of a trip from Iowa to California in 1865. Typed copy in California State Library, Sacramento.

BIBLIOGRAPHY 167

Bender, Flora Isabelle. "Notes by the Way, Memoranda of a Journey Across the Plains, from Bull Creek, Washington Co., Neb. to Virginia City, Nev. Terr. May 7 to August 4, 1863," ed. William C. Miller. *Nevada Historical Society Quarterly,* I (July, 1958), 144–74.

Benedict, Gilbert. Journal of a wagon trip to Montana in 1864. MS in Montana State Historical Society Library, Helena.

Bidwell, Charles T. *The Isthmus of Panama.* London, 1865.

Bixby, August S. Diary, 1855–64. Original MS at California State Library, Sacramento.

Blood, James A. Illinois to California by wagon in 1850. Original MS in Newberry Library, Chicago.

Boller, Henry A. *Among the Indians Eight Years in the Far West 1858–1866,* ed. Milo M. Quaife. Chicago, 1959.

Bond, ———. *Foot Travels Across the Plains.* Richmond, Ind., 1868.

Bonner, John Heath. Iowa to California by wagon in 1861. Original MS at Bancroft Library, U. of Cal., Berkeley.

Bowles, Samuel. *Across the Continent.* Springfield, Mass., 1865.

Brackett, William S. "Bonneville and Bridger," *Contributions to the Historical Society of Montana.* Vol. 3. Helena, 1900.

Brewer, William H. *Up and Down California in 1860–1864; The Journal of William H. Brewer,* ed. Francis P. Farquhar. New Haven, Conn., 1931.

Brown, J. Ross. *Adventures in the Apache Country: a tour through Arizona and Sonora with Notes on the Silver Regions of Nevada.* New York, 1869.

Brown, John G. "John M. Jacobs and the Bozeman Trail." Paper at Montana Historical Society Library, Helena.

Brownlee, Richard, ed. "Description of Train Leaving Fulton, Missouri, April 22, 1864." *Missouri Historical Review,* LVIII (October, 1963), 131–32.

Brown's Marysville Directory for the Year Commencing March 1861. Marysville, Cal., 1861.

Brundage, T. J. Diary of a wagon trip from Ohio to Virginia City, Montana, in 1864. Typed copy at Montana Historical Society Library, Helena.

Burlingame, Merrill G. "John M. Bozeman, Montana Trail Maker." *Mississippi Valley Historical Review*, XXVII (March, 1941), 541–68.

Burton, Richard F. *City of the Saints and Across the Rocky Mountains to California.* London, 1862.

Chicago Directory [1866]. Chicago, 1866.

Chillson, Lawrence D. Diary of a trip from Iowa to Nevada in 1865. Original MS in Huntington Library, San Marino, Calif.

Crackbon, Joseph. Narrative of a voyage from New York to California via Panama in 1849. MS in California State Library, Sacramento.

Cutting, A. Howard. "Journal of a Trip Overland to California" from Illinois in 1863. Original MS at Huntington Library, San Marino, California.

Daily Dramatic Chronicle (San Francisco), 1865.
Daily Union Vedette (Camp Douglas, Utah Territory), 1864.
The Deseret News (Salt Lake City), 1864.

Dickson, Albert J. *Covered Wagon Days,* ed. Arthur J. Dickson. Cleveland, 1929.

Dunham, E. Allene Taylor: See Taylor (Dunham), E. Allene.

Dunlap, Katherine. Journal of a trip from Council Bluffs, Iowa, to Bannack, Montana, in 1864. Microfilm of typed copy at Bancroft Library, Univ. of Calif., Berkeley.

Egan, (Maj.) Howard. *Pioneering the West 1846–1878.* Richmond, Utah, 1917.

Ence, Gottlieb. Journal of an 1860 trip to Utah and life in Salt Lake area in 1864. Original MS at Utah State Historical Society Library, Salt Lake City.

Fish, Lafayette. Iowa to California by wagon in 1860. Original MS at Bancroft Library, Univ. of Calif., Berkeley.

Fish, Mary C. Iowa to California by wagon in 1860. Original MS at Bancroft Library, Univ. of Calif., Berkeley.

Fisk, Andrew Jackson. Northern route to Montana, government troops. Original MS at Montana Historical Society Library, Helena.

BIBLIOGRAPHY

Fisk, James. Northern route to Montana, government troops. Original MS at Montana Historical Society Library, Helena.

Fulkerth, William L. Diary record of a wagon trip from Iowa to California in 1863. Photocopy in Bancroft Library, U. of Calif., Berkeley.

Gillis, William R. *The Nevada Directory for 1868–69*. San Francisco, 1868.

Grannis, John W. Life in Virginia City, Montana. Original MS at Montana Historical Society Library, Helena.

Greely, Horace. *An Overland Journey from New York to San Francisco in the Summer 1859*. New York, 1860.

Hafen, Leroy, ed. *Overland Routes to the Gold Fields 1859 from Contemporary Diaries*. Glendale, California, 1942.

Halpin & Bailey's Chicago City Directory for the Year 1862–63. Chicago, 1862.

Harter, George. Record of wagon trip from Michigan to Calif. in 1864. Transcribed by Doris Harter Chase. Mimeographed copy in California State Library, Sacramento.

Hebard, Grace and Brininstool, E. H. *The Bozeman Trail*. Introd. by Gen. Charles King. 2 vols. Cleveland, 1922.

Hedges, Cornelius. Diary of wagon trip from Iowa to Virginia City, in 1864. Original MS in Montana State Historical Society Library, Helena.

Herndon, Sarah Raymond. *Days on the Road; Crossing the Plains in 1865*. New York, 1902.

Hopper, Silas L. Diary record of a wagon trip from Nebraska to California in 1863. Typed copy at Huntington Library, San Marino, Cal.

Hosner, J. Allen. *Trip to the States in 1865*, ed. Edith M. Duncan. Missoula, Montana, 1932.

Inman, R. D. *Crossing the Plains in 1865*. [Portland? 1915?].

Jatta, Mary Hall. Diary of trip from Nebraska to California in 1865. Typed copy in Bancroft Library, U. of Cal., Berkeley.

Johnson, William G. *Overland to California*. Oakland, Cal., 1948.

Karchner, (Mrs.) Nicholas Harrison. Ohio to California by wagon in 1862. Original MS at California State Library, Sacramento.

Kelly, J. Wells. *Second Directory of Nevada Territory* [1863]. San Francisco, 1863.

Kirkpatrick, James. "A Reminiscence of John Bozeman." *The Frontier,* IX (May, 1929), 354-58.

Koch, Peter. "Historical Sketch," *Contributions to the Historical Society of Montana.* Vol. 2. Helena, 1896.

Larned, William L. Northern route to Montana by wagon in 1864. Original MS in Newberry Library, Chicago.

Leeper, David R. *The Argonauts of 'Forty-Nine.* South Bend, Ind., 1894.

Lewis, Edward M. Journal of train and wagon trip from New York to California in 1865. Original MS at California State Historical Society Library, San Francisco.

Lomas, Thomas J. *Recollections of a Busy Life.* n.p., n.d.

Los Angeles *Evening Herald and Express,* 1934.

Ludlow, Fitz-Hugh. "Among the Mormons," the *Atlantic Monthly,* April, 1864, pp. 479-95.

McConahay, A. P. *Incidents as I Remember Them Closing 1865.* Van Wert, Ohio, 1927.

McCormick, Henry. *Across the Continent in 1865.* . . . Harrisburg, Pa., 1937.

Maloon, Mary Eliza Warner: See Warner (Maloon), Mary Eliza.

Marye, George Thomas, Jr. *From '49 to '83 in California and Nevada.* San Francisco, 1923.

Marysville *Daily Appeal* (California), 1864, 1865.

Miller, James Knox Polk. *The Road to Virginia City: The Diary of James Polk Miller,* ed. Andrew F. Rolle. Norman, Oklahoma, 1960. (Original MS at Bancroft Library, U. of Cal., Berkeley.)

Mishawaka *Enterprise* (Ind.), 1864, 1865.

Montana *Post* (Virginia City), 1864.

Morris, Maurice O. *Rambles in the Rocky Mountains.* London, 1864.

BIBLIOGRAPHY   171

Muffly, Theophilus. Life in Virginia City, Montana, 1864. Original MS at Bancroft Library, U. of Cal., Berkeley.

Nash, Marie. Michigan to California by wagon in 1861. Original MS at California State Library, Sacramento.

Newcomb, Silas. Wisconsin to California by stage and wagon in 1850. Original MS at Newberry Library, Chicago.

Olmsted, John. *Trip to California in 1865.* New York, 1880.

Owen, Richard. Omaha to Virginia City. Original MS in Montana Historical Society Library, Helena.

Padden, Irene. *The Wake of the Prairie Schooner.* New York, 1943.

Park, Lucia Darling. Diary record of the wagon trip from Omaha to Bannack, Montana, in 1863. Typed copy in Montana Historical Society Library, Helena.

Pritchard, James A. *The Overland Diary of James A. Pritchard from Kentucky to California in 1849,* ed. Dale Morgan. San Francisco, 1949.

Purviance, M. C. Diary record of a wagon trip from Illinois to Calif. in 1863. Original MS at the Beinecke Rare Book and Manuscript Library of Yale University, New Haven, Conn.

Redman, J. T. Diary of a trip from Missouri to Calif. Original MS at Huntington Library, San Marino, Cal.

Remy, Jules and Brenchley, Julius. *A Journal to Great Salt Lake City.* 2 vols. London, 1861.

Richardson, Albert D. *Beyond the Mississippi.* Hartford, Conn., 1867.

Ryan, Benjamin W. "The Bozeman Trail to Virginia City, Montana, in 1864; A Diary by Benjamin W. Ryan 1826-1898." *Annals of Wyoming,* XIX (July, 1947), 77-104.

Sacramento *Daily Bee,* 1864, 1865.

The Salt Lake City Directory and Business Guide for 1869, compiled and arranged by E. L. Sloan. Salt Lake City, 1869.

Salt Lake *Telegraph,* 1864.

San Francisco *Daily Bulletin,* 1865.

San Francisco Directory for the Year Commencing October 1864, compiled by Henry G. Langley. San Francisco, 1864.

Sharwell, Samuel. *Old Recollections of An Old Boy.* New York, 1923.

Smith, I. M. Missouri to California by wagon in 1859. Original MS at Newberry Library, Chicago.

Smith, John T. The Bozeman Trail 1864. Typed copy in Montana Historical Society Library, Helena.

South Bend *Tribune,* 1922, 1923.

Spence, James M. 1864 diary record of a boat trip from San Francisco to Panama, from Panama to N. Y. Original MS at Huntington Library, San Marino, Cal.

Stuart, (Captain) James. "The Yellowstone Expedition of 1863 from the Journal of Captain James Stuart." *Contributions to the Historical Society of Montana,* I (1876), 149–233.

Taylor (Dunham), E. Allene. *Across the Plains in a Covered Wagon.* ([Milton?] Iowa, 192–).

Tomlinson, Fanny. Record of a stage trip from Kansas to California in 1864. Microfilm copy at Bancroft Library, U. of Cal., Berkeley.

Tourtillot, Jane Augusta Gould. Iowa to California by wagon in 1862. Original MS at Bancroft Library, U. of Cal., Berkeley.

"A Trip Through Silverland," Sacramento *Bee,* September 28, 1864, p. 2.

Udell, John. *Incidents of Travel to California Across the Great Plains together with the Return Trips through Central America and Jamica to which are added sketches of the Author's Life.* Jefferson, Ohio, 1856.

Vestal, Stanley. *Jim Bridger Mountain Man, a Biography.* New York, 1946.

Virginia *Daily Union* (Virginia City, Nevada Territory), 1864.

Warner (Maloon), Mary Eliza. Illinois to California in 1864. Original MS at California State Historical Society Library, San Francisco.

Watkins, Francis M. *Story of the Crow Emigrant Train of 1865 written by Ralph L. Milliken from conversations with Francis M. Watkins.* Livingston, Cal., 1935.

Wilkinson, J. A. Michigan to California by wagon in 1859. Original MS at Newberry Library, Chicago.

Winne, Peter. "Across the Plains in 1863: The Diary of Peter Winne." *Iowa Journal of History,* July, 1951, pp. 221–40.

Winther, Oscar O. *A Classified Bibliography of the Periodical Literature of the Trans-Mississippi West 1811–1957.* Social Science Series No. 19. Bloomington, Ind., 1961.

Wisner, (Mrs.) S. Missouri to Oregon by wagon in 1866. Original MS at Newberry Library, Chicago.

Wood, Joseph Warren. Wisconsin to California by wagon in 1849. Original MS at Huntington Library, San Marino, Cal.

APPENDIX I

The Indiana Train

On the inside front cover of the diary, Stanfield lists members of "The Indiana Train." These wagon immigrants at various times traveled toward Virginia City in the same group with Stanfield. Stanfield joined up with some of them just west of South Bend; others were not picked up until Fort Kearney. The names are listed below in Stanfield's order, the pairing apparently designating wagon companions. William S. Bartlett, included here, is not listed by Stanfield.

John Fowler, wife, and two boys

John Fowler was forty-five years old; his wife, Emiline, thirty-five. They had a son William M., fifteen. There is no information available about the other son. Fowler, who was a carpenter, had real estate worth $1,000 in 1850.

John Dunn and Dennis Brownfield

John Dunn, twenty-two years old, was the son of Reynolds Dunn, a retired farmer whose real estate in 1860 was worth $15,000 and whose personal property was worth $15,000. Dunn returned home from California by way of Cape Horn. He became a merchant in South Bend.

Dennis Brownfield, twenty-three years old, was the son of John Brownfield, a prominent merchant in South Bend. Dennis returned to South Bend.

Gerritt and Shellim Crockett and John Rose

Shellim Crockett was born in 1812 in Lexington, Kentucky, a descendant of Col. Davy Crockett. He moved to St. Joseph County, Indiana, in 1831 and to South Bend in 1848, where he engaged in various business enterprises. He crossed the plains in 1849. The 1850 *Census Reports* list him as a hemp maker worth $500. He was the father of seven children, including Elmer Crockett, one of the owners of the South Bend *Tribune*. He died August 7, 1893, in South Bend.

Gerritt Crockett, Shellim's son, remained in Oregon, where he was living in 1893.

John Rose, twenty-two years old, was the son of Elmer Rose, a farmer whose real estate was worth $16,000 in 1860 and whose personal property was worth $7,000. John had been employed as a clerk.

Hiram M. Moomaw and R. J. M. Locke

Hiram M. Moomaw, twenty-two years old, born in Virginia, was a farmer. He was the son of Christian and Frances Moomaw, whose real estate was worth $8,000 in 1860 and whose personal property was worth $1,500.

R. J. M. Locke, twenty-two years old, was born in Ohio. He was the son of George and Mary Locke, whose real estate in 1850 was worth $1,500.

C. W. Carleton and H. S. Stanfield

Charles William Carleton, twenty years old, was born in Indiana. He was the son of William Carleton, a cooper whose real estate in 1860 was worth $2,000 and whose personal property was worth $400.

Howard Stillwell Stanfield was born in South Bend, Indiana, April 17, 1846, and died there on November 18, 1923. He was the son of Judge Thomas S. Stanfield and Nancy Peebles Stanfield. He was educated in private and public schools, including the

Northern Indiana Academy in South Bend. Upon his return from the California trip in 1865, he entered the dry-goods business with John Dunn, who had also made the western trip, and several other men. After trying his hand at various other business ventures, Stanfield established with H. C. Dresden the lumber firm of Dresden and Stanfield, which remained his life work. In 1870 he married Flora Turner. He was a member of prominent South Bend social and literary clubs, including the Commercial Athletic Club, the Pickwick Club, and the Pleiades Club, and one of the founders of the Northern Indiana Historical Society in 1896. He spent each summer at his home on Cape Cod, Massachusetts, and in 1891 he revisited California.

His health was never robust, and he suffered from epilepsy. The family never fully understood why his father had permitted the strenuous western trip.

John Eberhart and Tom Norman

John Eberhart, thirty-nine years old, was born in New York. He was engaged in the lumbering business in 1860 and had real estate worth $8,000 and personal property worth $750. His wife, Mary, was twenty-eight years old and his daughter Hatty, four. When he returned from the west, he became a partner with his brother Adolphus Eberhart in the Ripple Flour Mill in Mishawaka. He died in 1902.

Tom Norman, thirty years old, was born in New York. His wife was twenty-six years old, and they had one child. Norman returned to Mishawaka and in 1870 was engaged in farming. His real estate was worth $1,200 and his personal property, $1,000.

John and Dan Pembroke

John Pembroke, thirty-seven years old, was born in New York. In 1860 his real estate was worth $3,300 and his personal property, $1,500. His wife Anna was twenty-four years old. In 1860 he was Constable for Mishawaka.

Dan Pembroke, thirty-two years old, was born in New York.

His real estate in 1860 was worth $1,500 and his personal property, $75. His wife Catherine was thirty-one years old.

These men were brothers of John Eberhart's first wife, Mary A. Pembroke Eberhart, who died in 1857.

John Rohrer and Pickett D. Hays

John Rohrer, twenty-five years old, was born in Indiana. In 1860 he had real estate worth $6,000, and his personal property was valued at $600. He was a farmer.

No information is available about Pickett D. Hays.

J. Stover and Len

John Stover, thirty-two years old, was born in Virginia. He was worth $400 in 1860.

No information is available about Len Stover.

Dr. and John Bowman

No information is available about Dr. Bowman.

John Bowman, twenty-nine years old, was born in Indiana and was a farmer. His real estate was worth $13,000 in 1860 and his personal property, $800. His wife May was twenty-five years old, and his son Frank, four.

W. D. Darby and John Haney

W. D. Darby was from Howard County; he became a traveling salesman in the West.

No information is available about John Haney.

Gerritt Mikesell and J. Smith

Gerritt Mikesell, thirty-eight years old, was born in Ohio. A farmer, he had real estate worth $800 in 1860 and personal property worth $200. His wife, Sarah, was thirty-two years old and his son Daniel, six. No information is available about J. Smith.

G. Donahue and F. Jackson

George Donahue, nineteen years old, born in Indiana, was the son of George Donahue, a farmer whose real estate was worth $4,000 in 1860 and whose personal property was worth $500.

No information is available about F. Jackson

Geo Mulks

No information is available about George Mulks.

A. McDermott and A. Mooney

No information is available about A. McDermott and A. Mooney.

William S. Bartlett

William S. Bartlett was born in South Bend in 1843, the son of Joseph G. Bartlett, and died in Los Angeles, California, in 1914. Before going to California, he had attended private and public schools in South Bend and worked as a clerk in his father's store. His mother died c. 1862. In 1864 his sister Anna was fourteen years old, and his brothers Joseph and Charles were, respectively, thirteen and ten. William later assisted his brother Joseph in settling in California. Charles remained in South Bend to become the high-school principal and an historian. The family home was at 720 West Washington Avenue, South Bend.

In Oakland, California, where he settled, Bartlett established himself very successfully in the banking business and in 1878 married the daughter of Franklin C. Gray, a prominent businessman who was a partner in the San Francisco banking firm of Graham and Gray and who served as an alderman of that city under its first charter. In 1882 Bartlett moved to Los Angeles, where he became president of the German American Trust and

Savings Company. Over the years he organized many banks in Orange County, and in 1904, he became president of the Union Bank of Savings in Los Angeles.

He had two children, Lanier Bartlett (who wrote historical novels about California) and Mrs. James H. French. Bartlett and his wife were among the founders of the West Adams Presbyterian Church of Los Angeles.

APPENDIX II

Calendar of Stanfield's Trip

1864

March 23	Left South Bend (by wagon) for Chicago
March 24	Through Plainfield, Carlisle Hill, Portland, Rolling Prairie
March 25	Through Springville, Michigan City, City West
March 26	Through Tolleston
March 27	Arrived Chicago
March 28	Chicago
March 29	Left Chicago (by railroad) for Grinnell
March 30	Through Davenport, arrived Grinnell
March 31	Left Grinnell (by wagon) for Virginia City, arrived Newton
April 1	Left Newton
April 2	Arrived Des Moines
April 3 and 4	Des Moines
April 5	Left Des Moines, arrived Adel
April 6	Adel
April 7	Left Adel, through Guthrie County
April 8	Arrived Dalmanutha
April 9	Dalmanutha
April 10	Left Dalmanutha, through Cass County

CALENDAR OF STANFIELD'S TRIP 181

April 11	Through Lewis
April 12	Through Pottawattamie County
April 13	Arrived Council Bluffs
April 14–22	Council Bluffs
April 23	Left Council Bluffs, through Omaha
April 24	Arrived Fremont
April 25	Left Fremont, arrived Shell Creek
April 26	Left Shell Creek, arrived Columbus, forded Loup River
April 27	Arrived Silver Creek
April 28	Left Silver Creek
April 29	Arrived opposite Fort Kearney
April 30–May 1	Fort Kearney
May 2	Left Fort Kearney
May 3–7	Along north bank of Platte River
May 8	Arrived Goose Creek
May 9	Goose Creek
May 10	Left Goose Creek, arrived Wolf Creek
May 11	Left Wolf Creek, passed Castle Creek, arrived Sand Hill Creek
May 12	Left Sand Hill Creek, along Platte River
May 13–15	Along North Platte, Chimney Rock and Court House Rock in sight
May 16	Passed North Platte Indian agency
May 17	Along North Platte
May 18	Arrived Fort Laramie, opposite side of river
May 19	Left Fort Laramie
May 20	Arrived Alder Clump
May 21–25	Left Alder Clump, along North Platte

May 26–29	Camped at Red Buttes, on the North Platte, train formed
May 30	Left Red Buttes, followed Bridger Route to Virginia City
May 31–June 6	Through Wind River area
June 7	Arrived Bighorn River
June 8–12	Along Bighorn River
June 13	Forded Greybull River
June 14	Along Greybull River
June 15–20	Along Stinking Water River
June 21–22	Through Pryor's Gap and Clarks Fork River
June 23–29	Along Clarks Fork
June 30	Arrived Divide Creek
July 1	Left Divide Creek
July 2	Arrived Rose Bud Creek
July 3	Arrived Yellowstone River
July 4	Along Yellowstone River
July 5–7	Left Yellowstone River and headed cross-country for Virginia City
July 8	Crossed Gallatin Fork
July 9	Crossed Madison Fork
July 10	Arrived Virginia City, Montana Territory
July 11–24	Virginia City
July 25	Left Virginia City (by stage) for Salt Lake City
July 26	Crossed Continental Divide
July 27	Along Snake River
July 28	Along Bear River
July 29	Through Ogden, arrived Salt Lake City

CALENDAR OF STANFIELD'S TRIP 183

July 30–Aug. 6	Salt Lake City
Aug. 7	Left Salt Lake City (by stage) for Virginia City, Nevada
Aug. 8	Crossed Great American Desert
Aug. 9	Through Ruby Valley, Diamond Mountains
Aug. 10	Through Austin
Aug. 11	Arrived Virginia City, Nevada
Aug. 12–14	Virginia City
Aug. 15	Left Virginia City (by stage) for Folsom, California
Aug. 16	Arrived Folsom, left (by railroad) for Sacramento, arrived Sacramento
Aug. 17–18	Sacramento
Aug. 19	Left Sacramento (by railroad) for Lincoln, arrived Lincoln, left (by stage) for Marysville, arrived Marysville
Aug. 20	Left Marysville (by stage) for Indiana Ranch, arrived Indiana Ranch

1864–65

Aug. 21–April 1	In the Indiana Ranch, Marysville, LaPorte area

1865

April 2	Left Indiana Ranch, through Oregon House, arrived Marysville
April 3–5	Marysville
April 6	Left Marysville (by steamer) for Sacramento, arrived Sacramento
April 7	Sacramento

April 8	Left Sacramento (by steamer) for San Francisco, arrived San Francisco
April 9–12	San Francisco
April 13	Left San Francisco (by steamer) for Nicaragua
April 14–26	At sea in the Pacific
April 19	passed Cape Lucas
April 21	crossed Gulf of California
April 23	entered Gulf of Tehuantepec
April 24	along Guatemalan coast
April 25	crossed Equator
April 26	along Nicaraguan coast
April 27	Arrived San Juan del Sur, Nicaragua
April 28	Left San Juan del Sur (by steamer) for Panama
April 29–30	At sea in the Pacific
May 1	Arrived Panama City
May 2	Left Panama City (by railroad) for Aspinwall, arrived Aspinwall, left by steamer for New York
May 3–10	At sea in the Atlantic
May 6	passed Cuba
May 7	passed South Carolina coast
May 9	passed Cape Hatteras
May 10	passed Cape Henlopen
May 11	Arrived New York

Notes

INTRODUCTION

1. Edward Peebles Stanfield was born December 25, 1842, in South Bend, Indiana, and died there on January 11, 1934. During the Civil War he participated in the siege of Vicksburg, the siege of Corinth, and Sherman's march to the sea. He was mustered out of the army December 24, 1864. Following the war, he completed his education at the University of Michigan where he received the law degree. After practicing law for several years, he entered the manufacturing and lumber business in South Bend.

His son Thomas Stanfield inherited Howard Stillwell Stanfield's diary and journal. These were preserved by his widow, Mrs. Thomas Stanfield of South Bend, and are now held by his daughter, Mrs. Lyndon Kirkley of Pittsburgh, Pennsylvania.

2. Judge Thomas Stillwell Stanfield was born in Ohio on October 17, 1816, and died in South Bend on September 12, 1885. In 1831 his parents moved to South Bend, where he was educated in the public schools, clerked in the store of Lathrop Taylor (co-founder of South Bend), and studied law in the offices of Samuel Sample, South Bend pioneer. He attended law school in Cincinnati, where he met and married Nancy Peebles. They had four children: Edward Peebles, Howard Stillwell, Eva Harper (Staley), 1851–89, and Mammie, 1861–66. He served several terms in the State Legislature and on the City Council. He was for a time Judge of the Circuit Court, and after retiring from the bench, he was engaged in law practice. He was instrumental in securing a railroad for South Bend. The family home was at 311 West Washington Avenue, South Bend.

3. Two of Stanfield's aunts were living in Yuba County, California, at the time of his visit. They were Mrs. Harriet Rosseter and Mrs. Mary Jane Smith. They had gone to California in 1852 with their

father William Stanfield, Howard Stillwell Stanfield's grandfather, who had died in 1859. William Stanfield was a native of Tennessee, born in 1792; he moved to Ohio and went on to Indiana in 1831. In South Bend he was engaged in manufacturing and trade. He later moved to California and settled in Yuba County. In 1856 he purchased 160 acres of land in Long Bar Township from John Freeman and F. C. Newton for $2,600. The land lay sixteen miles from Marysville on the road from Marysville to Oregon House (Yuba County Recorder's Book, No. 10, pp. 469–70). There he opened the Stanfield House which became a stage stop and a public inn. The site became known as Stanfield Hill.

4. Joseph G. Bartlett was born in 1815 in New England and died in South Bend in 1873. He was a prominent South Bend baker and merchant. In 1860 he held real estate worth $10,000 (including a handsome brick home at 720 West Washington Avenue, South Bend) and personal property worth $6,000. He was one of the founders of the Presbyterian Church in South Bend. His first wife died in about 1862 and he remarried shortly thereafter.

The family was strongly abolitionist. During the 1850's Mrs. Bartlett held abolitionist meetings in her home for the ladies of South Bend. The home was a stop on the underground railroad.

On the occasion of Lincoln's Emancipation Proclamation, Mr. Bartlett had all members of his family, and a Negro, Henry, who was in the household at the time, trace their fingers along Lincoln's signature to impress on them the importance of the document. The Negro, family legend recalls, failed to understand the meaning of the document and observed that "the man could write his name pretty."

5. See E. Allene Taylor (Dunham), *Across the Plains in a Covered Wagon* ([Milton?], Iowa, 192–), p. 4. The description is of an 1864 trip.

6. Studebaker Manufacturing Company advertisement in Mishawaka *Enterprise,* March 19, 1864, p. 3.

7. Lucia Darling Park, Journal of a trip across the plains to Montana in 1863, entry for July 29, 1863. Typed copy in Montana State Historical Society Library.

Thomas J. Lomas also describes the tensions which so easily brought on quarrels during his long overland journey in 1864. See *Recollections of a Busy Life* (n. p., n. d.), p. 48.

8. John M. Jacobs was a western mountain guide of considerable experience. In 1862–63 he left Bannack, Montana, with John M. Bozeman for the states with the idea of looking for a shorter route west than

the one up the Platte. In spite of serious Indian difficulties, they made their way to the Missouri River.

Jacobs is described as "a red-bearded Italian," able to spin a good story.

9. Schuyler Colfax was born in 1823 in New York and died in 1885 in South Bend. A newspaper man who became a professional politician, he was Vice President under U. S. Grant (1869–73). In 1865, accompanied by several newspaper men, he took a tour of the West to assess the resources of the region and to make recommendations concerning government support of the transcontinental railroad.

For further information see: Willard Smith, *Schuyler Colfax: The Changing Fortunes of a Political Idol* (Indianapolis, 1952).

10. *Daily Alta California* (San Francisco), September 2, 1865, p. 1.

CHAPTER ONE

1. South Bend was undergoing great economic growth. The Studebaker wagon manufacturers profited from war orders, and James Oliver, who had introduced his revolutionary "chilled" plow in the fifties, sold nearly 1,000 plows in 1864.

2. Studebaker Manufacturing Company advertisement in Mishawaka *Enterprise*, March 19, 1864, p. 3.

3. Clark was thirty-nine and married, and had two children.

4. Journal: The owner of the tavern is identified as Charley White (p. 13). The tavern was Stanfield's first stop on the road from South Bend to Chicago. The modern highways which approximate the route taken by Stanfield from South Bend to Chicago are as follows: From South Bend to Michigan City, US 20. From Michigan City to New City West, US 12 to the mouth of Salt Creek in the Little Calumet River, which Stanfield crossed on a bridge. Then, he angled southwest to Crisman (now Portage) and followed along the Michigan Central Railroad tracks to Lake Station (now East Gary); Tolleston (now Gary); Hammond—all in Indiana; and Harvey, Illinois. He then went north into Chicago. Many travelers followed a route nearer Lake Michigan.

5. Plainfield was the first platted town in Olive Township, St. Joseph County, Indiana; located on the LaPorte road one and one-half miles east of New Carlisle, and about thirteen miles west of South Bend. It was surveyed by Tyra W. Bray in 1833 and gradually disappeared after the railroad bypassed it.

6. New Carlisle is the name now given to Carlisle Hill. It was founded in 1835 by Richard R. Carlisle. He advertised the town in New York City through printed plats and lithographs. The Lake Shore Railroad came to the city in 1851, and its future was assured. It was not incorporated until 1866. The New Carlisle Collegiate Institute for boys and girls was erected in 1859 by the Methodist Episcopal Church and opened in 1861. It was housed in a substantial two-storied brick building.

7. The plat for Portland was recorded in 1853 by W. J. Walker, but the post office was called Rolling Prairie. The name "Bootjack" comes from the shape of the junction of the Old Chicago Trail (from Detroit to Chicago) and the Michigan Road (from Indianapolis to South Bend to Michigan City) at Portland.

8. Springville was located in Springfield Township, LaPorte County, on present US 20, where it is crossed by Indiana 39. It was surveyed in 1833 and platted in 1834; a post office was established there in 1840. The town was named for the spring of cool water flowing at the site. The population of the town was probably less than a hundred in 1864, but it had a tavern, a blacksmith shop, two grocery stores, and a steam sawmill. The settlement was on the road from Detroit to Chicago and declined after being bypassed by the railroad.

9. Michigan City is located on Lake Michigan at the mouth of Trail Creek. It was founded in 1832 as the northern terminal of the Michigan Road (which extended from Madison, Indiana, to Lake Michigan). It became an active lake port in the 1840's. Meat-packing plants, grain elevators, and flour mills were located along the beach and harbor in 1864. The population in 1860 was 3,320.

10. Stanfield passed through New City West, which was located about two miles south of the mouth of Fort Creek, at the site of the present town of Tremont on US 12. The city was never incorporated. The center of the settlement was Green's tavern, which was the stopping point on the Michigan City to Chicago road; the stages changed horses there. With the passing of stage travel, the city had declined by 1864.

11. Journal: At Michigan City, Holman train members "got on a big drunk and raised cain." Holman's train had left South Bend four hours ahead of Stanfield and Bartlett (p. 5).

H. C. Holman traveled the entire distance to California by wagon. For further information about him see *An Illustrated History of San Joaquin County, California* (Chicago, 1890), pp. 310–11.

12. Journal: The area appeared "beyond civilization," rather than just twenty miles from Chicago (p. 6).

13. The railroad which Stanfield crossed nine times was the Michigan Central (then called the Michigan Southern). The other railroads were the Chicago and Eastern Illinois, near Hammond, and the Illinois Central, west of Hammond.

14. This is the road and railroad which led through Lake Station (now East Gary) as far as Hammond, where higher ground was reached. Until the swamps were drained, the only way to reach East Gary was along US 6 or Indiana 51.

15. Journal: Leaving South Bend the day after Stanfield and Bartlett were John Fowler and family, Gerritt Crockett, Shellim Crockett, John Dunn, Dennis Brownfield, and John Rose (pp. 6–7).

16. Journal: The others remained at Tolleston Station overnight (pp. 6–7). Tolleston Station was a railroad construction town built in a swamp area nineteen miles from Chicago. Today it is a part of Gary. Although Stanfield did not stop over, his diary does reveal some concern, which was shared by other immigrants, about traveling on Sunday. For example, see Lucia Park, entry for June 14, 1863.

17. Journal: Three wagons were then traveling together, and Stanfield observed that it was not nearly as lonesome (p. 7).

18. Myrick House was located in Chicago, on Cottage Grove Avenue at 29th Street. Alexander Sherman was the proprietor. Its tavern was called the "Bull's Head."

19. Camp Douglas occupied sixty acres of land in the south section of Chicago, on the west side of Cottage Grove Avenue between 31st and 33rd streets. It was opened in 1861 and was used both as a recruiting and training station. It also served as a prison for Confederate soldiers, and late in 1862 between 5,000 and 7,000 prisoners were housed there. At the time Stanfield was in Chicago, rumors circulated that a plot was afoot to attack the prison and free the Confederates.

20. Joseph B. Arnold, 1839–1914. Arnold had studied law in Judge Thomas Stanfield's office and was attending law school in Chicago in 1864. He was later associated with Judge Stanfield in law practice.

21. Stanfield employs the words "horses" and "mules" interchangeably. He and Bartlett actually used mules.

22. The train was the Chicago and Rock Island Railroad, which went across Illinois to Rock Island, Illinois, on the Mississippi River. The road had been completed in 1854, and the bridge across the Mississippi to Davenport, Iowa, was completed in 1856. It there joined

the tracks of the Mississippi and Missouri Railroad, which, in 1864, extended as far as Grinnell, Iowa.

23. In 1864 the Sherman House was under the control of David A. Gage, Charles C. Waite, and John A. Rice, all experienced hotel men. It was a six-story luxury hotel made of brick.

24. Davenport was the seat of Scott County, Iowa, located on the Mississippi River and Lake Davenport. It had been a trading center of the American Fur Company and was founded in 1836 and grew rapidly in the 1850's, when many Germans migrated there. It was the first city in Iowa to have railroad service. In 1860 its population was 11,207.

Journal: Stanfield called it "quite a city" and was impressed by the diversity of manufacturing. The town was situated on gently rising land between the river and the high bluffs (p. 8).

CHAPTER TWO

1. Stanfield's experience and reaction were typical. "Iowa beats them all," Edward M. Lewis recorded in his diary a year later (entry for July 13, 1864). Original MS at California State Historical Society Library, San Francisco.

2. Grinnell, Iowa, was founded in 1854 by Joseph Grinnell, the man to whom Horace Greeley said "Go West young man." The town lies on the treeless prairie between the Iowa and Skunk rivers. Shortly after founding the town, Grinnell organized a college which became a strong abolitionist center. The place had the appearance of a New England village. The Mississippi and Missouri Railroad reached the city in 1863, and it grew rapidly thereafter. In 1860 the population was 522.
By 1864 the population was said to be 800. See Benjamin W. Ryan, "The Bozeman Trail to Virginia City, Montana, in 1864, A Diary by Benjamin W. Ryan 1826–1898," in *Annals of Wyoming*, XIX (January, 1947), 80.

3. The Bailey House had fourteen guest rooms, offices, and parlors and was located on Main Street, between Fourth and Fifth Avenues, across from the post office. It was also called the Hawk-Eye House. A. Bailey and Mrs. Bailey were the proprietors.

4. To follow Stanfield's trip from Grinnell to Council Bluffs today the following roads should be taken: From Grinnell to Des Moines, US 6. From Des Moines to Adel, Iowa 90—and continue on it to Wiota (Cass County). There rejoin US 6 through Lewis and on into Council Bluffs.

5. Newton was settled in 1846 and incorporated in 1857; in 1860 it had a population of about 1,200.

Ryan describes Newton as "quite a stiring little place, has a very nice court house" (p. 80).

6. Terre Coupee (also known as Hamilton), Indiana, is about seven miles west of South Bend. It was founded in 1837 and was an important trading post on the stage line between Detroit and Chicago. Its importance declined after the railroad bypassed it.

Journal: At Grinnell, Stanfield met travelers going everywhere in the West; the immigration, he felt, had just begun in volume and "bids fair to be large" (p. 10).

7. The Skunk River flows across the road from Grinnell to Newton. Stanfield apparently regarded much of the area between Grinnell and Des Moines as the Skunk River Bottom.

8. Journal: Des Moines was a flourishing business city. Stanfield's party stayed there until 4 P.M., when Fowler and Crockett joined them. The wagons then moved out of the city, planning to rest over Sunday in its outskirts.

Des Moines lies on the Des Moines and Raccoon rivers and is surrounded by rich prairie lands. Soldiers had been stationed at Fort Des Moines since the 1840's.

George Stone was Governor.

9. Ryan gives the toll as sixty cents (p. 80).

10. Journal: The wagons stayed on, longer than intended, waiting for some of the water to run off the road (p. 11).

11. The Savery House was located at Walnut and 4th streets and was the main banquet and guest house in the city.

12. Since wood was scarce, coal was used for fuel. A great coal-mining industry was just developing, and extensive operations began at this time. Coal was first mined in this region in 1843.

13. Journal: The Western Home was an inn owned by an Irish farmer.

14. Journal: Stanfield gives the population as 600 (p. 13).

The population in 1860 was actually 1,969. Adel is located at the confluence of the Butler and Raccoon rivers. These waterways made it a milling center for the surrounding grain-producing area.

15. Journal: There was no jail, Stanfield said, for there was nothing worth stealing (p. 13).

16. The Middle Raccoon is about ten miles west of Adel.

17. Journal: Dalmanutha was a "miserable place," with mud everywhere. Thirty Hoosiers stopped there at its dirty tavern (p. 16).

The town was founded in 1855; located in Thompson Township, Guthrie County. It gained importance as a stop on the Mormon Trail.

18. Lewis was an active station on the underground railroad with a population in 1860 of 1,612.

In this part of Iowa, corn was selling at from 75¢ to $1 a bushel and hay at $1 a cwt. (Ryan, p. 80).

19. Journal: At Council Bluffs the Stanfield group bought the items needed to complete their outfit: tent, stove, "and as the advertisements say other things to numerous to mention." Originally, they had intended to make their purchases at Omaha, but they found Council Bluffs was better as a commercial trading place. However, since they had told South Bend friends to write them in care of the Omaha Post Office, they had to go there to pick up their mail. The Missouri River is about half a mile wide at Omaha (p. 18).

Council Bluffs had its first boom as the supply center for immigrants of the '49 gold rush. In 1863 it was chosen as the terminus of the Union Pacific Railroad, and its prospects were bright.

Ryan gives the following prices charged at Council Bluffs in May, 1864: flour, $3 per cwt.; bacon and ham, 15¢ per lb.; sugar, 24¢ per lb.; and lard, 15¢ per lb. He also states that forty wagons were camped near him on May 12; on May 14, 180 wagons waited to cross the river. By nightfall, 300 wagons were waiting (p. 81).

It was an easy walk from Stanfield's camp site to the bluffs north of the city. Old Indian paths could still be followed to the bluffs.

CHAPTER THREE

1. Journal, p. 26. See also Ryan, pp. 81–82; Katherine Dunlap, 1864 Journal, entries for May 18 through May 24, 1864 (microfilm of typed copy at Bancroft Library, Berkeley); and Lomas, p. 37.

2. Journal, p. 30.

3. The city is described in the diary of James Polk Miller in the entry for September 9, 1864 (MS at Bancroft Library). This diary has been published as *The Road to Virginia City: The Diary of James Polk Miller,* ed. Andrew F. Rolle (Norman, Oklahoma, 1960).

4. The Scottsbluff area is in the western extremity of present-day Nebraska.

Those immigrants traveling on the south bank of the Platte found many ranches and stage stops scattered along the route. Stanfield found only a few along the north bank of the river.

NOTES FOR PAGES 36-39   193

5. These beauties are well described in Archie Argyle's overland journal in 1864: *Cupid's Album* (New York, 1866).

6. Journal: Also in the new company were H. Moomaw and R. J. M. Locke—both from South Bend. Stanfield bought a one-fourth interest in the outfit, which already had a "fine span of mules, a good wagon made for the purpose, and a tolerable outfit." The mules cost the new group $300 (p. 20).

7. That is, they left Council Bluffs.

The following modern roads approximate the trail Stanfield took: US 6 west from Omaha to junction with Nebraska 36 to junction with US 30; US 30 through Fremont, through Columbus and Kearney to junction with US 26; US 26 along the North Platte past Scottsbluff to Laramie. It should be noted that while the above roads follow the north side of the Platte, the main immigrant road was along the south side.

8. Journal: Five or six thousand inhabitants.

Going aboard the Council Bluffs ferry, the wagons were driven completely around the outer edge of the vessel so that they faced the entrance. In 1862 the ferry was the *Lizzy Bayles*. See Jane A. Gould Tourtillot, 1862 diary, entry for May 15, 1862. Microfilm of typed copy at Bancroft Library.

Thomas J. Lomas (pp. 39-40) reported that in May, 1864, the line waiting to cross the river in the ferry extended for two miles. He had to wait two days and two nights before getting across.

Omaha was opened to settlement after the government treaty with the Omaha Indians in 1854. It became the Territorial Capital the following year and grew rapidly after 1859. The capitol building is described as a handsome brick structure painted white and placed in a clearing so that it could be seen from a distance. See also: Lomas, p. 41; Martin Hardin, Trip Across the Continent 1860 (typed copy at Chicago Historical Society Library with Hardin family papers), p. 5; Leroy Hafen, ed., *Overland Route to the Gold Fields 1859 from Contemporary Diaries* (Glendale, Cal., 1942), pp. 103-104; and Alden Brooks, Grand Trip Across the Plains (1859) (MS at Newberry Library, Chicago), p. 1.

9. Journal: They traveled on Sunday to catch up with their friends' train (p. 21).

10. Shell Creek enters the Platte east of Schuyler, in Colfax County (or about twenty-five miles west of Fremont). It flows through Platte County about eight miles north of Columbus.

In this area the road was about one mile from the Platte. It was over generally level country bordered with lakes and spring sloughs. Timber was scarce but there were some cottonwoods, red cedars, and willows.

11. Fremont was the seat of Dodge County, on the Platte River, thirty-three miles west northwest of Omaha.

12. Journal: The Indians were of the Pawnee tribe. Stanfield knew that the next Indians encountered would be the more war-like Sioux. "They are or seem to be very quiet and peaceable this summer. I hope they may remain so" (p. 22).

13. Journal: "It is I think the most glorius sight I have ever witnessed. . . . The stars shining brightly look pale and insignificant when compared with the light of the burning grass" (p. 24).

14. Journal: The prairie fire blew into camp and would have burned them out except that the grass around the camp had been either eaten or burned off previously (p. 25).

15. Journal: Stanfield noted that Columbus was more advanced in both population and business activity than Eldorado (p. 26). A village with ten to twelve houses, a tavern, a store, a blacksmith shop, and a schoolhouse, Columbus was the seat of Platte County. It was founded in 1856 and existed as a supply stop on the western trail. However, the problem of crossing the Loup Fork was considered a major drawback to this route. The Loup River flows into the Platte near Columbus.

16. Ryan paid $1.50 on May 21, 1864, whereas on May 27, 1864, Katherine Dunlap paid only $1.00. Four wagons were ferried at a time; wagons waited for hours to get across. Lomas paid $5.00 per team in May.

17. Silver Creek lies seventeen miles west of Columbus along the Platte River. Its name was derived from the clearness, sparkle and color of the little stream which meanders over the prairies near the town. The town was not platted in 1864. Stanfield may have stayed at the ranch of Mr. Lathrop.

18. The Indians often dashed into the midst of a wagon train encamped for the night, and stampeded the horses with their war whoops. Wolves were another danger to the horses and livestock—once inside the animal corral, the wolves were as devastating as the Indians.

19. Journal: In this area the travelers looked for water, wood, and grass, but seldom found all three in one place. The water was always warm, frequently half sand; the grass at best was short and poor, except

for bunch grass, which was nearly as good as oats but not everywhere available. For the most part they fed the stock coarse flour which was brought along for that purpose. The wood, when found, was sage brush and grease wood, generally green. There was a great deal of this, but the animals would starve before eating it. For miles around prickly pear grew abundantly—in Indiana this was a house plant.

For three days the train saw no houses. Although on the plains now, Stanfield couldn't believe it: he had pictured them as a vast level prairie where the eye could see nothing but immense herds of buffalo and an occasional antelope pursued by wolves. In the distance, he had imagined majestic snow-capped mountains rising boldly from the plains. Instead he saw daily a rough, rugged line of low "miserable" sand hills covered with prickly pears. Only occasionally they came to a fertile little valley covered with grass. Of the Platte River Stanfield had this to say: "I have not the language at my command to express my contempt of this stream" (pp. 33–35).

20. Journal: No water was wasted. Stanfield says that by the time a pail of water settled, it was half sand (p. 35).

21. Goose Creek was approximately twenty-eight miles east of Wolf Creek. Cedars covered the bluffs along the Platte in this area, and earlier travelers had written their names on the buffalo skulls along the river bank. See Silas Newcomb, Journal, Madison, Wisconsin, Overland to California and Oregon, April 1, 1850, to March 31, 1851, p. 59. Photostatic copy of MS at Newberry Library, Chicago.

22. The area may be identified as about eight days west of Fort Kearney. Most travelers along the north bank of the Platte mention at this point, as does Stanfield, the great sand hill. See: Cornelius Hedges, Diary of a trip from Iowa to Montana in 1864, entry for May 19, 1864 (typed copy in Montana Historical Society Library); Richard Owen, Diary of a trip from Omaha, Nebraska, to the gold fields of Idaho in 1864, entry for June 14, 1864 (typed copy in Montana Historical Society Library); H. D. Barton, Diary kept in crossing the plains in 1865, entry for June 11, 1865 (typed copy in California State Library, Sacramento).

Often the immigrants double-teamed their animals to pull the wagons over this obstacle.

23. Wolf Creek was about three-days' travel (perhaps seventy miles) east of Chimney Rock and Court House Rock. Newcomb described it as a handsome creek, twenty feet wide, perhaps five miles long, flowing into the Platte (p. 60).

24. Castle Creek was about fourteen miles beyond Wolf Creek. It was six rods wide, two feet deep, swift, with a quicksand bottom. The huge rocks along the south side of the creek were said to resemble castles and were called the Castle Rocks.

Sand Hill Creek was six miles from Castle Creek. It was 100 feet wide, shallow (only two feet deep) and swift flowing, and had a quicksand bottom. See: Newcomb, pp. 62–70; Owen, entry for June 15, 1864; and Park, entry for June 13, 1863.

Sand hills were the outstanding landscape feature of this area. Prickly pear, scrubby sage plants, and greasewood were everywhere.

25. Journal: The place is identified as Raw Hide Creek (p. 39).

Raw Hide Creek begins near Raw Hide Butte in Wyoming and flows south into the North Platte near present-day Lingle, Wyoming, six miles east of Fort Laramie.

26. Journal: His business was to gather wood, secure water, get supper, and wash dishes. No one worked after dark (p. 39).

27. Journal: Chimney Rock was seen for a distance of from forty to fifty miles, Stanfield estimated. It was in sight for three days and Stanfield had a "fine View" of it through a telescope (p. 39–40). The Rock, a perpendicular, conical shaft of reddish sandstone, stood on an eroded plain about two and a half miles from the Platte. Further on, eight miles from the Platte, stood Court House Rock. It was of rough, hard marl substance in the shape of a rotunda. Its dimensions were imposing—300 feet high and one-half mile in circumference, with sides sloping thirty-five to forty-five degrees.

28. Journal: Stanfield was aware of the deceptiveness of distances. His practice in estimating was to put the figure at five times the appearance—then he found he was usually about one-quarter short (p. 40).

29. Journal: No houses had been seen since leaving Fort Kearney (p. 40).

In 1863 the Upper Platte Indian Agency buildings were moved to a point on the North Platte, twenty-five miles east of Fort Laramie. The Agency was in charge of the Northern Cheyennes, Northern Apaches, and the Sioux. John Loree was the agent from 1862 to 1865. Indians loafed around the agency buildings, stirring themselves only to beg from the passing immigrants or waiting for food to be offered during mealtimes. See George Harter, "Crossing the plains," 1864, p. 5. Mimeograph of transcribed copy at California State Library, Sacramento.

CHAPTER FOUR

1. R. D. Inman, entry for June 20, 1864, *Crossing the Plains in 1865* ([Portland?] 1915.)

Fort Laramie was especially important to the United States Government in its 1857 expeditions against the Mormons. The immigrant road split at Laramie—one branch went to the southwest and the other to the northwest.

2. Jacobs, with Jim Bozeman, had already explored this route to the northeast of the Bighorn Mountains, through the Powder River passes.

3. Jim Bridger (1804–81) has been called the West's most famous frontiersman. He went West while still a youth and became a skillful hunter and trapper. He was a trader, he established Fort Bridger, and he served as an Indian scout for the army and a guide for immigrants. His Indian knowledge was unequalled. He discovered Great Salt Lake.

The Bridger trip described in this diary was his famous race with the John M. Bozeman wagon train to see which could reach Virginia City first. Both arrived at about the same time. Simplified, the Bozeman route kept close to the eastern edge of the Bighorn Mountains, and Bridger's route kept to the west of the same mountains.

4. Virginia City was originally called Alder Gulch after the alders growing where Bill Fairweather and six other miners first discovered gold on May 26, 1863. When these men returned to Bannack for supplies, word of their discovery spread. The spring floods of 1864 had washed away the claim stakes of the previous summer, and the gulch filled with gravel. The damage was still being repaired while Stanfield was in the city. Virginia City was the first incorporated town in Montana (January, 1864) and the second Territorial Capital.

Other immigrants were also disappointed in the city. Mrs. Sarah Herndon in 1865 characterized it as a "shabby" town. *Days on the Road; crossing the Plains in 1865* (New York, 1902), p. 262.

5. By August, 1864, the Indian outbreaks along the South Platte had paralyzed travel, and the Indians controlled over 400 miles of the road Stanfield had just traveled.

6. Mrs. Sarah Herndon (p. 44) gives a good description of the difficulty in caring for the injured immigrant. Camphor, brandy, and ammonia were the only medicinal aids available. Other immigrants de-

scribed the problems created by the swarms of mosquitos, buffalo flies, and gnats. See Ellen Tompkins Adams, 1863 Diary, entry for May 24, 1863. Photocopy of original MS at Bancroft Library, Berkeley.

7. Because of the Civil War, the regular troops were withdrawn from Fort Laramie and detachments of the following volunteer units were stationed there: 4th and 7th Iowa Cavalry; 1st, 6th, 11th Ohio Cavalry; 6th Michigan Cavalry; and 8th Kansas Infantry (Francis W. Smith, "The Establishment and Early History of Ft. Laramie, Wyoming" [M. A. thesis, Univ. of Iowa, 1917], p. 44). Colonel Collins was the commanding officer. Katherine Dunlap (June 20, 1864) notes that in the spring of 1864 the Ohio 7th was stationed there.

Laramie City (settled in 1868) was located near the Fort as a trading post for Indians, the soldiers, and the immigrants. Generally, the whites purchased liquors and groceries, and the Indians purchased ornaments. Sometimes the site was called Badeau's Ranch.

The following modern roads approximate the trail Stanfield took: From the Wyoming-Nebraska border US 26 to Shoshone, Wyoming; then US 20 north to Greybull, Wyoming; then US 310 northwest to junction US 90 westward to junction with Montana 289; to junction Montana 287a southward. Turn west at Ennis, Montana, into Virginia City on Montana 287.

8. Laramie Peak was a landmark noted by all travelers along the North Platte. It was the first high mountain seen along the trail. Its snowy top emerged majestically above the clouds, rising from the treeless hills and barren plains. It is the highest point in the Laramie Mountains, 10,274 feet.

Mary Eliza Warner Maloon describes the large rock formations west of Fort Laramie as being "more like a picture than anything real" and the "most beautiful scenery we have yet seen" (entry for May 10, 1864). A typed copy of her 1864 diary is at Bancroft Library, Berkeley.

9. Alder Clump was always noted by travelers of this period and usually described in almost identical terms: fine grove of alders and a splendid spring. Hedges, camping at the spot just a week after Stanfield, says no good feed for the animals could be obtained there (May 27, 1864). Albert J. Dickson, at the site on June 5, speaks rapturously of the ". . . springs bubbling up clear and cold to form a sparkling riverlet along whose banks numerous thickets of alders contrasted the dark glossy green of their foliage with the red-tinted crags and the purple sage." *Covered Wagon Days,* ed. Arthur J. Dickson (Cleveland, 1924), p. 91. T. J. Brundage (1864 diary), who was there

on June 20, tells of a companion being shot by an Indian. (Typed copy of diary at Montana Historical Society Library, Helena.)

10. Journal: In the Black Hills, every day broke bright with sunshine; at noon it would cloud over and rain would start to fall, clearing for a beautiful sunset in the evening. The Black Hills were covered with cedar trees and appeared black (p. 42).

11. The Bighorn Mountains are a range in northern Wyoming, extending north and south from the Montana border.

Men in the Hedges train also went into the Bighorn Mountains to prospect and rejoined the train on the Yellowstone. See Hedges' diary, entry for June 19, 1864.

12. Journal: Major Bridger had located the road just ten days before. John Jacobs was to be paid $5.00 per wagon for guiding this train. The train assembled in three to four days at Red Buttes (ten miles up the North Platte River from present-day Casper, Wyoming) and expected to reach Virginia City in three or four weeks (p. 42).

13. Journal: The wagons which turned back belonged to Willard and Company. They arrived at Virginia City two weeks sooner than the Stanfield group and were engaged in mining when the latter got there (p. 44).

During this period the train was traveling through the area of the Wind River Canyon.

14. Journal: Each wagon was numbered so that each knew its place; the Stanfield wagon was in the middle of the train—number 35. In the evenings the wagons formed a corral with the wagon tongues pointing inward and the tents pitched inside (p. 45).

15. Hedges notes that on June 15 Captain Allensworth found a pony (entry for June 15, 1864).

16. The Bighorn River forms in west central Wyoming and flows north into the Yellowstone River.

The Bighorn was crossed in the vicinity of the present city of Basin, Wyoming. Grace Hebard and E. A. Brinistool, *The Bozeman Trail* (Glendale, 1960), p. 219.

Hedges describes the beautiful yellow flowers of the prickly pear in full bloom in this area in June (June 13, 1864).

17. Journal: The boat took only three or four wagons on each trip. The crossing took half an hour.

Hedges says that the ferry (which his train used a few days after Stanfield) could take two wagons on each trip (entry for June 12, 1864).

18. Journal: Sometimes Stanfield borrowed Mrs. John Fowler's wash-

board and was "as near happy as circumstances would permit." On this occasion he placed his clothes on a big boulder and pounded them with some smaller stones, using a little soap. The sage brush served as a clothes line. "I am not sure that it would have passed for clean in a nicely regulated household" (pp. 49–50).

19. The Greybull River rises in Park County, northwest Wyoming, and flows northeast into the Bighorn River.

20. Journal: Coarse flour had been used to feed the stock. Since Jacobs had promised them grass and water at this place, they had not made provision for a trip of more than twelve miles (p. 52).

21. Stinking Water is today called the Shoshone River. It is located about twenty-eight miles beyond the Greybull River in northwest Wyoming. It rises in present Park County and flows northeast into the Bighorn River.

22. Cornelius Hedges was in the Allensworth train. His diary tells of its progress as the train followed the Bridger and Jacobs trains into Virginia City. The train formed on June 1 after having passed Deer Creek (Glenrock) the day before. At that place on the North Platte, Hedges met Allensworth, who enthusiastically described the new (Bridger) route. The company elected Allensworth as Captain and hired a Frenchman, Rouleau, as guide for $5 per wagon. The train began with seventy-five wagons, but by June 4 had grown to ninety-five. The guide is described as a drunken, wrangling, undependable man. Allensworth had to ride out and search for him again and again. Allensworth was the effective leader.

Allensworth's train reached Virginia City July 10. Although Allensworth remained there until at least July 23, some of his men (still referred to as Allensworth's train) went on to Helena (Last Chance Gulch), where gold was discovered on July 14. Two of these men (C. L. Cutler and H. Bruce) were elected town commissioners of Helena in October, and another, John Somerville (Summerville), named the town Helena.

Hedges' diary supplements the Stanfield record and frequently refers to the Jacobs train. Hedges settled in Montana, became a probate judge and superintendent of public instruction, and was instrumental in the creation of Yellowstone National Park.

23. Journal: Two of Stanfield's partners went on this side expedition; each taking a mule and leaving Stanfield with one saddle mule, the wagon, and wheel mules. Their plan was to meet at the Yellowstone River (p. 54).

24. Journal: "There was one of the finest looking indians I have

NOTES FOR PAGES 64-71   201

ever seen with them. If he would go back to South Bend half of the girls in town would fall in love with him." The Indians told the train that they were on the war path to fight the Sioux, and that their main party of several hundred warriors was a few miles off (p. 55).

25. Journal: The Gap was an immense causeway just wide enough for a wagon. Huge, old rocks towered on every side (p. 55).

Pryor's Gap is located approximately thirty-five miles south of Billings, Montana.

26. Stanfield describes the Clarks Fork as a beautiful river. It rises in southern Montana and flows east through northwestern Wyoming, then north into Yellowstone River in south central Montana.

27. Journal: Clarks Fork.

28. Divide Creek was marked by each diarist traveling this route. It was noted for its clearness, cleanliness, and good trout fishing. See Hedges, entry for June 29, 1864. Journal: Several ponies were found running loose, and the men took possession of them (p. 61).

29. Journal: The returning prospectors reported that the mining prospects in the Bighorn Mountains were good but that the season was too late to develop them that year (p. 62).

30. Rose Bud Creek is a small stream which forks into the Stillwater River near Nye, Montana.

31. The Carson River is a small stream flowing into the Yellowstone River.

32. The charge for ferrying the river was $2.50 (Hedges, entry for July 4, 1864). The Allensworth train crossed as soon as the Jacobs train had gotten over. By July 4, the Bridger, Jacobs, and Allensworth trains were traveling in an unbroken line of wagons. Hedges writes of having caught up with the Bridger group, and this information confirms the disintegration of the Jacobs train as reported by Stanfield. It should be noted that the Allensworth train was also no longer operating effectively as such.

33. Journal: This train was under the guidance of Major Bridger (p. 64).

It consisted of the original Bridger train, remnants of the Jacobs and Allensworth trains, and independents.

34. The Gallatin River rises in the northwest corner of Wyoming and flows north to unite with the Jefferson and Madison rivers to form the Missouri River.

35. The Madison River rises in southwestern Montana, and flows west and north to unite with the Jefferson and Gallatin rivers to form the Missouri River.

36. Stanfield's estimate of the population is probably fairly accurate. Variant figures can be cited. For example, the population is given as 4,000 in *Powder River Campaigns and Sawyer's Expedition of 1865,* ed. LeRoy Hafen and Ann Hafen (Glendale, 1961), p. 220.

37. On May 26, 1864, Montana Territory was created by Congress with Sidney Edgerton as Governor. The territorial legislature did not meet until December 12, 1864, at Bannack.

CHAPTER FIVE

1. Lewis, entry for Nov. 15, 1865; Mary Fish, Daily journal, 1860, entry for August 1, 1860. Original MS at Bancroft Library, Berkeley.

2. Virginia City, Montana Territory, July 25, 1864: Stanfield took the Oliver and Conover Stage Line, which had been running between Virginia City and Salt Lake City since 1863 and was the only coach between the cities at this time. Not until July 27, 1864, did Ben Holladay begin his tri-weekly service over the same route. His Holladay Overland Mail and Express Company (Overland Stage Line) originally charged $100 for the trip. See the advertisement in the *Daily Union Vedette* (Camp Douglas, Utah Territory), July 26, 1864, p. 4. It may be assumed that Oliver and Conover charged substantially the same amount. On August 15, Holladay reduced the fare to $25 (advertisement, *Daily Union Vedette,* August 2, 1864, p. 3), and soon drove Oliver and Conover out of business. As the advertisements promised, the trip took less than four days. See the Montana *Post* (Virginia City), October 29, 1864, p. 4.

Journal: The stage was drawn by four horses—"miserable little mustangs," rounded up by Indians at the change stations. Meals were served at the stations, located every fifty to sixty miles, where both horses and drivers were changed. The meals were expensive but usually consisted of just bacon, bread, and coffee (p. 70).

Although the Indians were causing problems in other areas, they were quiet along this route at this time.

The stage line went through Idaho approximately along US 91 and US 191. By 1864, the route lay in Portneuf Canyon, and crossed the Bear River near the present town of Fielding, Utah. US 91 extends to Salt Lake City.

An employee of Holladay, E. M. Pollinger, in 1904, described the route taken by the stages as ". . . up through Cache Valley to Franklin then crossed Bear River at what was known as Stubbs Ferry which was a short distance above the battle field where Genl. Connors . . . shot . . . at the Bannack . . . then up through Fellos Valley then through Lincol Valley to the crossing of the Snake River known as Eagle Rock Ferry . . . about eight miles above the present Idaho Falls." From a letter of Pollinger to J. E. Calloway, 28 May 1904. Original at Montana State Historical Society Library, Helena.

Road agents, one of the great problems along the route, robbed the Oliver and Conover coach of $23,700 on August 20, 1864. Glade F. Howell, "Early History of Malad Valley" (M.A. thesis, Brigham Young University, 1960), p. 49.

3. Journal: The driver said he was no longer in the employment of the stage company. The passengers had agreed that if he did not go on, they would take possession of the coach and drive themselves to Salt Lake City (pp. 70–71).

On July 26, the stage crossed the Continental Divide.

When the road was lost, the passengers started looking for it in all directions. Fortunately, they soon found the track.

The danger of the travel is seen in the Montana *Post*, September 24, 1864, news report describing an Oliver coach overturning on this route.

4. The Snake River rises in Yellowstone National Park, northwest Wyoming, flows south, then southwest, west, and north in a big arc across Idaho, then turns north.

5. The Bear River rises in northern Utah and flows north crossing the Wyoming border, turns northwest into southeast Idaho, bends south and empties into Bear River Bay of Great Salt Lake.

6. Journal: After fording Bear River a large sage hen appeared, and everyone wanted to shoot it. It was finally killed by a man from St. Louis, but a man from Missouri also shot at it. He was sitting in the middle seat, and as he fired, a man in the front seat raised his shoulder and was hit. The wound was painful but not dangerous (p. 72).

7. Journal: On July 29, the stage reached Ogden City in time for breakfast. This area reminded Stanfield of Indiana with little houses and farms and an occasional town along the road. Arriving at Salt Lake City, Stanfield first bought a hat, then had supper, and set out to see the sights (p. 73).

Ogden—thirty-three miles north of Salt Lake City—resembled a pleasant midwestern village. It had been settled in 1847 by the Mormons at the forks of the Ogden and Weber rivers. The rivers provided the irrigation necessary for a prosperous agricultural region. Grain and vegetables grew in abundance. Its population in 1860 was 1,464.

8. Journal: Stanfield paid $3 a day for his hotel room, and it was

the only hotel fit to stay in. Each evening the boarders gathered at the dining-room door about a quarter of an hour prior to dinner. When the doors were opened, every seat was quickly filled. The second table had only what was left from the first, except for the meat. Stanfield described his bed as a poor one in a low room with five or six other men. Each evening before getting into bed, he hunted and burned the bed bugs. Many of the hotel guests slept on the verandah to avoid the pests (p. 77).

The Salt Lake City House was owned by the Church and managed by a son-in-law of Brigham Young, Feramorz Little. The House had a large yard for cattle, which added to the noise made by a generally rough-looking crowd which hung around it. The upstairs sitting rooms were comfortably furnished. Its bedrooms had very thin partitions. The hotel was located in the heart of the City, across the street from the post office and next door to the bath house and bakery. A verandah overlooked the main street. A sign board swaying from a tall flag staff attracted attention to the hotel.

William S. Bartlett arrived at the Salt Lake City House on August 13, 1864. Salt Lake *Telegraph*, August 13, 1864, p. 4.

9. Journal: On this morning (August 4) Stanfield met a member of his old train who had left Virginia City a week before Stanfield's departure. Stanfield had sent his trunk with two friends (Fowler and Crockett) in their wagon and now recovered it (p. 78).

10. The City was laid out by Brigham Young in 1847. The city blocks were in squares of about ten acres; each lot was one and a quarter acres; the streets, although unpaved in the residential areas, were eight rods wide. Ten acres were set aside for the Temple Square. The population in 1860 was 8,236. Some estimates place it as high as 20,000 by 1865. See Leonard Arrington and Thomas Alexander, "The U. S. Army Overlooks Fort Douglas 1862–1965," *Utah Historical Quarterly,* XXXIII (Fall 1965), 333.

11. Journal: Brigham Young's residence was described as a two-storied brick house surmounted by a lion's head. The weekly paper *Deseret* was printed on a press in Young's house. The paper reported passing events and contained articles relating to the arts and sciences (p. 75).

The entrance to Young's estate was through the famous Eagle Gate—a large impressive gateway topped by a huge carved eagle.

12. Journal: The Temple was to be built of enormous granite blocks which required forty yoke of oxen to transport each piece from

Little Cottonwood Canyon in the mountains (p. 75). The Temple was to be 186 feet by 199 feet; its cornerstone had been laid in 1853. The Temple Block was surrounded by a wall fifteen feet high.

13. The recently opened mines in Montana and the north provided a new business outlet for the city, and the economy was booming. Stanfield was incorrect if his evaluation—he had described the town as "dull"—referred to the business life of the thrifty community. Its downtown area included many shops and stores (a bakery, a butcher shop, a smithy; crockery, hardware, and shoe stores; grocery, liquor, furniture, and dry-goods stores). One of the stores in this part of town had a stock of goods valued at half a million dollars (Journal, p. 76).

Among the Gentiles, the leading merchants were Mr. Nixon and Mr. Gilbert; among the Mormons, the Walker brothers. Young tried to discourage commerce for it attracted Gentiles, who as merchants tended to dominate the business life of the Mormon capital. The shops had both luxurious imported goods and other, less pretentious, merchandise.

The Sacramento *Daily Bee* (September 28, 1864) said that Salt Lake City was the only place, other than the Atlantic coast, where there was any stir of business (p. 2). The *Daily Union Vedette* (Camp Douglas, Utah Territory), July 22, 1864, reported that "Utah is enjoying an unexampled prosperity . . ." (p 2).

14. Most diarists of the period confirm the sentiment that the Mormons did not like the Gentiles, and made them pay dearly for everything. General Conner, Commander of Fort Douglas, was so outraged at the prices the Mormons charged him that he freighted his own supplies into the city.

The diary of ——— Bond, on the other hand, demonstrates the helpfulness of the Mormons to a Gentile. *Foot Travels Across the Plains* (Richmond, Ind., 1868), pp. 6, 15.

15. Journal: Also on the fourth side was the Jordan River, the water of which was brackish and ill-flavored. The river was 100 feet wide with many wooden bridges across it within the city. Formerly, the city had been surrounded by an adobe wall which by 1864 had fallen into neglect (p. 76).

16. Camp Douglas was established by the United States Government to supervise the Mormons (this, following the trouble in 1857) and to watch the activities of Indians in Utah, Nevada, and part of Wyoming.

The fort was built around a square parade grounds with an area of 440 square feet and contained barracks, officers quarters, stores, magazines, a blacksmith shop, and the other buildings common to settlements of this kind. In the Battle of Bear River (January, 1863) Conner had inflicted losses on the Indians, and these account for the quietness of the Indians in the summer of 1864 in the areas of the Snake and the Bear rivers.

The enlistment terms of the 3rd Infantry Regiment of the California Volunteers were nearly ended, and recruits at Camp Douglas were promised a $100 bonus, good pay, and a large clothing allowance. See *Daily Union Vedette* (Camp Douglas), July 13, 1864, p. 3. Companies L and M of the 2nd Cavalry Regiment, California Volunteers were also stationed at the Camp. They were under Col. P. Edward Conner and Major Edward McGarry. (Conner was sometimes referred to as General, sometimes as Colonel.)

17. Journal: The theatre was not yet completed in 1864. The price of admission was fifty cents, and every performance was crowded. Although the parts were poorly played by amateurs (guests were brought in from time to time), the actors were cheered by the audience. The building was of brick, seated several thousand persons, and included a dress circle and three gallaries (pp. 75–76).

The theatre was built in 1861–62 and was formally opened in March, 1862. The amateur actors found their own costumes and never received a fixed remuneration. The 1,500 seats were usually filled, and tickets could be paid for with grain, chickens, or other merchandise. It was located at State and First South streets. Young believed that "the people must have amusement as well as religion." The architect was William H. Folson, and the scenery was designed by George M. Ottinger. The building was eighty feet by 144 feet, and the front was decorated with Doric columns.

In the summer of 1864, H. B. Clausen was the manager and John T. Caine was the director and stage manager.

18. Journal: One morning Stanfield went to the spring two miles distant with a friend. They rented a one-horse livery for $5 for the trip. Hearing that the mineral waters were healthy, he drank as well as bathed. He enjoyed the experience so much that he returned a number of times while in the city (pp. 77–78).

The Warm Springs were one mile north of the city. They were public baths, city owned and controlled, with private and public pool facilities. The usual temperature was 102°, and the waters contained a high concentration of sulphur. Two miles beyond were the Hot Springs, which emerged from the base of a mountain in a large stream. The water was boiling and formed the Hot Springs Lake.

19. Many church members at this time were beginning to refuse to tithe.

20. The Jordan River rises in Utah Lake in north central Utah and flows north through Salt Lake City and into Great Salt Lake.

21. The usual bathing place was at Black Rock. The beach was described as white sand with flakes of salt in it. In the neighborhood of the lake, the soil was thin—over gravel—with milkweed and greasewood the only vegetation.

22. Journal: Stanfield describes the Island as having mountains and valleys, and apparently fertile soil. Young reportedly kept the Church stock—thousands of cattle—on the Island (p. 82).

The Lake contained many islands, but the large island Stanfield mentions was Church (Antelope) Island. It was sixteen miles long and six miles wide, with a bold ridge rising 3,000 feet above the lake.

23. George Pauncefort played Hamlet, and Mrs. Florence Bell played Ophelia. Pauncefort, an Englishman, was an accomplished actor, having made his American debut in Boston in 1854 in *The Rivals*. He opened the Worcester, Massachusetts, Theatre in 1859 as the Pauncefort Athenaeum.

The theatre in Salt Lake City was sold out for the performance that Stanfield saw, and many people were turned away. The *Deseret News* (August 10, 1864) reviewed the performance: "Mr. Pauncefort's Hamlet was a decided success. In other parts he was less impulsive, in others not so dreamy as some eminent artists, yet his Hamlet was closely fashioned after the creation of Shakespeare's brain. The soliloquy . . . and the closet scene . . . were splendidly rendered. The whole character was carefully read and full of poetry of gesture and expression. Mrs. Bell's Ophelia was a very natural and fine piece of acting. Some of the other characters were carefully rendered, but the advice of Hamlet to the players might be studied to advantage very generally" (p. 4).

The Salt Lake *Telegraph* (August 13, 1864) also gave the performance a favorable review (p. 2).

CHAPTER SIX

1. Lomas (p. 66) notes that in 1864 Austin was at least one-half tent town and that every other building was a saloon or gambling house.

2. The economy in the Marysville area was depressed in 1864, as it was all along the coast. George Harter (p. 21) says the "universal cry" in Marysville was that there was no work. Mining operations had declined, and the farmers were suffering the results of a severe drought.

3. Journal: The trip was by stage. The only other passenger leaving Salt Lake City was a young woman going to California; other passengers were picked up during the first day of travel (p. 85).

The coach was a "regular" one swinging on leather straps, suitable for short trips. It was pulled by from four to six horses—depending on the terrain— which were changed every twenty miles. The coaches were changed every sixty miles, at coach stations, and each driver had his regular coach, which he drove between two stations. This necessitated passengers changing coaches every sixty miles, but the company believed that this practice gave the driver pride in keeping the equipment in good order. Since the company held a monopoly, Stanfield felt that it was unconcerned with passenger convenience.

From Salt Lake City to Virginia City Stanfield took the Overland Mail Company Stage (owned by Wells Fargo). Bela M. Hughes was Acting President and Hiram S. Rumfield the Assistant Treasurer stationed at Salt Lake City. The company advertised the trip as taking less than five days—and made the trip in Stanfield's case in four days, sixteen hours. The distance was 518 miles. The company profited most from its express business, and may well have been guilty of Stanfield's charge of neglecting the passengers. Its advertisements claimed it gave special attention to the comfort and convenience of passengers. *Daily Union Vedette* (Camp Douglas, Utah Territory), July 26, 1864, p. 4.

The general route followed by the stage was from Salt Lake City to Ruby Valley, across the Diamond Mountains to Austin, and into Virginia City. The specific stations which were major posts were Joe's Dug Out, Rush Valley, Ft. Crittenden, Black Rock, Canon Station (all in Utah); Spring Valley, Ruby Valley, Camp Station, Reese River (Austin), Mount Airey, Middle Gate, Fair View, Odd River, Dayton, and Carson City (all in Nevada). On this route the stations usually supplied good and full meals with a variety of meats, vegetables, fruits, and breads. The prices ranged from 50¢ to $2. Many passengers preferred to carry their own food—to the annoyance of their fellow passengers.

Passenger fare changed frequently depending upon the Indian situation, toll charges, and highway holdups. Root and Connelley give the 1863 fare from Salt Lake City to Placerville as $75 and the 1865 fare as $100. See Frank A. Root and William E. Connelley, *The Overland Stage to California* (Columbus, Ohio, 1950), p. 50. James F. Rushing gives the 1865 fare from Salt Lake City to Nevada as $150 and from Nevada to California as $50. See *The Great West and Pacific Coast* (New York, 1877), p. 41.

NOTES FOR PAGE 90

Modern highways which in general follow Stanfield's stage trip from Salt Lake City to Folsom, California, are: From Salt Lake City west over US 80 to junction with US 40. US 40 to junction with US 93 and south on US 93 to the branch of Nevada 11 which passes through Ruby Valley and southward to Nevada 46. Nevada 46 until it meets US 50 and US 50 into Austin, through Austin, to Nevada 79 just outside Virginia City. Take 79 into Virginia City. Leaving Virginia City take US 50 just south of it through Carson City, follow it around the south end of Lake Tahoe. Then westward through Placerville to Folsom.

The railroad which Stanfield took from Folsom for the most part followed present-day US 50 into Sacramento. The railroad that he took from Sacramento to Lincoln followed in a general way US 40. From Lincoln to Marysville US 99; from Marysville to Browns Valley on California 20; from there to Indiana Ranch on county roads to Dobbins, which is just two and one-half miles from the site of Indiana Ranch.

4. Journal: Ruby Valley was described as a beautiful little vale, rich and fertile, surrounded by a desert. Its farms reminded Stanfield of Indiana. It was an overnight stop for the Overland Stage (p. 86).

The Ruby Mountains are chiefly in south Elko County, northeast Nevada, and extend south. The Diamond Mountains are a range in east central Nevada, extending from southwest Elko County southward.

The Overland Mail Company cultivated hundreds of acres in Ruby Valley and employed several hundred farmers. They thus tried to supply themselves and avoid the exorbitant prices charged by the Mormons.

Ruby Valley Station was sometimes described as "Half-way House," since it was approximately 300 miles from both Salt Lake City and Carson City.

The area through which they traveled for several days was covered with soil of powdered alkali which supported no vegetation and irritated the skin. In some spots the horses could hardly draw the coaches, which would sink up to their hubs in potash.

5. Journal: Silver was the metal mined in Austin (p. 86).

Austin, in the Reese River district, had a number of silver veins (unlike Virginia City, which centered about the Comstock Lode). It was the chief mining operation in central Nevada. The town was five miles long and a mile wide with mines operating throughout this area. All mines took their ore to centrally located mills for crushing and roasting. Hundreds of little dwellings of stone and brick or adobe were scattered up the hillside among hundreds of piles of reddish dirt, showing the activity of the miners. The town had no trees or bushes, but there were the usual stores and accommodations, and all transactions were in gold and silver. Gambling was carried on day and night with women handling the tables.

Silver was first discovered there in 1862, and the population by 1864 was perhaps 10,000. It became the seat of Lander County in 1863 and is 145 miles northeast of Carson City.

6. The "weary" trip from Austin to Virginia City is described in an unsigned article appearing in the Sacramento *Daily Bee,* September 28, 1864, p. 2.

7. Journal: His breakfast cost 75¢, but in change for a two-dollar greenback he received just 25¢ in silver. All transactions were on a specie basis (p. 88).

8. Virginia City had many banking establishments: Wells Fargo, Arnold and Blanvelt, B. F. Hastings and Company, Stateler and Airrington, and Paxton and Thornburgh. In 1863 they had formed an association to bring about uniform business procedures. In that same year California had passed the Specific Act, which provided that contracts could specify the type of currency to be used in the transaction. Nevada businessmen approved of the act for they, too, preferred gold and silver to greenbacks. By 1864 there was general distress over the use of paper money in Virginia City, and most business establishments there refused to accept anything but gold and silver. The Virginia *Daily Union,* August 12, 1864, editorialized "Now you can not get credit with the best security, because the banker and merchant are afraid you will give them paper dollars for their gold dollars . . ." (p. 2). The newspaper felt that the economic decline in the West was caused by the lack of circulating currency, brought about by the business community's insistence on using only gold and silver. This background offers the explanation of why Stanfield was unable to cash his draft on a New York bank: the Virginia City bankers feared repayment in greenbacks.

9. Stanfield, like most travelers, probably stayed at the International Hotel. It was filled with noise and confusion—crowds of mingling miners, visitors and gamblers, occupying the lobby and flowing out onto the street. Its gas lights added a touch of style to the establishment. The Hotel was rebuilt in 1860 by Isaac Bateman and had twelve sleeping rooms, a barroom, dining room, parlor, and even an elevator. "The house is in every respect a first class hotel." See William R. Gillis,

The Nevada Directory for 1868–69, (San Francisco, 1868), p. 43. All important visitors stayed at this hotel, and it was the center of the town's social activity.

10. Journal: Stanfield considered writing to friends in California for assistance, but since none of them knew he was coming, he believed they would consider him an imposter. Humorously, he noted that he had pondered the idea of stealing, but dismissed this, for men were "choked" (hanged) for this deed. Since employment was not available, he became discouraged with his situation (pp. 88–89).

11. Wilson S. Bender was twenty-two years old, the son of Jacob Bender a forty-seven-year-old tailor. Jacob Bender with his wife and four children had moved to South Bend from Ohio prior to 1850. In 1859 they started for Pike's Peak but abandoned the trip and took up farming at Bell Creek, Washington County, Nebraska. In 1862 the two oldest boys, Wilse and Almon, went to Virginia City, Nevada, in response to the silver strikes. In 1863 the rest of the family joined them, and Jacob hoped to establish himself as a tailor. His health declined and with the high cost of living, it was necessary for the family to move to Sacramento with Mrs. Bender's sister, Mrs. Margaret (Edwin B.) Crocker. Edwin B. Crocker was the attorney for the Central Pacific Railroad, and through him Wilson S. Bender obtained his position in the Virginia City Telegraph Office. See J. Wells Kelly, *Second Directory of Nevada Territory* [1863] (San Francisco, 1863), p. 173.

The Bender trip of 1863 to Virginia City is described in Flora Isabelle Bender, "Notes by the Way, Memoranda of a Journey Across the Plains from Bull Creek, Washington County, Neb., to Virginia City, Nev. Terr., May 7 to August 4, 1863," ed. William C. Miller, *Nevada Historical Society Quarterly,* I (July, 1958), 144–74.

12. Journal: Although the city was just four or five years old, it contained both fine stores and homes. The economy centered about the ten to fifteen large silver-mining companies. Until the previous summer, when the mining fever subsided, the population had been 20,000. It was much less than this by the summer of 1864. In the mines the men worked in small niches and tunnels which spread out from the main tunnel. The miners "presented a very wierd singular picture, with their haggard bearded faces." They loaded the ore into cars which ran to the surface over tracks laid in each tunnel. Stanfield was not impressed with the city and concluded: "I do not care about coming back very soon" (pp. 89–91).

Virginia City began with the silver strike of 1859–60, when the

Comstock Lode was uncovered. By 1862, the mines were in full production. The city presented a picturesque sight, perched half way up the side of Mount Davidson (then called Sun Mountain). Below it lay the ravines and canyons, above it the mountain peak.

The value of mines was calculated by the foot. Whereas the Gould and Curry property had once commanded $6,000 per foot, the value had declined by this date. The silver vein was several hundred feet wide with smaller veins slanting off in all directions. Stout timbers held the tunnels open. Descent into the mines was in a cage on a pulley. At the bottom, level tracks for the rail cars extended into the working veins. The yield was from $1,000 to $2,000 per ton of ore. Some 500 men were employed by Gould and Curry.

The city had begun to shed the rawness of a wild western town—well-built brick stores lined the main street; the Sabbath was beginning to be observed with many churches growing strong; and gambling and vice were less in evidence. Theatres, newspapers, and telegraph lines gave the city an eastern look. Especially noteworthy were the Piper Opera House, the Maguire Opera House, the office of the *Territorial Enterprise,* and the Wells Fargo building. The communities of Silver City and Gold Hill adjoined Virginia City and the casual traveler could not tell where the city boundaries began.

The year 1864–65 was a depression period for the city. Mine production was down, and the economic ruin of the town seemed at hand. Many people were moving away, and immigrants could not sell their surplus goods. Auctions were held day and night. Still, prices remained high (Mary Eliza Warner Maloon, entry for July 12, 1864).

13. Journal: Stanfield attended a Presbyterian church and reported that it seemed just like his home church (p. 91).

The church had been organized in 1862 with Rev. D. H. Palmer of New York as the minister. Services were held on Sunday at 11 A.M. and at 7 P.M. in the District Court Room, Post Office Building.

14. The County Hospital was under the supervision of visiting physician Dr. Thomas H. Pinkerton. It was a three-story brick building with a Male Department (sixty patients) and a Female Department (fourteen patients).

The nearby Flowery Hill Cemetery, which Stanfield visited, covered twenty-seven acres. To visit the graves of the town's outlaws was considered the thing to do.

15. Journal: The stage was drawn by a team of four to six horses, according to the state of the road. The horses were kept on a trot or a run. The trip "made my blood run cold," when the stage would whirl

NOTES FOR PAGE 93   213

along roads bounded on one side by a steep mountain and on the other by an equally deep crevice. In narrow places the driver would blow his horn before proceeding (p. 93).

From Virginia City to Folsom the Pioneer Stage Line passed through Carson City, along the eastern shore of Lake Tahoe with its usual stop at the Lake House. Then, it descended the western slopes of the Sierra Nevadas to Placerville and went on to Folsom, where railroad connections could be made with Sacramento. Specific station stops on the run were Carson City, Genoa, Fridays, Yanks, Strawberry, Weber, Moos, Sportsman's Hall, and Placerville. Altogether over 100 stations lined the road to take care of the heavy traffic.

Stanfield took one of the two Pioneer coaches which left Virginia City on August 15. Each was filled, and together they carried twelve men, six women, and two children (Virginia *Daily Union,* August 16, 1864, p. 3). The Pioneer Line is sometimes called Crandall's Pioneer Line for its founder J. B. Crandall; but after 1860 it was owned and operated by Wells Fargo. Louis McLane was in charge of this line between Virginia City and Folsom.

Stanfield does not mention Placerville as most travelers do. No doubt this is because the coach passed through the town at night. It had a population of between 3,000 and 4,000, was located in the western foothills of the Sierras, and was a trading center for mine supplies.

It took Stanfield's coach just twenty-three hours to travel from Virginia City to Folsom. Good time was possible largely because of the improved toll roads and the nerveless drivers. The toll road was well graded, kept in top condition, even watered to keep the dust down. The Pioneer drivers were considered an elite group. They wore long dusters of white linen, yellow kid gloves, and flat-crowned wide brim hats. They lorded over the passengers and demanded respect and obedience. They needed full control, for road agents still operated along this route. As recently as June 30, 1864, the stage had been robbed near Placerville. John Young, *San Francisco* (San Francisco, n. d.), p. 38.

The coach used on this run was a "Concord Coach" that swung, swayed, pitched, and jolted the eight or nine passengers. Mail, bullion, and baggage were piled on top, making it top-heavy. Express materials were also loaded on the front and rear boots. Two drivers were assigned, one serving as an armed express agent. The coaches were painted in brilliant colors. Sociability reigned as the intimacy of the accommodations ruled out formality. Passengers learned to doze throughout day and night. There was no overnight stop on this trip, and the hooting of the driver as he approached a station effectively prevented sleep.

16. Journal: Lake Bigler was also called Lake Tahoe. The Swiss lake referred to by Stanfield is Lake Lucerne. The rise of the road, as the summit of the Sierra Nevadas was approached, was the most beautiful scene Stanfield had ever seen (p. 92). Some travelers took a boat across the Lake, for the water had an extraordinary transparency, but Stanfield remained on the stage.

17. Journal: The freight wagons were pulled by teams of eight, ten, and twelve mules and weighed from ten to fifteen tons (p. 93).

Wagon freight transportation on the Placerville-Virginia City road was at its height in 1864. So crowded were conditions that travelers were frequently forced off the road for hours by a string of freight wagons. See Byron Pugh, "History of Utah-California Wagon Freighting" (M.A. thesis, University of California, Berkeley, 1949), p. 142.

18. Folsom was founded in 1855 and is located on the American River. Gold was discovered at the site in 1849, and the Coloma road through it was the first route to the gold fields. The railroad from Sacramento to Folsom had been engineered, layed out, and constructed by Theodore D. Judah. In 1856 Folsom became the temporary terminus of the Sacramento Valley Railroad, and the town prospered as the point of departure for the miners and travelers going to the mines in northeastern California.

The Pioneer Stage Line advertised that it made connections with the 7 A.M. train for Sacramento (the Virginia *Daily Union,* July 28, 1864, p. 1). The fare from Folsom to Sacramento, about twenty-two miles, was probably about $2 (Sacramento *Bee,* May 5, 1939, Sec. A, p. 6).

19. Journal: "The capitol is rather a common looking ediface, but I suppose it answers all purposes." The city had constructed large levees to contain the river and prevent the floods which had been disastrous in the past (p. 94).

Sacramento lies on a loop of the Sacramento River at its confluence with the American River. It is seventy-eight miles northeast of San Francisco. Red-brick buildings, the older part of the city, lay along the river banks. With their tall narrow windows and tin-roofed awnings projecting over the sidewalks they made a picturesque scene. The residential sections of the city had wide streets, and its substantial houses were surrounded with masses of shrubs, flowers, and trees.

Platted in 1848 on John Sutter's farm, the town became a supply center for miners. In 1856 the Sacramento Railroad was built—the first in California. The population in 1860 was 13,785, including 988 Asians.

20. Indiana Ranch was a mining-site settlement, after 1851, on Indiana Creek, a tributary to Dry Creek. Originally known as Indiana Creek or Tolles' New Diggins, the settlement was founded by the Page Brothers and A. P. Labadie and John Tolles. Francis Page and Labadie, both from South Bend, had gone to California in 1849; and the town which they founded became a center for many gold seekers from South Bend. In 1851–52 it had a population of about 500 miners with a large mill for melting the gold ore. The town had hotels (one of which was run by Labadie), stores, and even a race track. After 1860 mining declined in the vicinity, although rich pockets were discovered from time to time. In 1864 M. G. Morey owned the hotel.

The Indiana Ranch area was called "indescribable" in the 1850's by George Baker. He wrote in his diary of the beautiful streams, mountains, trees, and wild flowers (p. 125). See the diary of George Baker (original MS at Society of California Pioneers Library, San Francisco).

The Federal Census Reports for 1860 (Yuba County, p. 157) show that Stanfield's aunt, Mrs. Mary Jane Stanfield Smith, and her husband, William Smith, a butcher by trade, were living at Indiana Ranch. The Stanfield family had moved there from Stanfield Hill in Long Bar Township, Yuba County. The latter site was named for William Stanfield, who had opened there the hotel and tavern, Stanfield House, in 1856. He sold the hotel in 1858 and died in 1859. The House was on the main Marysville-LaPorte road (see n. 24).

21. Lincoln was as far northeastward as the California Central Railroad had extended from Sacramento toward Marysville by 1864. It lay on the road to the mines, twenty-five miles from Sacramento. Although not yet incorporated, the settlement flourished as a trade and supply center. It was founded under the auspices of C. L. Wilson, who had built the railroad to that point by 1861.

22. Journal: Stanfield called Marysville a played-out city; it had 6,000 residents, many from South Bend (p. 94).

Marysville was the seat of Yuba County, located at the confluence of the Feather and Yuba rivers, forty miles north of Sacramento. A trading post from 1842 and a station on the Oregon-California trail, it was incorporated as a city in 1851. Freight and passengers in the 1850's flooded through it on the way to the Feather and Yuba river diggings. By 1864 the city still had life as a business community. The 1860 population was 4,740. Marysville was surrounded by levees built to protect it from the floods of the Feather and Yuba rivers.

As Stanfield learned in his visits to the city, it had several fine churches, a substantial city hall, firehouse, schoolhouse, courthouse, hospital, and a large business district. Most of the buildings were less than ten years old. As Stanfield notes, the great boom had ended.

From Lincoln to Marysville and from Marysville to Indiana Ranch Stanfield probably took a California Stage Company coach. These ran daily and offered the best stage service in the area. See *Brown's Marysville Directory for the Year Commencing March 1861* . . . (Marysville, 1861), pp. 94–96. James Haworth was the agent in Marysville (Marysville *Daily Appeal,* October 7, 1864, p. 1).

23. On January 16, 1863, D. R. Sample purchased a thirty-acre farm from A. H. Julian for $500. The farm was located in Park Bar Township, Yuba County. (See Yuba County Recorder Book Number 16, p. 209.) Sample was a leader of the socially significant Marysville Volunteer Firemen's Brigade, the Eureka Engine Company Number 1 (Minutes of Marysville Common Council, August 1, 1864).

24. LaPorte (known as Rabbit Creek 1850–57) was a mining camp on Rabbit Creek, a tributary of Slate Creek, located sixty-one miles from Marysville. Gold was discovered there in 1850, and it was a flourishing community in the 1860's, when it became a major center for hydraulic mining. It had many inns and the usual stores and saloons.

Stanfield remained at LaPorte until at least February 25, 1865. See the letter of Edward P. Stanfield to Howard Stillwell Stanfield, 1 January 1864 [5?]. (The letter is dated 1864, but was actually written in 1865.) Original copy in the possession of the Indiana State Historical Society, Indianapolis.

25. Edward P. Stanfield was mustered out of the army December 20, 1864 (Ibid.).

26. It had not been a pleasant spring, and the March 4, 1865, report of snow flurries and rain showers was typical (Marysville *Daily Appeal,* p. 3). Yet beginning early in April summer-like weather suddenly arrived. See the Marysville *Daily Appeal,* April 1, 1865, p. 3; and the Sacramento *Daily Bee,* April 6, 1865, p. 2.

27. Oregon House, twenty-four miles northeast of Marysville on the

NOTES FOR PAGES 99–102   217

road to Camptonville, was built in 1852. It was an unusually popular house known for its hospitality and a community developed around it. In 1854 a post office was located there.

28. The Yuba House was a stage stop.

29. The United States Hotel was a brick building, erected in 1856 at the corner of C and Third streets. It was opened by Lee and Hoffman, had fifty-two rooms, a lobby, and dining rooms.

In 1865 the Hotel was operated by W. C. Stokes. An advertisement in the Marysville *Daily Appeal* (October 2, 1864) claimed for it "The best beds, well lighted, ventilated and cheerful rooms, and a table equal in its variety and quality of things good to the sight and taste to any in this city or any other city in this State . . ." (p. 1). The Hotel also provided omnibus service for guests to the coaches and boats.

30. There were Episcopal, Catholic, and Presbyterian churches. Stanfield, no doubt, attended the Presbyterian services which Rev. E. B. Walsworth conducted on Sunday mornings and Wednesday evenings. The church had been built in 1859 at a cost of $33,000.

31. On April 5, 1865, the Marysville *Daily Appeal* reported this celebration: "A truce was given to business. In a short time the Stars and Stripes were seen floating to the breeze from every flag-staff in the city. . . . Arrangements were also immediately made for firing 100 guns. At about half-past 2 o'clock the bells began to ring, and the whistles of our machine shops and the fire-engine began to blow. The Firemen were on the *qui vive,* and soon drew their machines into procession, which was headed by the Marysville Brass Band. This impromptu procession was under command of Marshall Bockius, who with a long wooden sword managed his somewhat demoralized troops with commendable skill. The procession moved through all the principal streets in about the following *dis*-order. . . ." Included in the procession were California Volunteer troops, two pieces of artillery, fire-engine companies, hose companies, a steam fire engine "with a powerful head of steam on the engine," the U.S. Hotel omnibus, and horses and buggies. The fire engines were decorated with flags and flowers. Flags were carried by everyone. The crowd gathered then to listen to brief remarks by J. G. Eastman, C. V. D. Hubbard, and D. R. Sample (Stanfield's friend). "A happier, jollier and more patriotic demonstration was never made in this city." After dark bonfires were lighted, and the "Union boys" came out with a marshall band. ". . . everybody was out on the streets" (p. 3).

32. The *Gov. Dana* was built in about 1850 and owned by the California Steam Navigation Company. It was a light-draft steamer suitable for the Yuba and upper Sacramento rivers, and it carried passengers and cargo. It is described as an eighty-ton stern-wheeler. The boat made daily trips from Marysville to Sacramento, leaving at 6 A.M. and making connections with the *Chrysopolis* for San Francisco. W. D. Shallcross was the Captain, and G. P. Jessup was the Marysville agent for the company.

The Sacramento River was turbulent and frequently overflowed its banks at Sacramento. As a consequence of the floods of 1862, which had inundated the city, levees were built to line the shores, along which rows of large cottonwoods grew.

33. The Golden Eagle Hotel was a three-story brick structure built in 1853. It had thirty-eight sleeping rooms, parlors, and a dining room, and was the principal headquarters for politicians and travelers. It was comfortably furnished, well ventilated, and set a good table. Its proprietor was D. E. Callahan.

34. The Chinese population of Sacramento County was 1,731; of Yuba County 1,781; and of San Francisco 2,719. See Mary Roberts Coolidge, *Chinese Immigration* (New York, 1909), p. 503.

35. The *Chrysopolis* was 250 feet long, built in 1860 for Captain John G. North, a partner in the California Steam Navigation Company. He picked the lumber specifically for it, and it was regarded as a beautiful ship. Its sumptuous fittings were gold and white, paintings hung in each cabin; its cuisine was superb. For a decade it was the fashionable way to travel between Sacramento and San Francisco. The ship cost $250,000.

The Captain of the ship was Mr. Chadwick. It sailed from Sacramento to San Francisco on Tuesdays, Thursdays, and Saturdays at 1 P.M. (Sacramento *Daily Bee*, August 15, 1864, p. 1).

36. The Sacramento River rises near Mt. Shasta in northern California and flows south into Suisan Bay. Between Sacramento and San Francisco its banks were lined with fine farms growing immense cabbages, squash, and potatoes. It was thought that the tailings from the mines were so filling the river as to soon render it unnavigable. Willows hung over the muddy river in many places. See (Col.) Henry McCormick, *Across the Continent in 1865* (Harrisburg, Pa., 1937), p. 38.

37. The American Exchange Hotel, a fireproof building, was erected in 1852 in the heart of the business district at 319–325 Sampson Street.

NOTES FOR PAGES 104–6   219

Its rates were $1 to $1.50 per day for board and room. It had 165 guest rooms and dining and parlor facilities. J. W. Sargent was the proprietor. See *The San Francisco Directory for the Year Commencing October 1864* (San Francisco, 1864), p. 460.

38. Montgomery Street skirted the base of the San Francisco hills and ended at Telegraph Hill.

The city was admired by all visitors. They often commented on the wide cobblestone streets cut into the hillsides; on the colorful wharf area; the substantial blocks of brick stores and stylish wooden dwellings; the cosmopolitan character of the town with its large Chinese population. A good-natured tolerance characterized the city. The population in 1860 was 56,802.

39. Calvary Presbyterian Church was organized in 1854 by Rev. William A. Scott. His sympathies with the South made this church a center of controversy.

Rev. Charles Wadsworth was the minister in 1865. Sunday services were held at 11 A.M. and 7:30 P.M. The Church, built in 1854 at a cost of $70,000, seated 1,000. Its $8,000 organ was the largest and costliest on the Pacific coast.

The San Francisco *Daily Bulletin* (April 10, 1865) reported that all ministers had preached the day before on the theme of the Union victory—Lee's surrender to Grant. "The recent triumphs of the Union armies were averted to by nearly all the clergy of the city in their pulpit ministrations yesterday" (p. 5).

40. The Lone Mountain Cemetery was a popular tourist attraction. It was three miles from the heart of the city on high land between the ocean and the Bay, of which it commanded an impressive view. The view, the expanse of grass, the dense scrub oaks, evergreens, and flowers—amid the waste of sand and gravel—made the cemetery an attractive place. It was opened in 1854 with 300 acres, and many prominent San Francisco people were subsequently buried there.

41. The Cliff House was built in 1863 and was the third hotel-restaurant of that name built on the same site. It was a plain square structure with a terrace overlooking the Pacific Ocean and the Seal Rocks. It was seven miles west of the center of the city.

42. Oakland had been chartered in 1854 and in 1860 had a population of 1,543. On the east side of San Francisco Bay, opposite the Golden Gate, the city extended over a sandy plain between the Bay and the hills. In 1864 the sandy streets were planked or graveled in the

areas of the costly residences of San Francisco businessmen. The well-cared-for gardens and fine trees were notable, especially the oaks.

The four-mile trip across the Bay was a pleasant excursion ride on the Larue Line for 25¢. From the pier (Larue's Wharf) visitors were taken into Oakland, two miles away, on a steam car.

Stanfield does not mention his early partner, William S. Bartlett, who had settled in Oakland.

43. Maguire's Opera House was owned by Thomas Maguire, a native of Ireland who opened the San Francisco Hall in 1853 and in 1856 changed its name to Maguire's Opera House. It was located on Washington Street near Montgomery. He owned all of the principal theatres in San Francisco and always placed them near a good bar. The theatre had its own stock company and imported visiting stars. All types of plays, musicals, and performers appeared on his bills.

Charles Wheatleigh, distinguished American actor, appeared in San Francisco regularly after 1860. He played Maguire's on April 11, 1865, in two comedies: *Nine Points of the Law* and *A Bull in a China Shop*. On that date the San Francisco Minstrels were appearing at the Eureka Music Hall. They were noted for combining "sweet warblings" and fun (San Francisco *Daily Evening Bulletin,* April 11, 1865, p. 3).

Jacobs may have been Jacobs the Wizard, a magician who was appearing in the San Francisco area at this time.

CHAPTER SEVEN

1. The *Moses Taylor* was a wooden, side-wheel steamer. It had three decks and two masts, was 246 feet long and thirty-four feet wide, and weighed approximately 1,400 tons. It was built to carry 600 passengers with state-rooms to accommodate 100. It cost $250,000 when built (by William H. Webb) in 1858. From 1860 it operated in the Pacific. Beginning in September, 1864, it was run by the Central American Transit Company between San Francisco and San Juan del Sur, Nicaragua (Panama in the case of Stanfield's trip). As Stanfield noted, the ship was also known as the "Rolling" *Moses*—a nickname which, he said, was deserved. His voyage began on April 13, 1865, and the captain was J. H. Blethen.

The trip from San Francisco to New York usually took from twenty-two to twenty-four days.

2. Ernest A. Wiltsee, *Gold Rush Steamers of the Pacific* (San Francisco, 1938), pp. 301–303.

3. Sacramento *Daily Bee*, August 15, 1864, p. 1.

4. The Department of State passport division has no record of a passport for Howard Stillwell Stanfield. Passports were not required by law for travel abroad by United States citizens until World War I, except for the period from August 19, 1861, to March 17, 1862.

The Provost Marshal at San Francisco was Captain Hugh B. Fleming, who had succeeded Brigadier General John S. Mason on March 28, 1865. With the United States on war footing, it was not uncommon for the Provost Marshal to require a passport as a means of obtaining information about people in transit. The army regarded this check as a military decision based on military necessity.

The Provost Marshal's primary function was to supervise the operation of the draft laws, but he was also charged with apprehending deserters, arresting disloyal persons, inquiring into and reporting treasonable practices, seizing stolen government property, and detecting spies.

5. The trip was approximately 3,300 miles from San Francisco to Panama, and 2,000 miles from Panama to New York.

6. The Pacific Mail Steamship Company added the *Sacramento* to its fleet in September, 1864. It weighed 2,640 tons and was—until May, 1865—one of the three ships to sail each month for the Company between San Francisco and Panama. It carried about 1,000 passengers, and W. H. Hudson was the Captain. See the San Francisco *Evening Bulletin,* April 12, 1865, p. 3.

7. The situation described also held true on the ships of the Pacific Mail Steamship Company. See the Virginia *Daily Union* (Virginia City, Nev.), August 11, 1864, p. 1.

8. Families tried to screen off their berths for privacy, but the heat and the lack of ventilation made this impractical.

9. Digger Indian referred in popular terminology to the plains Indians who were ". . . a type chiefly distinguished for their filthy habits, repulsive appearance, and pilfering propensities." This description was written by Stanfield's neighbor David R. Leeper in his *Argonauts of 'Forty-Nine* (South Bend, Ind., 1894), p. 57.

10. Hot tar and sulphur were also used as disinfectants.

11. The Lower California Coast, along which the boat was steaming, was a monotonous sight with its parched and barren shores. This was the reaction of every diarist of the trip. See, for example, John Olmsted, *Trip to California in 1868* (New York, 1880), p. 21.

12. Cape St. Lucas was the southern extremity of Lower California. The passengers saw it as a mountain with a white sandy beach.

13. The Gulf of California is an arm of the Pacific Ocean, extending northwest between the Mexican district of Lower California on the west and the Mexican states of Sonora and Sinaloa on the east.

14. Stanfield does not mention stopping at Acapulco, although he must have done so. All ships docked there, usually about one week out of San Francisco, to replenish supplies. The city is usually described (as in John Olmsted, p. 21) in idyllic terms: a perfect sheltered harbor, cobblestoned narrow streets, plaza, cathedral, tile-roofed adobe buildings, happy, brown natives eager to sell tourists trinkets and fruits.

15. The *Golden Gate* of the Pacific Mail Steamship Company Line burned four miles off the coast of Mexico (fourteen miles from Manzanillo) on July 27, 1862. One hundred ninety-eight lives were lost; one hundred and forty were saved. Only the bed plate, wheels and attachments remained above water and could be seen from passing boats.

16. In this latitude Stanfield could see the Southern Cross. The Gulf of Tehuantepec is a wide-mouth inlet of the Pacific Ocean in southeast Mexico bounded by the states of Oaxaca and Chiapas.

17. Central American Transit Company.

18. Stanfield may have been describing the Volcano of Pecaya, which was in eruption at that time. See William H. Brewer, *Up and Down California in 1860–1864. The Journal of William H. Brewer*, ed. Francis Farquhar (New Haven, Conn., 1931), pp. 565–69.

Generally, Stanfield was observing a low plain, much swamp land, extending ten to twenty-five miles inland and rising from the sea with mountains in the background. The coastline had no natural harbors.

19. San Juan del Sur was a poor harbor, and vessels had to anchor offshore—usually one and one-half miles—to prevent the dragging of anchor when the wind was high. It was established during the 1849 gold rush as the western Nicaraguan departure point for California. It deteriorated after the Panama Railroad was completed in 1855, for the railroad eliminated the time advantage of the route across Nicaragua from New York to California. The hotels Stanfield speaks of date from the earlier period. The Opposition Line tried to revive the route beginning in the fall of 1864.

20. Petroleum V. Nasby was the pseudonym of David Ross Locke (1833–88). Locke was an American political satirist, journalist, and opponent of slavery. Beginning in 1861, he published in the Findlay, Ohio, *Jeffersonian* letters signed by Nasby, who was represented as a

dissolute, stupid, hypocritical, and corrupt Copperhead preacher and whose championing of slavery was discredited accordingly.

21. Lake Nicaragua was about 100 miles long and covered 2,972 square miles. The San Juan River flowed from it to Greytown (or San Juan del Norte) on the Carribbean Sea. Greytown was the Atlantic Nicaraguan port for sailings to and from New York.

22. General William Walker, an American citizen, just prior to the American Civil War entered Nicaragua and with fifty-eight men defeated large armies. He was accepted by the Indians as a savior and became a dictator. His downfall came in part as a result of the opposition to him by the American government. His eyes were a steel grey, almost without pupils, and he was popularly called "the grey eyed man of destiny." See: Albert Z. Carr, *The World and William Walker* (New York, 1963); Laurence Green, *The Filibuster: The Career of William Walker* (Indianapolis, 1937); and James J. Roche, *The Story of the Filibusters* (New York, 1891).

23. The U.S.S. *Wateree* was an iron gunboat 205 feet long, armed with two hundred-pound guns and smaller armament. It had been commissioned in January, 1864, and was ordered to join the Pacific squadron. It was under the command of Commander F. K. Murray and carried nineteen officers and 160 enlisted men. On April 3, 1865, the ship was ordered to remain in ports of Central America, especially El Realejo, until the Commander of the Pacific Coast Squadron could learn something definite relative to a suspicious steamer said to be bound for some of those ports.

24. While Stanfield attributed the phrase "living waters" to David in the Psalms, the Biblical passage appears in John 4:10, 11; Jeremiah 2:13 and 17:13; Song of Solomon (Songs) 4:15; and Zechariah 14:8. It is probable that he has reference to the familiar story from John of the Woman from Samaria offering Jesus a drink at the well.

25. The term "flying fish" is a common name given to some fifty species of fish all in the family Exocoetidae. They are blue or green above with silver bottoms and are found in warm seas, usually far from land. Their glide over the water is made possible by the enlargement of the pectoral fins and is ordinarily a means of escaping enemies. Flight may be stimulated by any large body, such as a ship, cutting through the water. The fish shoot into the air at a speed of from thirty to forty miles an hour, and a glide may last up to thirty seconds and cover 300 yards.

26. Sea-serpent stories enlivened most trips. See for example Archie Argyle, p. 227.

CHAPTER EIGHT

1. Stanfield does not mention the fire which had destroyed much of Panama City in July, 1864, but he does give evidence of the rapid encroachment of the tropical growth in certain parts of the city.

The population of Panama City was perhaps from 6,000 to 8,000. See Charles T. Bidwell, *The Isthmus of Panama* (London, 1865), p. 179; and Albert D. Richardson, *Beyond the Mississippi from the Great River to the Great Ocean . . . 1857–1867* (Hartford, Conn., 1867), p. 537.

2. The *Moses Taylor* did not use the 450-foot pier built by the railroad company, probably because it was reserved for the steamers of the Pacific Mail Steamship Company.

3. The Aspinwall House was considered the best hotel. It charged $3 a day.

4. The soldiers were dressed in dirty white linen shirts and pants with a blue-cloth skull cap with a red band in front. They wore no shoes, and their guns were old English muskets. The main function of the soldiers was to guard the bullion sent across the Isthmus.

5. Lincoln was assassinated on April 14, 1865.

6. The Captain of the *Golden Rule* was Mr. Babcock. The ship of 3,500 tons usually ran between New York and Greytown, the Atlantic port city for Nicaragua. It was owned by the Central American Transit Company.

7. Alexander R. McKee was the United States Consul at Panama, Columbia, from May 15, 1861, to September 3, 1865. His home was Somerset, Pulaski County, Kentucky.

This incident took place on Cathedral Plaza, which was dominated by the twin-towered church on one end and the Hotel Centrale with its open-air cafe on the other.

8. The Panama Railroad route was built 1850–55 under the supervision of William Aspinwall, a New York capitalist and owner of the Pacific Mail Line. The railroad ran from Panama City to Aspinwall, approximately forty-nine miles over difficult terrain: through swamps, over rivers, across mountains, and into jungle growth. For twenty-five miles the road followed the Chagres River. The fare was twenty-five gold dollars. The officials were Americans, and the laborers were natives.

9. Aspinwall, now Colón, is built on Navy Island (or Manzanillo Island), which was originally covered by mangrove and mahogany

NOTES FOR PAGES 138-40   225

forests. Creeping vines and tropical growth reclaim any land not carefully kept cleared. It is the eastern terminal of the Panama Railroad, founded in 1850, and named for William Aspinwall, one of the builders of the railroad. In 1865 it had about 200 wooden houses, and its shops fronted the bay along a wide street. These whitewashed buildings usually had balconies extending over the sidewalks. Its business activity centered about the tourists, to whom the Jamaican and Negro shopkeepers tried to sell the usual variety of trinkets and fruit. The population was probably between 1,500 and 2,000. This figure is from Bidwell, p. 125.

10. Francis W. Rice was the United States Consul in Aspinwall from August 1, 1861, to May 31, 1869. He was a resident of Maine and the Special Panama Correspondent of the New York *Times*. His dispatches to Washington make no mention of Stanfield or of the practice of collecting one silver dollar before permitting a traveler to leave the port.

Commander Thomas H. Patterson, USN, commanded the U.S.S. *James Adger* assigned to Aspinwall at this time.

11. Turks Island is a dependency of Jamaica, located in the southeastern part of the Bahama Islands.

12. The steamer *Ariel* traveled between New York and Panama and was owned by Commodore Cornelius Vanderbilt. It had been seized by the Confederate raider *Alabama* in December, 1862, and was released after the Captain gave bond for $200,000.

13. Cape Hatteras is southeast of Hatteras Island, North Carolina. It is a long narrow sand bar extending into the Atlantic and is considered a dangerous navigational point.

14. Cape Henlopen is on the east coast of Sussex County, Delaware, and south of the entrance of Delaware Bay.

INDEX

Adel, Iowa, 23, 28–29
Alder Clump, Wyoming, 51, 55
Allensworth's train, 63
American Pacific Line, The. *See* Steamship companies
Areil (of the Pacific Mail Steamship Company), 139. *See also* Steamship companies
Arnold, Joseph B., 20
Aspinwall (Colón), 131, 136–37
Aspinwall House, 134
Atlantic voyage: Cape Hatteras, 131, 140; Cape Henlopen, 131, 140; Caribbean, 138, 139; Cuba, 131, 139; New York City, 131, 139, 140; Round Island, 139; South Carolina, 140; travel experiences, 131; Turks Island, 131, 139
Austin, Nevada Territory, 87, 90

Bailey House, Grinnell, Iowa, 22, 25
Bartlett, Joseph, 2
Bartlett, William S., 2, 11, 16, 19, 27, 30, 33, 34, 38
Bear River, 74
Bender, W. S., 92
Bighorn Mountains, 51, 56, 61, 64, 68
Bighorn River, 57, 59, 60
Bigler, Lake (Tahoe), 88, 93–94

Black Hills, Wyoming, 55
Black Rock, Great Salt Lake, 76
Bozeman, John M., 51
Bozeman Trail, 51
Bridger, Jim, 51–52, 56, 57–58, 59, 60, 63, 70; his route to Virginia City, Montana Territory, 51–52, 56, 57–58, 59, 60, 63, 70, 71, 72
Brownfield, Dennis, 19

California. *See* names of cities in state
Camp Douglas, Chicago, 20
Camp Douglas, Salt Lake City, 77, 87; and the California Cavalry, 81
Carleton, C. W., 38
Carlisle Hill, Indiana, 13, 17
Carson River, 69
Cass County, Iowa, 23, 30
Castle Creek, Nebraska Territory, 48
Castle Rocks, Nebraska Territory, 36, 48
Chagres River, Panama, 137
Chicago, Illinois, 13, 20
Chimney Rock, Nebraska Territory, 36, 48
Chinese population, 105
Chrysopolis (Sacramento River steamer), 89, 104
City West, Indiana, 19

Civil War: reactions to, 101–102, 135, 136
Clarks Fork River, 51, 58, 64, 65–67, 70
Cliff House, San Francisco, 89, 105–106
Colfax, Schuyler, 9
Columbus, Nebraska Territory, 34–35, 40
Comstock Lode, 88. *See also* Mining
Conner, General P. E., 77
Council Bluffs, Iowa, 23–24, 31, 32–33, 34, 38, 40, 42
Courthouse Rock, Nebraska Territory, 36, 48
Crockett, Gerritt, 19, 29, 38, 40
Cuba, 131, 139

Dallas County, Iowa, 28
Dalmanutha, Iowa, 29, 30
Davenport, Iowa, 14, 20
Deseret News (Salt Lake City), 77
Des Moines, Iowa, 22, 23, 26–28
Diamond Mountains, 87, 90
Divide Creek, 67
Dunn, John, 26, 27, 30, 32, 55

East Nishnabotna River, Iowa, 23
Eldorado, Nebraska Territory, 34, 41

Folsom, California, 9, 88, 94
Fort Kearney, 34, 35, 36–37, 42, 43, 45, 47, 49; Ohio Cavalry stationed at, 35
Fort Laramie, 49, 51, 53, 55
Fowler, John, 19, 27, 38, 39, 40
Fowler, William, 55
Freight wagons, 87, 88, 94

Fremont, Nebraska Territory, 34, 38, 39

Gallatin Fork (river), 51, 71
Gold: mining in Virginia City, Montana Territory, 52, 72, 73. *See also* Mining
Golden Eagle Hotel. *See* Sacramento
Golden Gate (Pacific Mail Steamship Company), 118
Golden Rule, 9, 131, 136, 138; accommodations on, 131, 138; food, 138–39
Goose Creek, Nebraska Territory, 46
Gould and Curry Mine, 88, 93. *See also* Mining
Gov. Dana (Sacramento River steamer), 103
Great Salt Lake, 76, 81, 82–84, 123
Great Salt Lake Desert, 87, 90
Great Salt Lake House, 79
Greybull River, 51, 61
Grinnell, Iowa, 14, 22, 25, 26, 27, 94
Guthrie County, Iowa, 23, 29

Hatteras, Cape, 131, 140
Havana, Cuba, 139
Henlopen, Cape, 131, 140
Holman, H. C., 19, 28

Idaho, 16, 38, 73, 74
Indiana Ranch, California, 9, 88, 89, 95, 96, 98, 99
Indiana train, 70, 71
Indians: characterized, 4, 35, 53; the Cheyenne, 53; the Crow, 58; the Flathead, 53, 64; in Iowa,

INDEX 229

22, 26, 33; in Nebraska Territory, 35, 36–37, 38, 39, 47, 48; the Pawnee, 36–37; the Sioux, 36–37, 53; the Snake, 58; in Wyoming-Montana, 49, 51, 53, 57, 58, 64
Iowa: attitude of residents toward immigrants, 4; coal mines, 28; farms, 21, 26, 28; prairies, 21–22; roads, 21, 22, 23, 25, 26, 28, 29, 31, 32. *See* names of cities in state

Jacobs (San Francisco violinist), 106
Jacobs, John M., 8, 51–52, 53, 56, 58, 63, 70; and the wagon trip to Virginia City, Montana Territory, 51–52, 56, 57–58, 59, 60, 70, 71, 72
Jordan River, 75, 82

LaPorte (Rabbit Creek), California, 96
Laramie River, 49
Laramie's Peak, Wyoming, 55, 56
Lewis, Iowa, 23, 31
Lincoln, California, 88, 95
Lone Mountain Cemetery. *See* San Francisco
Loup River, Nebraska Territory, 35

Madison Fork River, 51, 71
Maguire's Opera House. *See* San Francisco
Marysville, California, 88, 89, 95, 96, 99, 100–103, 110
Michigan, Lake, 20
Michigan City, Ind., 13, 17, 19
Mining: in Austin, Nevada Territory, 90; in Virginia City, Montana Territory, 53, 73
Mission Street Wharf. *See* San Francisco
Mississippi River, 20
Missouri River, 23, 33, 38, 51, 67, 71, 72
Montana, 49, 51, 72, 73, 74
Montana *Post* (Virginia City), 52
Montgomery Street. *See* San Francisco
Mormons: antagonism toward, 77; in Iowa, 23; women, 74, 75. *See also* Brigham Young
Moses Taylor, 9, 107, 108, 109, 110–11, 121, 131, 133, 136, 138; accommodations on, 112, 113, 114, 116, 128; fire, 117; food, 112–13, 114, 115–16; rolls, 119; sanitation, 115; water, 126–27. *See also* Steamship companies
Myrick House, Chicago, 13, 20

Nebraska: farms, 39–40; houses, 42, 45; roads, 36. *See also* Fort Kearney; Indians; names of cities in state
Nevada City, Montana Territory, 53
Newton, Iowa, 22, 25–26
New York City, 107, 131, 139, 140, 141
Nicaragua, 107, 108, 109, 111, 121–25, 130, 135; Lake Nicaragua, 121–22; natives, 124–25; San Juan del Sur, 109, 121–25, 126, 128. *See also* William Walker
Nishnabotna River, 23
North Platte River, 49, 51, 53, 55. *See also* Platte River

Oakland, California, 89, 106
Ogden, Utah, 74
Oliver and Conover Company. *See* Stagecoach
Omaha, Nebraska Territory, 32, 34, 38, 39, 40
Oregon, 16, 49
Oregon House, California, 99

Pacific voyage: amusements, 114–15, 117, 119, 127–28; Cape St. Lucas, 117; Guatemala shoreline, 120; Gulf of California, 117–18; Gulf of Tehuantepec, 119; Lower California, 114; Mexican coast, 118; travel experiences, 108–109, 112–14; Volcano of Pecaya, 121
Panama, 107, 109, 112, 122, 126, 130–31, 133–38; Aspinwall (Colón), 131, 136–37; Chagres River, 137; countryside, 136–37; natives, 130, 135, 137; Panama City, 130, 133–36; train, 136–37
Passport, 107, 110–11, 131, 137–38
Pioneer Stage, 88, 93
Plainfield, Indiana, 13, 16
Platte River, 34, 35, 36, 39, 42, 43, 45, 46, 47, 48. *See also* North Platte River
Portland, Indiana (Bootjack), 17
Pryor's Gap, 64

Rabbit Creek. *See* LaPorte
Raccoon River, 23, 29
Railroads: Lake Shore and Michigan Southern, 13; Mississippi and Missouri, 14; in Panama, 131, 136; Rock Island, 14
Red Buttes, Wyoming, 51

Roads: in Iowa, 21, 22, 23, 25, 26, 28, 29, 31, 32; in Nebraska Territory, 36; in Great Salt Lake Desert, 90; in Wyoming-Montana, 62. *See also* Trails
Rolling Prairie, Indiana, 17
Rose, John, 19, 27
Rose Bud Creek, 68
Route of Stanfield, 7, 9, 13–14
Ruby Valley, 87, 90

Sacramento, 108, 112. *See also* Steamship companies
Sacramento, California, 88, 89, 92, 95; capitol, 103; Chinatown, 103; Golden Eagle Hotel, 103
Sacramento River, 95, 103, 104
Salt Lake. *See* Great Salt Lake
Salt Lake City, 72, 73, 74, 75, 77, 78, 79–81, 90, 104; Civic Theatre, 75, 81, 85; hotels, 76, 79, 84; Mormon Temple, 75, 80; Sulphur Springs, 75–76, 81; Tabernacle, 76, 80; Young's home, 80
Sample, Rench, 95
Sand Hill Creek, Nebraska Territory, 46
San Francisco, 89, 104, 107, 118, 122, 126, 141; American Exchange Hotel, 104; Bush Street Presbyterian Church, 89, 104; Chinese, 105; Cliff House, 89, 105–106; Lone Mountain Cemetery, 104; Maguire's Opera House, 89, 106; Mission Street Wharf, 111; Montgomery Street, 89, 104, 105, 106
San Francisco Evening Bulletin, 108
San Juan del Sur. *See* Nicaragua

INDEX

Savery House, Des Moines, Iowa, 27
Scottsbluff, Nebraska Territory, 36, 48, 49
Shell Creek, Nebraska Territory, 34, 39
Sherman House, Chicago, 14, 20
Shoshone River. *See* Stinking Water River
Sierra Nevadas, 88, 94
Silver Creek, Nebraska Territory, 41
Skunk rivers, 21, 22, 26
Snake River, 74, 79
Soldiers: characterized, 4, 49
South Bend, Indiana, 11, 132
Springville, Indiana, 17
Stagecoach: accidents, 78, 79; described, 74, 78; drivers, 74; Oliver and Conover Company, 74; Pioneer Stage, 88, 93; Stanfield's stage trip, 87–89, 90; travel conditions, 74, 78–79; travel through Idaho and Utah, 74–75
Stanfield, Edward, 1, 96
Stanfield, Eva, 14, 20, 97
Stanfield, Howard Stillwell, 1; self description, 16
Stanfield, Judge Thomas, 1, 14, 20, 96, 97
Stanfield, Mammie, 97
Stanfield, Mrs. Thomas, 96–97
Steamship companies: Central American Transit Company (American Pacific Line; People's Opposition Steamship Line), 107–108, 111, 119; Pacific Mail Steamship Company, 107, 108, 139. *See also Moses Taylor; Sacramento*

Stinking Water River (Shoshone), 51, 62, 63
Studebaker wagons, 4, 11–12
Sun Mountain, Virginia City, Nevada Territory, 88

Tahoe, Lake. *See* Lake Bigler
Terre Coupee, Indiana, 13, 26
Toiyabe Canyon, Nevada Territory, 87
Tolleston, Indiana, 13
Trails: animals, 11, 25, 38, 44; conditions, 5, 17; followed by Stanfield, 7–9, 10, 13–14, 50, 86; hardships, 5, 13; in Indiana, 16–20; pleasures, 6–7; supplies, 11, 17, 32
—*in Iowa:* and hunting, 25, 27, 31, 32; and Indians, 26, 33; roads, 25, 26, 28, 29, 31; Stanfield's experiences, 21–24
—*in Nebraska:* death on plains, 41; guard duty, 43; hunting, 36, 43–44, 45–46, 47; prairie fires, 40; roads, 36, 45, 47; rope ferry, 35; routine described, 36, 42; sand storm, 46; trains organized, 35; Stanfield's experiences, 34–37
—*in Wyoming-Montana:* death, 55–56, 61, 64; feeding of animals, 62, 63; fording rivers, 59–60, 65, 69–70; health problems, 53–54, 60, 61, 64; hunting, 61, 65–67; mining, 53; roads, 62; routine, 56–57, 60; vegetation, 58; wagon trains, 51, 53, 57; Stanfield's experiences, 49–54
Turks Island, 131, 139

U.S. Hotel, Marysville, California, 100

Virginia City, Montana Territory, 51–53, 56, 65, 67, 70, 71–73, 74
Virginia City, Nevada Territory, 87–88, 90, 92, 94; described, 93; greenback problem, 87, 92; hospital, 93. *See also* Comstock Lode; Gould and Curry Mine

Wagons. *See* Studebaker wagons; Freight wagons
Walker, William, 109, 123
Wateree (U.S. gunboat), 126

Western House, Adel, Iowa, 28
Wolf Creek, Nebraska Territory, 47

Yellowstone Cut-off, 51, 56
Yellowstone River, 51, 69–70
Young, Brigham, 75, 76–77, 79–80, 104
Yuba County, California, 56, 88, 100
Yuba County House, California, 99
Yuba River, 103